GREAT WARSHIPS
FROM THE AGE OF STEAM

GREAT WARSHIPS
FROM THE AGE OF STEAM

AN ILLUSTRATED GUIDE TO GREAT WARSHIPS
FROM 1860 TO 1945

DAVID ROSS

METRO BOOKS
New York

METRO BOOKS
New York

An Imprint of Sterling Publishing
387 Park Avenue South
New York, NY 10016

Editorial and design by
Amber Books Ltd
74–77 White Lion Street
London N1 9PF
www.amberbooks.co.uk

Project Editor: Michael Spilling
Designer: Andrew Easton
Picture Research: Terry Forshaw

All artworks courtesy of Tony Gibbons © Amber Books and Art-Tech

Picture Credits:
Cody Images: 7, 12; Library of Congress: 5, 8, 13–15
Photos.com: 9; Public domain: 10
U.S. Department of Defense: 6, 16, 17

ISBN: 978-1-4351-5487-2

For information about custom editions, special sales, and premium and corporate purchases,
please contact Sterling Special Sales at 800-805-5489 or specialsales@sterlingpublishing.com.

Manufactured in China

2 4 6 8 10 9 7 5 3 1

www.sterlingpublishing.com

Contents

Introduction

THE GREAT ERA OF THE STEAM WARSHIP WAS FROM THE MID-1860S TO THE MID-1940S—AN 80-YEAR PERIOD IN WHICH A HUGE VARIETY OF LARGE SHIPS WAS BUILT, EVER-GREATER IN SIZE, FIREPOWER, AND TECHNICAL SOPHISTICATION. CAPITAL SHIPS WERE THE MOST EXPENSIVE AND DESTRUCTIVE WEAPONRY PRIOR TO THE ATOMIC BOMB, AND THEIR DEVELOPMENT CAN BE TRACED DECADE BY DECADE, THOUGH SHIP DESIGNERS WERE OFTEN CONFUSED AND IN DISPUTE ABOUT THE BEST WAY FORWARD.

The capital ship was always a specialized implement of warfare. Its great size and draft restricted the number of ports where it could be docked, and the areas of sea—particularly in coastal zones—where it could be deployed. Its original and prime purpose was to fight other ships of the same type, and this continued for as long as rival navies continued to build battleships, though from the 1930s some were also seen as commerce raiders. Its main usefulness was to countries that possessed large merchant fleets, or far-off colonies, or both. Great Britain was the most prominent example of this, and its Royal Navy had the largest battleship contingent through the 19th century and up to the early 1940s. Countries that claimed influence or control over adjacent seas also felt a need for major warships in order to demonstrate and exercise that control.

Germany's High Seas Fleet of the 1900s was intended to contest Britain's dominance in the North Sea, just as France and Italy both sought to be the chief naval powers in the Mediterranean Sea; while in the Adriatic Sea Italian and Austro-Hungarian battleship squadrons confronted each other. The United States at first considered its battleships as defenders of the coastal waters, but they assumed a wider role from 1907–08, with a world cruise deliberately intended to show America's new

RIGHT: *The First and Second Battleship Squadrons of the German High Seas Fleet, moored at Kiel, 1911.*

OPPOSITE: *Battleships of the High Seas Fleet steaming in line. Nearest is a ship of the pre-dreadnought Deutschland class, perhaps* Pommern *(1906), sunk at Jutland by torpedoes from the British submarine* Onslaught.

naval strength. Imperial Russia built battleships for its Baltic, Black Sea, and Pacific fleets. In Japan, construction of battleships paralleled and demonstrated the country's emergence in the late 19th century as a major power. Although many other countries possessed two or three battleships, these were the only powers to build and maintain capital ships in significant numbers.

OPPOSITE: *The close-range duel at Hampton Roads, March 9, 1862, between CSS* Virginia *(formerly USS* Merrimack*) and USS* Monitor. *The grounded USS* Minnesota *is on the right.*

LEFT: *USS* Iowa *("Battleship No. 4") some time after 1910 when the "basket" mainmast was fitted. At this time it was a training ship for midshipmen.*

eye on the ever-increasing naval budgets. Every step forward in technology added to the cost. Japan, after victory in the sea war against Russia in 1905, found its financial reserves so depleted that the specifications for its next generation of battleships had to be reduced. Russia, its ships sunk or captured, had to find the resources to build a new battle fleet.

In the 1860s, battleships were still wooden-hulled, though sheathed in armor of wrought iron or iron plates, and a really big ship might displace around 7,000 tons/tonnes. They still carried multiple masts and sailing rig. Even though engines were installed, mechanical power was still considered as supplementary to the sails; partly through worries about reliability but more through concerns about their lack of power and the possibility of running out of fuel on a long-range mission (eventually naval coaling stations were set up at key bases round the globe, particularly by the British Navy). Guns in warships of the 1860s were carried in the

CHARACTERISTICS

Three basic considerations underlay the design of the steam-driven, iron- or steel-hulled battleship: gun power, staying power, and speed. For designers, the task was to combine these elements in the most effective form, a challenge which brought together every branch of engineering and industrial science. A broad national industrial base, founded on steel and chemicals, was a prerequisite. Another vital consideration was cost. Capital ships were hugely expensive to build and to maintain in fighting condition, and politicians in all countries kept an anxious

OPPOSITE: *A scene from the Battle of Lissa, July 20, 1866, with the Austrian* Erzherzog Ferdinand Max *bearing down on the Italian* Re D'Italia, *which it sank by ramming.*

traditional broadside formation, though from the late 1850s experiments were being made with guns placed in revolving turrets. The famous duel between CSS *Virginia* and USS *Monitor* in Hampton Roads, Virginia, on March 9, 1862, in the American Civil War, confirmed the future of iron-protected hulls and turreted guns, but much work had to be done before these could be successfully incorporated in sea-going ships.

The concept of end-on firing took a long time for conservative-minded naval authorities to accept; bows and sterns had historically been lightly armed, with the main firepower amidships. This tradition led naturally to the central battery ship, with a heavily armored area which also protected the boilers and engines. For a period the proponents of the central battery arrangement prevailed over those of the turret, partly because the central battery kept the guns relatively low down, while turrets had to be mounted on an upper deck, leading to stability problems, especially when the ship also had tall masts and a full rig of sail. A separate but related controversy about the use of sail, especially in turret ships, was dividing opinion, sometimes bitterly, at the same time. It took the disastrous capsizing in 1870 of the British HMS *Captain*, carrying both gun turrets and a full sailing rig, to show that this was not the way forward.

EARLY COMBAT

Hostile actions between fleets were a rarity in the 19th century after 1815. The first time ironclad capital ships were tested in battle was in the Battle of Lissa, fought between the Italian and Austrian navies on July 20, 1866, off the island of Lissa (Vis) in the Adriatic Sea. This was at a period when armor development had temporarily outpaced advances in gunnery. It resulted in an Austrian victory for Admiral Wilhelm von Tegetthoff, whose tactics outmatched those of the Italian admiral Carlo Pellion di Persano. Much of the fighting was conducted at close quarters, and both sides attempted to ram opposing ships. Only one ship was sunk this way—the only one ever in warfare, though several were lost by accidental rammings in peacetime maneuvers—but the ram, with the concept of the whole ship as a weapon in itself, remained a feature of capital ships for another 40 years despite many criticisms by experienced officers.

The impregnability of armor plate did not last long. Advances in gun and shell design put an end to that. A new controversy arose, over the advantages and disadvantages of muzzle-loading (pushing the shell down the barrel, like an old-style cannonball) and breech-loading (inserting the shell and the propulsive charge from the inner end of the barrel). Eventually the superiority of breech-loading guns was so evident that muzzle-loading was abandoned, and the guns of numerous older but still viable ships were changed. From 1871 the growth in the destructive power of naval guns vastly exceeded the capacity for resistance of the armor opposed to them. Twenty- or even 24-inch (500–610 mm) armor was unavailing against the guns being developed by Armstrong, which could fire explosive shells weighing half a ton, and similar guns were built by Krupp in Germany.

THE TORPEDO

From around 1880 warship designers had also had to consider the self-propelled torpedo, with a warhead of high explosive power, which traveled under water. Influential figures in the French Navy thought that the day of the battleship was over. But torpedo boats, at least until they grew into "destroyers," could only operate near land, while the battleship was intended to rule the open sea. Other navies tackled the threat by new protection methods, with "torpedo bulkheads" intended to absorb and localize the effect of a torpedo strike, and steel-mesh torpedo nets, hung out from the sides on booms, to stop the torpedo well away from the hull. Inevitably, the mesh-cutting torpedo was introduced, to pierce the nets. Light guns had scarcely been used on battleships before, but the advent of the fast, light torpedo boat brought a new range of small guns that could be rapidly brought to bear and fired shells of sufficient power to pierce a torpedo boat's hull. Fighting tops, known from the 16th century, gained a new importance both for high-level spotting of torpedo boats, and as firing platforms for fending off attack.

For a time, torpedoes themselves became a conventional part of a battleship's armament. The advance from clumsy spar launchers to the underwater torpedo tube took only a few years. Battleships might have as many as six torpedo tubes, mounted on deck, or in the hull both above and below the waterline, but their use by capital ships in battle was extremely rare. Some battleships carried their own torpedo boats, as an additional, highly maneuverable offensive weapon. By World War II it was unusual for battleships to be armed with torpedoes.

There was a good deal to be said in favor of the French anti-battleship view of the 1880s. Battleships were immensely expensive and every technical innovation—electric power, radio, optical instrumentation, hydraulics—increased the cost. Regular maintenance and

OPPOSITE: *British steam torpedo boats docked, probably at Portsmouth. Note the coal stack and coal chutes for filling up the bunkers.*

RIGHT: *The Russian battleship* Tsesarevitch *makes a friendly visit to Portsmouth, England, in 1913. The armored belt, bow torpedo tube, and tumblehome sides are all clearly visible.*

periodic refits were essential. Dockyard and dry-dock facilities built for ships of around 60 ft (18 m) beam had to be extended to hold ships of 90 ft (27 m) beam and double the displacement of their predecessors. Political protests about the cost were common in all parliaments. The fact that this enormous investment, not to mention the need for a trained crew of around 1,000 men and boys, could be lost in a few minutes by a torpedo strike, deterred navies from hazarding their battleships.

ARMORED INNOVATIONS

In the 1890s the armor-makers again seemed to hold the advantage. New hardened steels, and steel alloys, were developed, which promised for a time to make the battleship an unsinkable floating fortress. In 1890 Hayward Augustus Harvey devised his "Harveyized" nickel steel armor in the United States. The Le Creusot Steelworks in France also developed a nickel-steel armor. A few years later, Krupp, Germany's huge new steel-and-munitions company, developed their cemented armor. In response the gun makers and ammunition suppliers produced new guns with high muzzle velocity and armor-piercing shells that penetrated armor plate and then exploded, rather than bursting on impact. By 1900 it had become obvious that the future effectiveness of battleships was to be based on long-range and accurate gunnery. This was confirmed by the Battle of Tsushima in 1905, between the Russian and Japanese fleets, when long-range gunnery and radio communication were decisive. Admiral Togo Heihachiro and Admiral Zinovy Rozhestvensky were the men who would win or lose the war for their respective nations. Togo's tactics triumphed, with Russia's fleet either sunk or captured, and the usefulness of the capital ship as a military instrument seemed to be confirmed. Just at this time naval rivalry between Germany and Great Britain was reaching a peak. The British and Germans were not alone in pursuing this policy. Across the Atlantic, Brazil, Chile, and Argentina were all in the market for battleships. It was Brazil's fleet-building, in particular, that prompted the United States to commence a program of

Opposite: HMS Dreadnought's *after-deck cleared for action, preparatory to firing the 12-inch (305mm)/45 cal. guns.*

Left: USS South Carolina *(BB 26), commissioned in 1910, the first battleship to have superfiring turrets. It also introduced cage or "basket" masts.*

Below left: USS Indiana, *commissioned in 1895 and classed as "Battleship No. 1," took part in the Battle of Santiago de Cuba on July 3, 1898.*

battleship construction. And Japan, racing to make itself a modern industrial nation and to dominate its own area of the globe, after acquiring ships from the United States, France, and especially Britain, was engaged in its own capital ship building program by 1910.

Although Japan contributed no major new ideas to the technicalities of battleship construction, the United States came up with several important innovations. A key one was the super-firing turret, enabling a doubling of the field of fire both fore and aft. First used on USS *South Carolina* (1910), it was very quickly adopted by other navies. The American approach to armoring was also influential: although individual battleships had always had most protection round the vital parts—magazines and machine rooms—the US Navy brought matters to

the logical conclusion of "all or nothing," concentrating the armor while ensuring that damage to unprotected bow and stern areas could not hazard the entire ship. In this way a battleship like the German *Scharnhorst* could be flooded with thousands of tons of water and still remain mobile and effective.

Study of the specifications given for each vessel will reveal the progress of mechanical propulsion from basic simple-expansion marine steam engines to the compound engines of the 1870s, culminating in the various triple-expansion types used through the 1890s and into the 1900s. These made bigger ships possible: Italy's *Re Umberto* of 1893 had a displacement a third greater than Britain's HMS *Royal Sovereign* of 1892, double the propulsive power, and was slightly faster. But Britain's use of the steam turbine in HMS *Dreadnought* (1906) made all previous engines obsolescent. By 1910 the concept of the "super-dreadnought," heavily armed, heavily armored and capable of up to 30 knots (34.5 mph; 55.5 km/h), dominated naval thinking.

It was ships of this type, British and German, that met at the Battle of Jutland, in May 1916. From 1920, the rate of development slowed. New developments were primarily in the fields of light weapons, especially anti-aircraft and anti-submarine; of telecommunications;

RIGHT: *The two 16-inch (406mm)/50 cal. forward triple turrets of USS* Missouri *(BB 63) fire simultaneously during a gunnery exercise.*

OPPOSITE: *An aerial view of USS* Iowa *(BB 61) with modernized AA defence systems and afterdeck laid out for helicopter operations.*

of electronic equipment to assist in range finding and gun control; and finally in the use of radar detection equipment.

TWO WORLD WARS

The torpedo threat to battleships took on a new significance once the oceangoing submarine became a reality. Now a capital ship could be struck almost anywhere. The speed provided by steam turbines came at just the right moment to reduce, if not to remove, the risk. In fact submarines proved generally more valuable, to the German war effort in particular, during 1914–18 by attacking slow-moving merchant vessels rather than alert and well-defended warships. By 1918 attention had shifted towards a new threat, that of attack from the air.

At the onset of World War II, in September 1939, capital ships still dominated the major navies. By 1942 their vulnerability to attack by bombs and aerial torpedoes was a major disadvantage, despite the provision of ever-larger AA batteries. Their prime role came to be as protectors of aircraft carriers, now the

key to ascendancy at sea. The final great encounter between battleships was in the Surigao Straits episode of the great Leyte Gulf battle on October 23–26, 1944, when the Japanese *Fuso* and *Yamashiro* were sunk, and USS *Mississippi* delivered the last full salvo in an engagement between capital ships.

After 1945 the battleship remained such a symbol of power and prestige that navies were reluctant to give them up, even though their role in naval warfare had been taken over by the carrier and the submarine. The development of the nuclear submarine and the guided missile confirmed the position.

Nevertheless, the United States deployed four of its *Iowa*-class ships in the Korean War (1950–53): USS *Iowa*, *New Jersey*, *Wisconsin*, and *Missouri*, using their long-range artillery against land targets, before placing them in reserve. *New Jersey* was reactivated during 1968–69 in the Vietnam War. In 1990–91, *New Jersey*, *Wisconsin*, and *Missouri* were in action in the Persian Gulf and the "Desert Storm" war. USS *Missouri* was the last battleship to fire its guns in war, against Iraqi positions in Kuwait, in January–February 1991.

Note: All specifications relate to the ship's original condition unless otherwise noted. Lengths given are overall length.

USS *Monadnock* (1864)

THE FIRST *MONADNOCK* WAS THE ONLY MONITOR OF THE *MIANTONOMOH* CLASS TO SEE ACTION DURING THE AMERICAN CIVIL WAR. LATER IT PASSED THROUGH THE STRAITS OF MAGELLAN ON A CRUISE FROM PHILADELPHIA TO SAN FRANCISCO.

A twin-screw, double-turreted, wooden-hulled, ironclad monitor, it was laid down at the Boston Navy Yard, Charlestown, Massachusetts, in 1862, launched on March 23, 1863, and commissioned on October 4, 1864. *Monadnock* steamed to Norfolk, Virginia, where Commander Enoch G. Parrott took command on November 20, and on December 13 left for the assault against Fort Fisher, in North Carolina, joining Rear-Admiral David Porter's North Atlantic Blockading Squadron on December 15, and four days later joined the fleet assembled to attack Confederate defenses on the Cape Fear River. On the morning of Christmas Eve, it closed the entrance of the river and bombarded Fort Fisher throughout the day. The following morning it resumed shelling as 2,000 Union troops landed north of the fort.

The attack failed but was renewed on January 13, 1865, with *Monadnock* again shelling the fort's defenses. Firing continued until the last gun on the sea face was silenced. During the action, *Monadnock* was struck five times.

Having aided in the closing of the port of Wilmington, North Carolina, *Monadnock* turned toward Charleston, South Carolina, crossing the bar on January 20, after the city's evacuation by Confederate troops. After a stay at Port Royal, South Carolina, *Monadnock* returned to Hampton Roads, Virginia, March 15. On April 2, it joined the final assault on Richmond and assisted in clearing the James River of torpedoes. A final wartime duty was to watch over CSS *Stonewall* at Havana, Cuba. Back at Norfolk by June 12, it entered the Philadelphia Navy Yard on June 20 to fit out for a cruise to the West Coast.

West to California

Monadnock left Philadelphia for the West Coast on October 5 with USS *Vanderbilt*, *Tuscarora*, and *Powhatan*, passing under its own power through the Straits of Magellan and reaching San Francisco on June 21, 1866. On June 26 it proceeded to Vallejo, California, and entered the Mare Island Navy Yard where it decommissioned on June 30. It remained there, its wooden hull gradually decaying, until it was broken up in 1874–75.

SPECIFICATIONS

DISPLACEMENT: 3,400 tons (3,454.5 tonnes)

DIMENSIONS: 285 ft 6 in x 52 ft 9 in x 12 ft 8 in (78.8 m x 16 m x 3.86 m)

PROPULSION: Twin shafts, horizontal return connecting rod engines, four Martin boilers

ARMAMENT: Four 15-in (375 mm) SB guns

ARMOR: Sides 5 in (125 mm); turrets 10 in (250 mm), deck 1.5 in (37 mm)

SPEED: 10 knots (11.5 mph; 18.5 km/h)

CREW: 150

USS *Monadnock*

VENTILATION
A VENTILATION SHAFT FOR THE ENGINE ROOM WAS PLACED ABAFT OF THE FUNNEL.

PILOT HOUSES
PILOT HOUSES WERE MOUNTED ON EACH TURRET, WITH A LIGHT HURRICANE DECK BETWEEN.

DECK
THE DECK WAS 31 IN (0.79 M) ABOVE THE WATERLINE.

TURRETS
INTERNAL DIAMETER OF THE TURRETS WAS 23 FT (7 M).

HMS *Cerberus* (1870)

THE FIRST OF GREAT BRITAIN'S "BREASTWORK MONITORS," SMALL BUT ARMORED AND HEAVILY GUNNED SHIPS DESIGNED FOR COASTAL AND HARBOR PROTECTION, WITH GUN TURRETS MOUNTED ON A RAISED BREASTWORK. *CERBERUS*, BASED ON A DESIGN BY SIR EDWARD REED, WAS INTENDED SPECIFICALLY AS A GUARD SHIP FOR THE PORT OF MELBOURNE, AUSTRALIA.

Chief constructor at the Admiralty since 1862, Reed was closely involved in the technical, but also the financial and political, aspects of warship design in a period of radical change and development. British naval vessels traditionally had a high freeboard to enable them to meet all sea conditions, but several reasons combined to make the ship sit low in the water: this made for a more stable gun platform, it saved on armor plating, and was adequate for operations in relatively sheltered waters. In addition, the design dispensed with conventional masts and yards, which required a higher freeboard. The armored breastwork raised the turrets to a suitable firing level and enclosed the funnel uptakes, ventilation shafts, and hatchways that would otherwise have had to have their own protective armor.

Melbourne Harbor Guard Ship
Built by Palmers of London, the ship was laid down on September 1, 1867, launched on December 2, 1868, and completed in September 1870, at a cost of £117,556.

A central superstructure rose above the breastwork, the gun turrets were mounted on the centerline at each end of the breastwork, each with a 180° angle of fire, and there was a single pole mast, used only for signaling purposes. These were novel, indeed revolutionary features that made *Cerberus* different from any predecessor.

Throughout its career the ship mounted four 18-ton (18.3 tonne) 10-in (254 mm) guns. Machine guns were placed on the hurricane deck at a later stage. Twin screws, each powered by separate engines, made up for the lack of sail power, and a balanced rudder was fitted.

For its only long voyage, out to Melbourne, temporary bulwarks extended fore and aft from the breastwork, and a full three-masted rig was fitted. As coal capacity was only 210 tons (213 tonnes) the voyage was made largely under sail. *Cerberus*'s entire career was spent at Melbourne, and a very similar sister ship, HMS *Magdala*, commissioned in November 1870, performed the same duties at Bombay (Mumbai). In later years *Cerberus* was a depot ship at Williamstown naval base in Victoria, Australia. In 1936 it was scuttled and incorporated into a breakwater.

SPECIFICATIONS

DISPLACEMENT: 3,340 tons (3,393.6 tonnes)

DIMENSIONS: 225 ft x 45 ft x 14 ft 4 in (68.6 m x 13.7 m x 4.4 m)

PROPULSION: Twin shafts, Maudslay engines, 1,370 ihp (1,022 kW)

ARMAMENT: Sides 8 in–6 in (203–152 mm); breastwork 9 in–8 in (228–203mm); turrets 10 in–9 in (254–228mm)

ARMOR: Four 10-in (254 mm) MLR guns

SPEED: 9.75 knots (11.2 mph; 18 km/h)

CREW: 155

HMS *Cerberus*

DECK
THIS WAS THE ROYAL NAVY'S FIRST LOW-FREEBOARD SHIP, WITH THE OPEN DECK ONLY 42 IN (1.06 M) ABOVE THE WATERLINE.

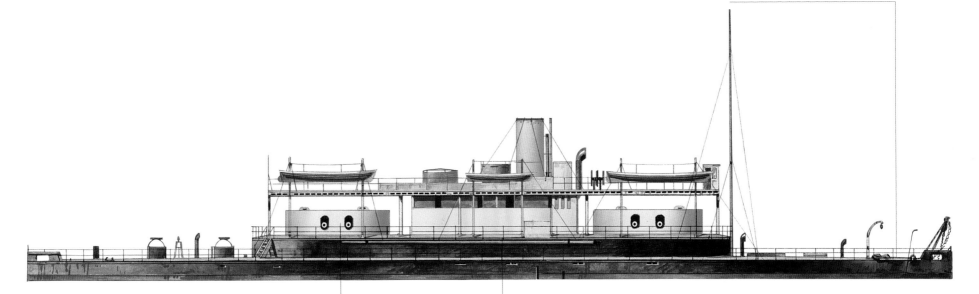

TURRETS
CERBERUS WAS ALSO THE FIRST ROYAL NAVY SHIP WITH FORE AND AFT GUN TURRETS.

ARMOR
1-IN (25 MM) DECK ARMOR COVERED THE WEATHER DECK AND THE BREASTWORK DECK.

HMS *Devastation* (1873)

DEVASTATION, THE FIRST SEA-GOING TURRET SHIP, CARRYING THE HEAVIEST GUNS YET, WAS A CONTROVERSIAL DESIGN WITH ITS BIG-GUN LAYOUT, AND ITS RELIANCE ON ENGINES ONLY. BUT IT SHOWED THE FUTURE OF WARSHIP DEVELOPMENT. *DEVASTATION* WAS DESIGNED BY SIR EDWARD REED, AND ITS RESEMBLANCES TO HIS *CERBERUS* ARE NOTICEABLE.

Laid down at Portsmouth on November 12, 1869, launched on July 12, 1871, it was completed on April 19, 1873, at a total cost of £361,438. The capsizing of the turret ship HMS *Captain* with the loss of almost all its crew in September 1870 held up construction, though *Captain*'s instability had been caused by inflicting three masts and a full set of sails on the design.

On commissioning, it caused a sensation. The freeboard was only 4 ft 6 in (1.37 m), allowing waves to wash over the weather deck. The hull was virtually square in section, a vast box with rounded ends, and a short ram was placed below the waterline. Internally it was divided into 68 compartments, with a double bottom capable of holding 1,000 tons (1,016 tonnes) of water ballast. Fore and aft, protected by an armored breastwork, a massive gun turret, 30 ft 6 in (9.3 m) in diameter, held two 12-in (305 mm) ML guns, firing 706-lb (320 kg) shells. Despite forecasts of disaster, *Devastation* behaved in rough seas exactly as its designers had predicted, and proved to be a steady gun platform. In an 1879 refit, six Nordenfelt guns were mounted on the hurricane deck and a Gatling gun placed in a fighting top on the mast. Ports for 14 in (356 mm) torpedoes were cut in the breastwork armor on each side. Further modifications in 1891–92 included new 10-in (254 mm) breech-loading guns, and replacement of the Nordenfelts with six 6-pounder and eight 3-pounders. New inverted triple-expansion engines were installed. This was the first complete application to a seagoing battleship of the principle of mounting the guns on top of the hull rather than inside it. *Devastation*'s original 12-in (305 mm) guns could be depressed for loading within the protective breastwork.

Heavy but Seaworthy

Though *Devastation* never fought a battle, its performance in exercises confirmed the merits of the design. Attached to the Channel Fleet in 1874–75, it transferred to the Mediterranean until November 1878. After refit it remained in reserve until April 1885, and from August 1885 to May 1890 was port guard ship at Queensferry, Wales. After completion of the second refit (1892) it had further spells as a port guard ship, including at Gibraltar from November 1898 to April 1902, and on reserve. Stricken in 1907, it was sold for scrapping in 1908.

SPECIFICATIONS

DISPLACEMENT: 9,330 tons (9,480 tonnes)

DIMENSIONS: 285 ft x 62 ft 4 in x 27 ft 6 in (86.9 m x 19 m x 8.4 m)

PROPULSION: Twin shafts, Penn direct–acting trunk engines, 6,650 ihp (4,959 kW)

ARMAMENT: Belt 12 in–8.5 in (305–216 mm), breastwork 12–10 in (305–250 mm), turrets 14–10 in (356–250 mm), conning tower 9 in (228 mm), deck 3–2 in (76–50 mm)

ARMOR: (1873): Four 12-in (305 mm) MLR guns

SPEED: 13.84 knots (16 mph; 25.6 km/h)

CREW: 358

HMS *Devastation*

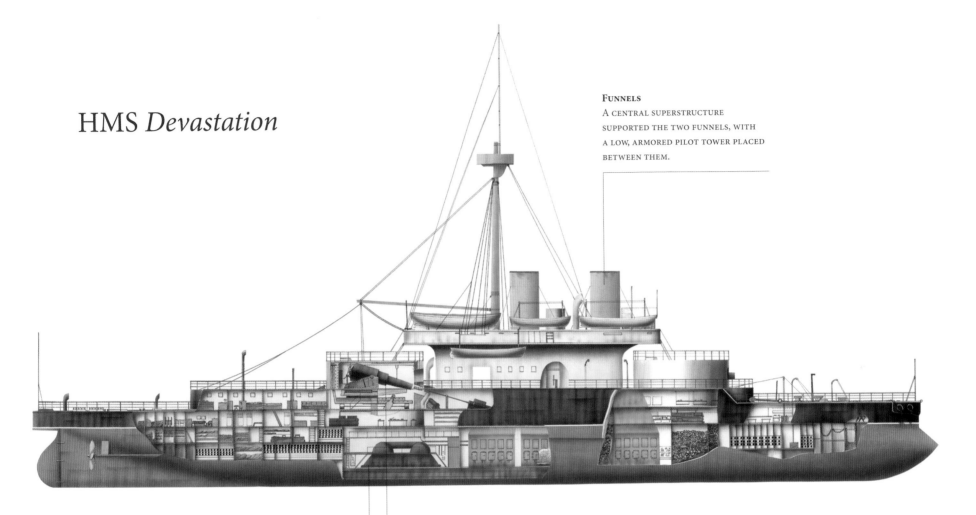

FUNNELS
A CENTRAL SUPERSTRUCTURE
SUPPORTED THE TWO FUNNELS, WITH
A LOW, ARMORED PILOT TOWER PLACED
BETWEEN THEM.

ENGINES
PENN DIRECT-ACTING TRUNK-TYPE ENGINES
WERE ORIGINALLY FITTED, FOR THE LAST
TIME IN A BRITISH BATTLESHIP, DRIVING
TWIN FOUR-BLADED PROPELLERS.

GUNS
IN 1886 THE ROYAL NAVY READOPTED THE PRINCIPLE OF BREECH-
LOADING, AND THE WHITWORTH 10-IN (250 MM) BREECH-LOADING
GUNS OF 1892, FIRING 500-LB (227 KG) SHELLS, DOUBLED THE RANGE
AND TRIPLED THE RATE OF FIRE.

Koning der Nederlanden (1874)

THE DUTCH NAVY'S LARGEST SHIP UNTIL THE 20TH CENTURY, IT WAS BUILT NOT FOR SERVICE IN THE BRITISH-DOMINATED NORTH SEA BUT TO HELP POLICE AND DEFEND THE NETHERLANDS' COLONIES IN THE EAST INDIES.

Laid down at the Rijkswerf, Amsterdam, on December 31, 1871, as *Matador* before renaming, it was launched on October 20, 1874, and commissioned on February 16, 1877, at a cost of 3,220,170 florins. Incorporated in the design was a 4-ft (1.22 m) ram, and a full-length waterline wrought-iron armored belt was fitted. Armor plating on the turrets was 9.1 in (230 mm), with 12 in (305 mm) at the gun ports. The deck was unarmored, but at this time the limitations of naval artillery did not allow for long-range fire with a high trajectory, and "plunging fire" was not yet a problem to be coped with. Its freeboard, at 10 ft 10 in (3.3 m) was relatively low, but the bulwarks could be raised on hinges if the ship was facing into a heavy sea.

The main guns were 25-ton (25.4 tonne) Armstrong Whitworth rifled muzzle-loaders, mounted in pairs in hydraulically operated turrets. The 4.7-in (120-mm) guns were Krupp breech-loaders. Six 1.5-in (37 mm) Hotchkiss 5-barrelled revolvers were also fitted in the superstructure. Spar torpedoes, initially installed, were later removed. During a refit in the later 1880s, the revolving guns were replaced by two 3-in (75mm) and four 1.5-in (37-mm) QF guns.

Service in the East Indies

On April 1, 1895, the ship was decommissioned and afterwards served as a barrack and guard ship at Surabaya, Indonesia, the Royal Netherlands Navy's main base in the East Indies. The rig was removed but the three masts were retained. Recommissioned on December 1, 1899, despite its virtually obsolete condition, with secondary armament only, it served as a "stand-by" ship until 1916, when, again at Surabaya, it was converted to a submarine tender and served as such until 1923. In World War II, as the Japanese advanced on Java, the old ship was set on fire and scuttled on March 2, 1942, to prevent its capture.

SPECIFICATIONS

DISPLACEMENT: 5,315 tons (5,400 tonnes)

DIMENSIONS: 279 ft x 49 ft 8 in x 19 ft 6 in (85.03 m x 15.14 m x 5.94 m)

RIG: Three masts, barkentine rig

PROPULSION: Twin shafts, Penn compound reciprocating engines, 4,630 ihp (3,450 kW)

ARMAMENT: Four 11-in (280 mm) MLR, four 4.7-in (120 mm) BL guns

ARMOR: Belt 8–6 in (200–150 mm); turrets 12–9 in (305–230 mm)

SPEED: 12 knots (22 mph; 14 km/h)

CREW: 256

Koning der Nederlanden

SAILS
TOTAL SAIL AREA WAS 9,120 SQ FT
(847 SQ M).

MASTS
DESPITE THE TURRET POSITIONING,
FORE AND AFT FIRE WAS IMPRACTICABLE
BECAUSE OF THE MASTS AND YARDS.

GUNS
THE 4.7-IN (120 MM) GUNS WERE MOUNTED
ON THE UPPER DECK.

TURRETS
DETACHABLE GANGWAYS LED ON TO THE
TURRET TOPS.

25

Petr Veliki (1876)

NAMED FOR TSAR PETER THE GREAT, ORIGINALLY INTENDED AS A BREASTWORK MONITOR FOR COASTAL DEFENSE, THE SHIP'S DESIGN PASSED THROUGH MANY ALTERATIONS AND ENLARGEMENTS. DURING A LONG CAREER THE MAIN EVENTS WERE RECONSTRUCTIONS AND REPLACEMENTS RATHER THAN NAVAL ACTION.

Originally named *Kreiser*, or "cruiser," *Petr Veliki* was laid down at the Galernii Island shipyard, St. Petersburg, on June 1, 1869, launched on August 27, 1872, and completed on October 14, 1876, at a cost of over 5,500,000 rubles. Its planning went back to 1867 and was characterized by afterthoughts and additions, including the name, changed to its final form shortly before the launch. In final design it was a turret ship, with a turret at each end of a short but massively protected citadel surrounding the single funnel and the ventilators. Other protection included a complete waterline belt of English wrought iron, backed by layers of teak and iron, and 14 in (356 mm) on the citadel, which was quite short at 160 ft (48.8 m) and the main magazines had to be placed outside it and armored separately. Internally there were nine transverse and two wing watertight bulkheads, and a longitudinal center bulkhead separating the boilers and engine rooms. The original boilers and engines were defective and replaced by vertical compound engines at Elder's Yard in Glasgow in 1881–82.

Russian-made 12-in (305 mm) 20-caliber rifled guns, based on a Krupp design, were installed. Six 3.4-in (86 mm) 4 pounder guns were intended as anti-torpedo boat armament, along with two Palmcrantz 1-inch (25 mm) machine guns. The ship also carried two 15-in (375 mm) spar-mounted torpedoes below the waterline at the bow.

Peaceful Service on the Baltic

Apart from a Mediterranean cruise in 1882, *Petr Veliki* served entirely with the Baltic Fleet. By the late 1890s, despite occasional updating of the secondary armament, the ship was obsolescent and the turrets were taken out in 1898. In 1903 it was marked for conversion into a gunnery training ship, and by 1908 this was complete. An entirely new superstructure, new side armor, two funnels, two pole masts with fighting tops, and four 8-in (203 mm) sponson-mounted guns forward of the superstructure made it look a completely different ship. Assigned to the Gunnery Training Detachment until 1917, after the Russian Revolution it was used as a submarine depot ship, first at Kronstadt, then Helsinki, returning to Kronstadt in April 1918. Hulked on May 21, 1921, it was used as a stores and accommodation vessel until its final disposal in 1959 for scrap.

SPECIFICATIONS

DISPLACEMENT: 10,406 tons (10,573 tonnes)

DIMENSIONS: 333 ft 8 in x 63 ft x 24 ft 9 in (101.7 m x 19.2 m x 7.5 m)

RIG: Three masts, partial barkentine rig

PROPULSION: Two shafts, horizontal return connecting rod engines

ARMAMENT: Four 12-in (305 mm)/ 20-caliber, six 3.4-in (86 mm), six 4-pounder guns; one 1-in (25 mm) machine gun; 4 spar torpedoes

ARMOR: Belt 14 in–8 in (356 mm–203 mm), turrets 14 in (356 mm), citadel 14 in (356 mm)

SPEED: 13 knots (15 mph; 24 km/h)

CREW: 441

Petr Veliki

MASTS
THOUGH FULL RIGGING WAS ABANDONED
DURING BUILDING, THREE MASTS WERE
RETAINED UNTIL 1905.

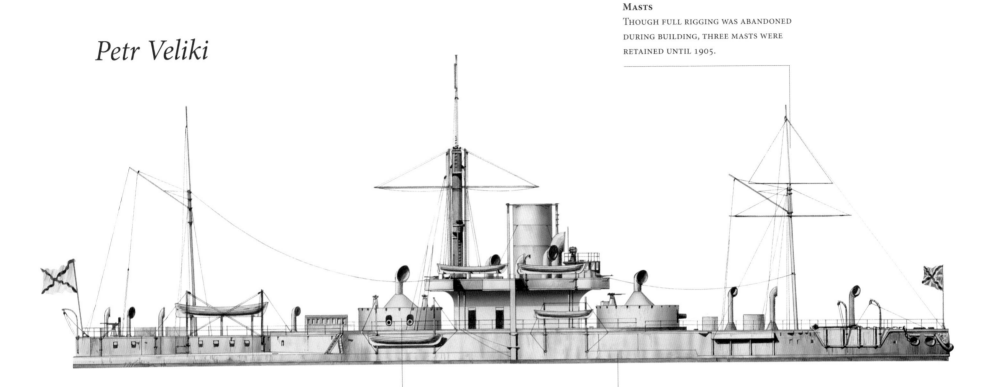

TURRETS
VENTILATION FANS HAD TO BE INSTALLED
ON THE TURRET ROOFS TO DISPERSE FUMES
CAUSED BY THE GUNS RECOILING AFTER
FIRING.

DESIGN
IN THE 1905–06 RECONSTRUCTION A SECOND
FUNNEL WAS ADDED AND THE SIDES HEIGHTENED,
HELPING TO GIVE THE SHIP A RADICALLY
DIFFERENT APPEARANCE.

HMS *Alexandra* (1877)

As a central battery ironclad, *Alexandra* was effectively obsolescent even when commissioned, with turreted warships already afloat. But it also had new features and served in the Royal Navy, frequently as a flagship, for 23 years, mostly with the Mediterranean Fleet.

By the mid-1870s the efficiency and power of marine steam engines had greatly improved, but the British Admiralty was not yet prepared to give up the practice of fully rigging the ships intended for blue-water service, and *Alexandra* was rigged as a three-masted barque. Laid down at Chatham Dockyard, in England, on March 5, 1873, launched on April 7, 1875, and completed on January 31, 1877, it was regarded as one of the most successful central-battery ships. The iron hull was divided into 115 watertight compartments, with a central longitudinal bulkhead 245 ft (74.7 m) long, and a double bottom.

The first RN ship to have vertical compound engines, making it the fastest large warship of its day, it was also a good sailer, though somewhat slow under sail alone, as all central battery ships seem to have been. An innovation was two 600 ihp (450 kW) auxiliary engines which kept the screws turning while the ship was under sail. It was the last British battleship to carry its main guns below the top deck, with the typical box-battery arrangement.

Flagship of the Mediterranean Fleet

From January 2, 1877, it was flagship of the Mediterranean Fleet and kept the role to 1889. It participated in the show of force off Istanbul in 1878, grounding in the Dardanelles Strait but quickly towed off by HMS *Sultan*; and was one of the ships bombarding Alexandria, Egypt, in June 1882. Refits were made in 1884 and on a larger scale in 1889–91 when breech-loaders and QF guns replaced MLR guns in the upper battery level, and four 16-in (408 mm) torpedo tubes were fitted. A control tower, with 12-in (305 mm) armor was also installed. At this time, too, the rig was cut back with the uppermost masts removed, and light topmasts fitted, with fighting-tops on the fore and mizzen masts. From 1891 to 1901, with a reduced armament, it was flagship of the Reserve at Portsmouth. In 1903 it became a training vessel for artificers, and was sold for breaking in 1908.

SPECIFICATIONS

DISPLACEMENT: 9,490 tons (9,642 tonnes)

DIMENSIONS: 344 ft x 63 ft 8 in x 26 ft 6 in (104.8 m x 19.4 m x 8.1 m)

RIG: Three masts, barque rig

PROPULSION: Sails, two shafts, vertical inverted compound engine, 8498 ihp (6337 kW)

ARMAMENT: Two 11-in (280 mm), ten 10-in (254 mm) MLR guns

ARMOR: Belt 12–6 in (305–152 mm), main battery 12 in (305 mm), upper 8 in (200 mm), deck 1.5–1in (38–25 mm)

SPEED: 15.09 knots (17.4 mph; 28 km/h)

CREW: 674

HMS *Alexandra*

SAILS
Alexandra'S BARQUE RIG GAVE A SAIL
AREA OF 27,000 SQ FT (2,508 SQ M).

ARMOR
THE PROTECTIVE BELT WAS 10 FT 6 IN
(3.2 M) HIGH AND COVERED THE WHOLE
WATERLINE LENGTH.

BATTERY
THE SIDE-BATTERY ARRANGEMENT, HARKING
BACK TO THE OLD WOODEN WARSHIP, WAS
USED HERE FOR THE LAST TIME.

ANCHOR
THE DAVIT WAS REQUIRED TO HELP IN RAISING
AND STOWING THE OLD-TYPE STOCKED ANCHOR.

Redoutable (1878)

FRENCH NAVAL DESIGNERS COULD ALWAYS BE RELIED UPON TO BE ORIGINAL IN THEIR APPROACH, AND *REDOUTABLE* WAS A VERY DISTINCTIVE SHIP OF THE CENTRAL BATTERY TYPE IN APPEARANCE AND DIMENSIONS BUT WAS ALSO THE FIRST WARSHIP TO BE BUILT LARGELY OF STEEL. IT SAW MUCH SERVICE IN ASIAN WATERS IN THE COURSE OF ITS CAREER.

Laid down at Lorient naval yard in August 1873, launched in September 1876, *Redoutable*, a celebrated name in the French Navy, was completed in December 1878. Its designer was the engineer Louis de Bussy. France led the world in steelmaking with the Siemens process at that time, and only the bottom plates of the vessel were of iron, the rest of the hull being steel, with consequent improvement in structural strength and reduction in weight.

Compared to other central battery ships, it was of wider beam and with a shortened battery, holding only four main guns, corner-mounted. The armor belt, 9 ft 10 in (3 m) high, was of wrought iron, and completely enclosed the hull, which had a marked tumblehome. The ship was full-rigged at first, with 24,000 sq ft (2,229.7 sq m) of sail, but was later altered to barkentine rig. Its service was mostly with the Mediterranean and Indo-China squadrons, based at Toulon, France, and Saigon, Vietnam, respectively. *Redoutable* had fifteen captains from 1879 to 1909.

Modernized and Electrified

In the mid-1890s a major modernization and reconstruction was done, with new guns, new boilers, and a revised superstructure. Electric circuits were installed. The rig was dismantled and replaced by two military masts, and torpedo defense netting was fitted.

From 1894 it carried seven 10.6-in (270 mm) and six 5.5-in (140 mm) breech-loading rifled guns, and Hotchkiss machine guns, four of these being mounted on a platform running round the outside of the funnel. Four torpedo tubes were mounted, two on each side. In the early 1900s the ship was deployed in the Far East during a period of high international tension, with war between Japan and Russia. In 1909 *Redoutable* completed its final tour of service at Saigon. Stricken in 1910, it was broken up in 1912.

SPECIFICATIONS

DISPLACEMENT: 9,224 tons (9,372 tonnes)

DIMENSIONS: 318 ft 8 in x 64 ft 6 in x 25 ft 7 in (97.13 m x 19.6 m x 7.8 m)

RIG: Three masts, square rig, later barkentine rig

PROPULSION: Sails, screw propeller, horizontal compound engine, 6,200 ihp (4,623 kW)

ARMAMENT: Eight 10.8-in (274 mm), six 5.5-in (140 mm), twelve 1-pounder guns

ARMOR: Belt 13.8 in (350 mm), battery 11.8–9.5 in (300–240 mm), deck 2.4–1.8 in (60–45 mm)

SPEED: 14.7 knots (17 mph; 27.2 km/h)

CREW: 705

Redoutable

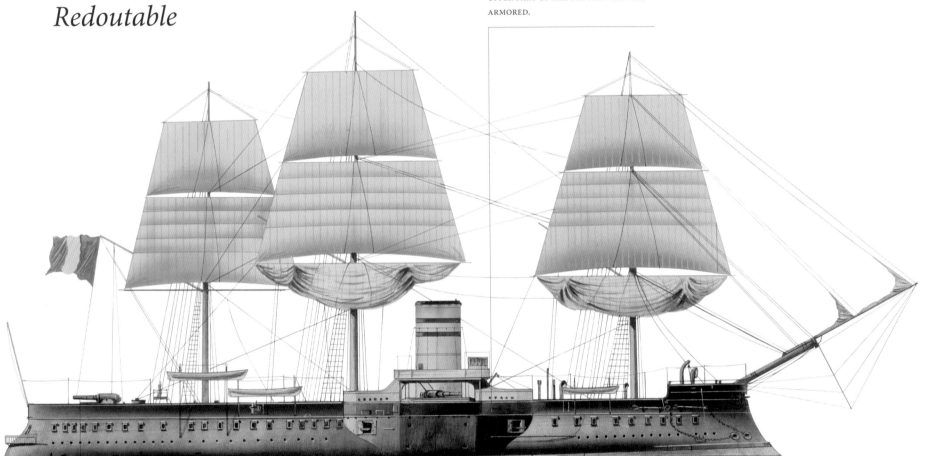

ARMOR
Redoutable HAD A PARTIAL ARMORED DECK, 2.4 IN (61 MM) THICK ON EACH SIDE OF THE BATTERY, BUT THE UPPER PART OF THE BATTERY WAS NOT ARMORED.

GUNS
TWO OF THE 10.8-IN (274 MM) GUNS WERE PLACED IN THE BOW AND STERN RESPECTIVELY, WITH NO PROTECTION.

BATTERY
THE MAGAZINES FOR THE BATTERY WERE CONSIDERED BY SOME EXPERTS TO BE DANGEROUSLY CLOSE TO THE BOILER ROOMS.

BRIDGE
THIS WAS AMONG THE FIRST WARSHIPS TO HAVE A RAISED NAVIGATION BRIDGE.

Fuso (1878)

JAPAN'S MOST POWERFUL SHIP OF WAR IN ITS NEW NAVY WAS DESIGNED AND BUILT IN ENGLAND, AND FITTED WITH GERMAN GUNS. AT FIRST AN IMPERIAL FLAGSHIP, BY THE TIME OF ITS DISCARDING IN 1908 JAPAN HAD A SUBSTANTIAL AND PROVEN BATTLE FLEET.

The modern Japanese Navy began with the American-built *Adzuma* of 1869 but it was with the program of 1875 that development got seriously under way, spurred by the prospect of a Japanese–Korean war. Most powerful of a trio of new vessels, *Fuso* was designed in London by Sir Edward Reed and laid down in September 1875 at Samuda Brothers' yard at Poplar on the Thames. Launched on April 14, 1877, it was completed in January 1878.

A central-battery ironclad typical of the time, it was modeled on the Royal Navy's *Audacious* class of 1870–71, though smaller and more lightly armed. The gun layout was very similar to that of *Redoutable*, with the four main guns at the corners of the battery, which protruded from the sides in order to widen the field of fire.

A refit in 1894, just before the Japanese–Chinese war, saw the mainmast removed, and military tops placed on the fore and mizzen masts. The 6.7-in (170 mm) guns were replaced by two 6-in (152 mm)/50-caliber QF guns, with two more, protected by shields, at the bow and stern; also eleven 3-pounder QF guns and two 18-in (457 mm) deck-mounted torpedo tubes. At the Battle of the Yalu River, September 17, 1894, the ship took eight hits, and was also involved in the Wei-Hai-Wei campaign of January–February 1895 when the Japanese ships supported land forces.

Veteran of Two Wars

On October 29, 1897, following a collision with the protected cruiser *Matsushima*, *Fuso* sank off the coast of Shikoku, but was refloated in 1898 and repaired at Kure Naval Arsenal. Its main guns were replaced by 6-in (152 mm) QF guns. Returned to service in 1900 as a second-class battleship, it took part in the blockade of Port Arthur in the Russo–Japanese war of 1904–05, and made patrols along the Korean coast. Reduced to the status of a coastal defense ship in December 1905, it was withdrawn from service on April 1, 1908, and scrapped in 1910.

SPECIFICATIONS

DISPLACEMENT: 3,717 tons (3,777 tonnes)

DIMENSIONS: 220 ft x 48 ft x 18 ft 4 in (67 m x 14.6 m x 5.5 m)

RIG: Three masts, barque rig

PROPULSION: Twin shafts, two pairs Penn reciprocating engines, 3,932 ihp (2,932 kW)

ARMAMENT: Four 9.4-in (240 mm), two 6.7-in (170 mm), six 3-in (76 mm) guns; 1 Nordenfelt 4-barrel machine gun

ARMOR: Belt 9 in–6.4 in (229–163 mm), battery 8 in (203 mm), bulkheads 7 in (178 mm)

SPEED: 13 knots (15 mph; 24 km/h)

CREW: 295

Fuso

MASTS
REMOVAL OF THE MAINMAST AND RE-GUNNING WOULD GIVE THE SHIP A VERY DIFFERENT LOOK AFTER 1895.

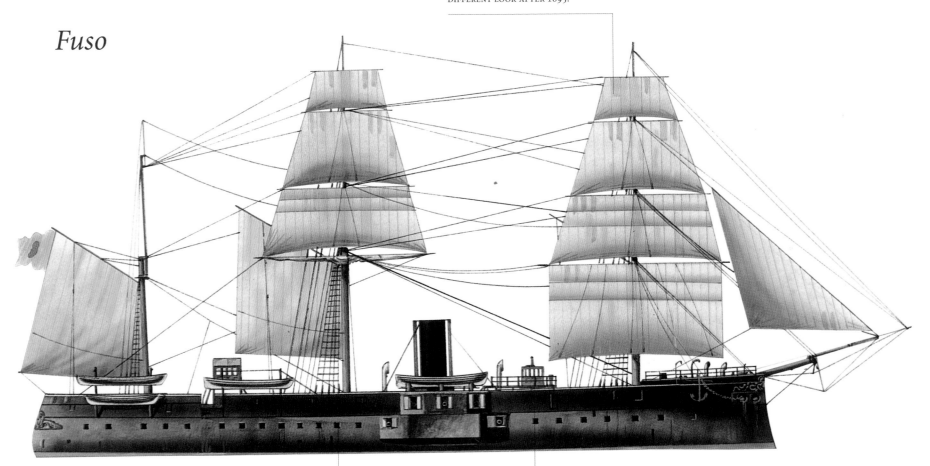

GUNS
THE POSITIONING OF THE LOWER GUNS CLOSE TO THE WATERLINE DID NOT HELP THEIR EFFECTIVENESS.

COMMUNICATION
TRADITIONALLY WARSHIPS WERE COMMANDED AND NAVIGATED FROM THE AFTERDECK, BUT *FUSO* SHOWS A FORWARD CONTROL CABIN MOUNTED ON A PLATFORM. THIS ALLOWED FOR VOICE-PIPE COMMUNICATION WITH THE ENGINE ROOM.

HMS *Belleisle* (1878)

ORDERED BY THE IMPERIAL OTTOMAN NAVY, BOUGHT BY THE BRITISH GOVERNMENT DURING A "WAR PANIC," *BELLEISLE* WAS INTENDED AS A RAM FOR COASTAL OPERATIONS IN THE BLACK SEA UNTIL ITS SUDDEN TRANSFER TO THE BRITISH FLEET.

As *Peik-i-Sherif* the ship was launched on February 12, 1876, and was almost completed at Samuda Brothers' yard on the Thames in mid-1878. The Turkish and Russian empires were at war, and the possibility of Great Britain being drawn into the conflict prompted a rush of naval activity. Renamed *Belleisle*, the ship was commissioned into the Royal Navy on July 2 and sent as guard ship to Kingstown, Ireland (now Dun Laoghaire). The Russian war scare soon abated and *Belleisle* remained on the Kingstown station for 14 years.

Broad-beamed in relation to its length, it had an octagon-shaped central battery, whose ports were enlarged to accommodate 12-in (305 mm) 25-ton (25.4 tonne) guns, mounted in the corners. With a sister ship HMS *Orion* (ordered by Turkey as *Bourdjou-Zaffer*) it was the last in the Royal Navy to have big guns mounted in a central battery. British battle tactics required broadsides, and these vessels, with guns placed to support their prime role as rams, were not suitable for fleet actions. The ship was well-armored and twin screws made it maneuverable in calm water at least: in rough weather, especially against a head sea, it was a different story. Making headway was extremely difficult and excessive rolling made use of the guns impossible. Its bunker space was modest, allowing for some 200 tons, giving it a cruising capacity of around 1,000 miles (1,580 km).

For its crew, *Belleisle* had the unwanted distinction of being the only British capital ship never to have steam-powered capstans and steering. In original form it had a stubby funnel and two masts, square-rigged on the fore. Modifications were made in 1886 when six 3-pounder guns and two searchlights were mounted on the battery. The funnel was greatly heightened and the yards were removed from the foremast, leaving a theoretical schooner rig which was rarely if ever used.

Into Reserve as a Target Ship

From April 1893 *Belleisle* went into reserve and was finally paid off in May 1900. It was then used as a target ship for testing Lyddite-filled shells, and torpedoes. Sunk on September 3, 1903, it was raised on October 8 and the battered hulk was sold off.

SPECIFICATIONS

DISPLACEMENT: 4,870 tons (4,948 tonnes)

DIMENSIONS: 245 ft x 52 ft x 21 ft (74.68 m x 15.85 m x 6.4 m)

RIG: Two masts, square rig on foremast

PROPULSION: Twin shafts, Maudslay 2-cylinder horizontal direct acting engine, four boilers, 4,040 ihp (3,013 kW)

ARMAMENT: Four 12-in (305 mm) MLR, four 20-pounder guns; two 14-in (356 mm) torpedo launchers

ARMOR: Belt 12 in–6 in (305–152 mm), battery 10.5 in–8 in (266–203 mm), conning tower 9 in (228 mm), main deck 3 in–2 in (76–52 mm)

SPEED: 13 knots (15 mph; 24 km/h)

CREW: 250

HMS *Belleisle*

FUNNEL
MOST BRITISH WARSHIPS HAD VERTICAL
FUNNELS, BUT *BELLEISLE*'S HAD A
PRONOUNCED RAKE.

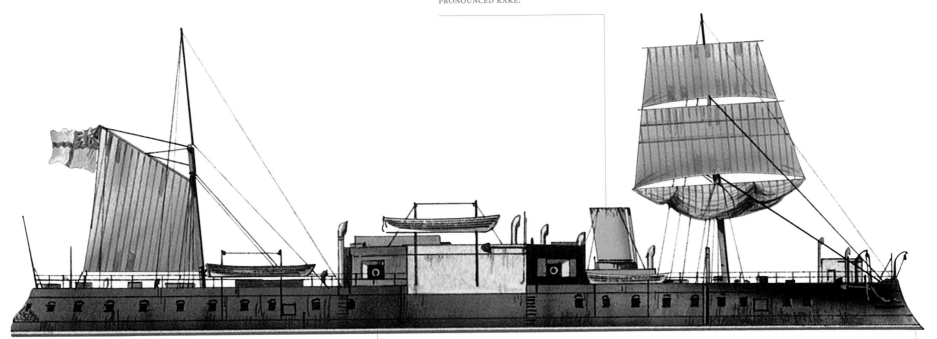

GUNS
IN THE MID-1880S THE SHIP ACQUIRED
SIX 3-POUNDER QF GUNS AND TWO
SEARCHLIGHTS.

RAM
THE RAM PROJECTED 10 FT (3 M) FORWARD
UNDERWATER, SUPPORTED BY EXTENSION OF
THE SIDE ARMOR.

HMS *Dreadnought* (1879)

COMMENCED AS *HMS* FURY, THEN ADAPTED AND RENAMED TO A CONSIDERABLY ALTERED DESIGN, *DREADNOUGHT* INCORPORATED IMPORTANT NEW FEATURES, INCLUDING COMPOUND ENGINES. *FURY* WAS LAID DOWN IN PEMBROKE DOCK, WALES, ON SEPTEMBER 10, 1870, AND CANCELLED THE FOLLOWING YEAR.

Construction was resumed to a new plan in 1872 and *Dreadnought* was launched on March 8, 1875, and completed on February 15, 1879, at a cost of £619,739. The hiatus was due to the appointment of an Admiralty Committee on Designs. The resultant ship was an enlarged and in all respects more powerful *Dreadnought*, with the breastwork extended to the full beam (in this form regarded as a "citadel") and the hull sides fore and aft raised to its height, giving a full-length flush deck. The narrow superstructure carried a broad platform with a clutter of ventilators, boats, and davits, above which rose a stubby mast with a fighting top, and two funnels. The navigation bridge extended forward, partially over the bow turret. Hydraulic machinery operated the 38-ton (38.6 tonne) 12.5-in (318 mm) MLR guns, and the turrets were revolved on the main deck by steam power.

Dreadnought was the first warship to have a longitudinal bulkhead amidships, and armor accounted for almost 34 percent of its displacement, though despite its thickness, the iron plating was inadequate by the time the ship was launched. This was the first capital ship to be equipped with compound engines, with vertical rather than horizontal cylinders, and in addition steam power worked ventilation (first warship with artificial ventilation), fire pumps, steering, capstans, and gun turrets.

In the Mediterranean

On commissioning, the ship was fitted with torpedo-launching gear and went into reserve at Portsmouth until 1884, when it was deployed in the Mediterranean until 1894. In September 1904 it had a refit at Chatham and from March 1895–March 1897 was guard ship at Bantry, Ireland. A second refit that year at Chatham gave it new boilers and heightened funnels. From July 1902 until 1905 it was a tender at Devonport, England, then placed on reserve. It was sold in July 1908 for £23,000.

SPECIFICATIONS

DISPLACEMENT: 10,886 tons (11,061 tonnes)

DIMENSIONS: 343 ft x 63 ft 8 in x 26 ft 8 in (105 m x 19.4 m x 8.2 m)

PROPULSION: Twin shafts, 12 boilers, two triple expansion engines, 8,210 shp (6,120 kW)

ARMAMENT: Four 12.5-in (318 mm) MLR guns

ARMOR: Belt 14–8in (356–203mm), turrets and conning tower 14 in (356 mm), deck 3 in (76 mm)

SPEED: 14.5 knots (16.7 mph; 26.9 km/h)

CREW: 369

HMS *Dreadnought*

MASTS
POSITIONING OF THE SINGLE MAST BEHIND THE FUNNELS WAS NOT IDEAL BECAUSE OF SMOKE, AND LATER SHIPS, LIKE THE *VICTORIA* CLASS, HAD THE MAST FORWARD OF THE FUNNELS.

ARMOR
DREADNOUGHT CARRIED THE THICKEST COMPLETE ARMOR BELT OF ANY BRITISH BATTLESHIP.

GUNS
TEN NORDENFELT MACHINE GUNS WERE ADDED IN 1884, REPLACED IN 1894 BY SIX 6-POUNDER AND TEN 3-POUNDER GUNS.

GRAY PAINT
IN 1903 GRAY PAINT REPLACED THE BLACK, WHITE, AND BUFF OF THE 19TH-CENTURY BRITISH WARSHIPS.

Caio Duilio (1880)

IN THE 1880S AND 1890S THE NAVAL ENGINEER BENEDETTO BRIN DESIGNED A SERIES OF DISTINCTIVE AND POWERFUL BATTLESHIPS FOR THE ITALIAN NAVY, PRESENTING A CHALLENGE TO DESIGNERS IN OTHER COUNTRIES.

Its name often shortened to *Duilio*, the ship was laid down at Castellammare Navy Yard, Naples, on January 6, 1873, launched on May 8, 1876, and completed on January 6, 1880. During these seven years many modifications were made to the original plan, which was for a large armored turret ship. Determination to provide it with the largest possible guns meant a sacrifice of armor weight, making the ship, and its sister *Dandolo*, vulnerable to guns of the same caliber. Even if other navies did not yet possess the 100-ton, 17.7-in (449 mm) gun, they would certainly hasten to catch up. *Duilio* had a long hull with the guns mounted centrally, but in echelon formation, the forward turret to starboard, the after one to port, between a massive military mast.

The two funnels were widely separated, rising from forward and aft superstructures. A flying walkway linked the fore and aft sections above the turrets, with a transverse bridge at the mast. Heavy armor was confined to the citadel, and was made of steel for the first time. Outside this, a system of 83 watertight compartments provided protection. A protective deck was fitted, and altogether armor accounted for 22.8 percent of displacement. A stern compartment carried a small torpedo boat, *Clio*, of 26.5 tons (27 tonnes).

Innovative Design

The fighting qualities of the class were never tested in battle. Naval experts have suggested that the hulls would not have withstood the effects of continuous firing, though the slow process of muzzle loading would have been a more obvious disadvantage in combat. Nevertheless the design of *Caio Duilio* caused naval designers in Britain and the United States to revise their ideas and future plans. In 1890 the main guns were supplemented by three 4.7-in (120 mm) guns, and in 1900 anti-torpedo boat armament was provided by two 3-in (75 mm), eight 2.2 in (57 mm)/40-caliber QF, and four 1.5-in (37 mm)/20-caliber revolving guns. *Duilio* was based primarily at Taranto, Italy. It was disarmed in June 1909, and hulked. Renumbered GM40, it was used as a floating fuel bunker, with coal and oil, before scrapping in the 1920s.

SPECIFICATIONS

DISPLACEMENT: 10,962 tons (11,138 tonnes); 12,071 tons (12,265 tonnes) full load

DIMENSIONS: 358 ft 1 in x 64 ft 9 in x 27 ft 3 in (109.16 m x 19.74 m x 8.31 m)

PROPULSION: Twin shafts, Penn vertical compound engines; 7,711 ihp (5,750 kW)

ARMAMENT: Four 17.7-in (449 mm) 20-caliber MLR guns; three 14-in (356 mm) torpedo tubes

ARMOR: Side 21.5 in (546 mm), turrets 17 in (432 mm), citadel 17 in (432 mm), deck 2 in–1.2 in (50–30 mm)

SPEED: 15.6 knots (18 mph; 29 km/h)

CREW: 420

Caio Duilio

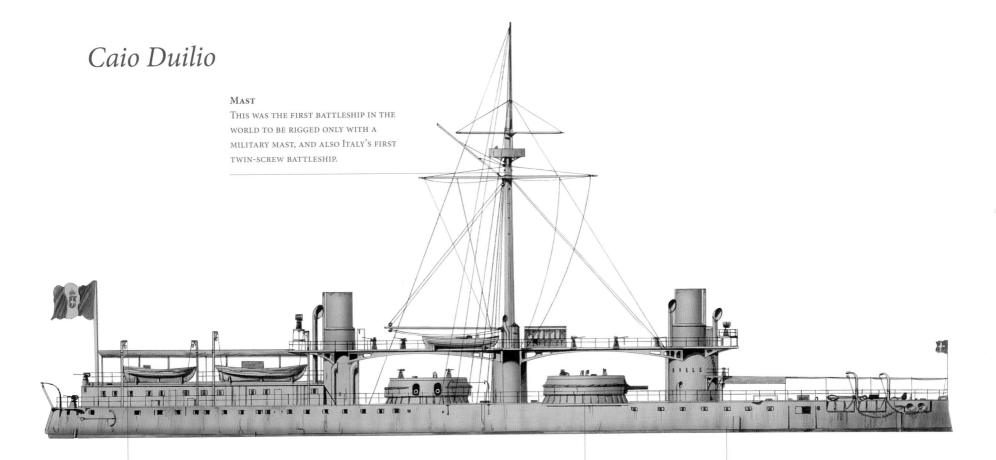

MAST
THIS WAS THE FIRST BATTLESHIP IN THE WORLD TO BE RIGGED ONLY WITH A MILITARY MAST, AND ALSO ITALY'S FIRST TWIN-SCREW BATTLESHIP.

TORPEDO BOAT
THE TORPEDO BOAT COMPARTMENT WAS A SIGNIFICANT FORERUNNER OF LATER NAVAL SHIPS WITH A STERN-DOCK FOR LANDING CRAFT.

GUNS
LOADING ARRANGEMENTS FOR THE HUGE GUNS WERE CUMBERSOME, AND RATE OF FIRE WAS SLOW: ONE SALVO EVERY 15 MINUTES.

OPERATIONAL RADIUS
THE OPERATIONAL RADIUS WAS 3,760 NAUTICAL MILES (4,327 MILES; 6,964 KM) AT 10 KNOTS (11.5 MPH; 18.5 KM/H).

Italia *(1880)*

On commissioning, *Italia* was the world's largest and fastest warship, mounting the heaviest guns yet taken to sea. It was the lead ship in the *Italia* class. She and her sister ship *Lepanto* were the largest and fastest warships in the world for years after they entered service.

Defeat by the Austrians at the Battle of Lissa, 1866, drove the Italians to further expansion of their fleet. Laid down at Castellammare in 1877 and launched in 1880, *Italia* was Brin's answer to the brief for a very fast ship, heavily armed, which could also carry an infantry division of 10,000 men and its equipment. The guns were mounted in echelon, with a main armament of four 17-in (432 mm) guns each weighing 103 tons (104.6 tonnes), firing 2,000-lb (907 kg) shells. The guns were mounted in a huge barbette of oval shape extending beyond the sides, forming an armored redoubt set diagonally across the hull. *Italia*'s sides carried no armor, relying on gun power and high speed to avoid attack.

Six funnels in sets of three, linked by high catwalks with the conning tower, a lofty central mast, and a large curved crane on the afterdeck, gave *Italia* a unique appearance. Built largely of steel, the ship internally had the now-standard armored deck, curving upwards slightly from the sides 6 ft (1.83 m) below the waterline. Above it a cellular raft ran the entire length of the ship. The space between them was lined laterally with cork-filled watertight cells separating the hull plating from an inner cofferdam on each side, and two transverse levels, one of empty cells, with coal storage space below. A double bottom was also fitted.

Obsolete in the 20th Century

Between 1905 and 1908 *Italia* was rebuilt, losing two funnels and with the tall single mast replaced by two, forward and aft of the funnels. By this time battleship development had caught up and moved on. Improved armor had disproved Brin's theory that gun power had made side-armor pointless, and the formidable guns were sadly out of date. By the 1890s the ship really ranked with armored cruisers. The secondary armament was changed and reduced in quantity. In 1909–10 it was used for torpedo training. Still in commission during World War I, but renamed as *Stella d'Italia*, it was based at Taranto and Brindisi, Italy, for gunnery training until 1917, when it was disarmed and transferred to the mercantile marine as a grain transport. It was returned to the Regia Marina in 1921, but was almost immediately sold for scrapping.

SPECIFICATIONS

DISPLACEMENT: 15,654 tons (15,900 tonnes) full load

DIMENSIONS: 409 ft x 74 ft x 28 ft 8 in (124.7 m x 22.5 m x 8.7 m)

PROPULSION: Twin shafts, 24 boilers, two vertical compound engines, 15,797 ihp (11,780 kW)

ARMAMENT: Four 17-in (432 mm) BL, seven 5.9-in (150 mm), four 4.7-in (119 mm) guns; four 14-in (356 mm) torpedo tubes

ARMOR: Redoubt 19 in (483 mm), boiler uptakes 16 in (406 mm), conning tower 4 in (102 mm), deck 4–3 in (102–76 mm)

SPEED: 17.8 knots (20.5 mph; 33 km/h)

CREW: 701

Italia

CRANE
THE MASSIVE CRANE PLACED ON THE
CENTERLINE BEHIND THE AFT FUNNELS
WAS REMOVED BY 1898 AND THE LARGER
BOATS MOUNTED IN DAVITS.

ANTI-TORPEDO DEFENSE
THE SPOTTING-TOP, WITH MACHINE GUN
AND SEARCHLIGHT, WAS PART OF THE
ANTI-TORPEDO BOAT DEFENSE.

RATE OF FIRE
THE MAIN GUNS COULD BE INDEPENDENTLY
TRAINED AND AIMED, BUT AS WITH OTHER
VERY LARGE GUNS OF THE TIME, THE RATE
OF FIRE WAS SLOW, NO MORE THAN ONE
ROUND EVERY FOUR OR FIVE MINUTES.

GUNS
UNLIKE THOSE OF HMS *INFLEXIBLE*, *ITALIA*'S BIG
GUNS WERE NOT ENCLOSED IN TURRETS BUT ROSE
ABOVE THE RIM OF THE BARBETTE.

HMS *Neptune* (1881)

ORDERED BY THE BRAZILIAN NAVY TO MAINTAIN PARITY WITH CHILE, THIS WAS ANOTHER SHIP BOUGHT IN A HURRY BY THE ROYAL NAVY IN THE WAR SCARE OF 1878. UNLIKE THE OTHERS, IT WAS A FULLY SEAGOING BATTLESHIP, BUT NOT A SUCCESSFUL ONE.

Independencia, ordered by a Brazilian naval commission from J & W Dudgeon of Millwall, London, in 1873, was laid down in 1874 but not launched until February 1878. The British government bought it for £600,000, a high price compared to the new HMS *Devastation*. Renamed *Neptune*, the ship was not finally completed until September 3, 1881, by which time a further £89,172 had been spent on it, including the cost for electric lighting.

It was something of a hybrid, a fully rigged steam turret ship, whose masts, rigging and built-up forecastle, specified by the Brazilians, seriously restricted the usefulness of the guns. These had been planned as four Whitworth 35-ton (35.5 tonne) 12-in (305 mm) in the turrets and two 8-in (203 mm) guns under the forecastle. No other Royal Navy ship had these and they were supplanted by Woolwich-built 38-ton (38.6 tonne) and 12-ton (12.2 tonne) MLR guns. Ten 20-pounder Armstrong breech-loaders were also changed for Nordenfelt guns, later themselves replaced by a final secondary battery of fourteen 6-pounder and 3-pounder QF guns spread between the forecastle, flying and poop decks. A single torpedo tube was installed on each side: originally for 16 in (406 mm) and later adapted to 14 in (356 mm).

A citadel extending the full width of the ship and 112 ft (34.1 m) long enclosed the turret bases, magazines, hatches, scuttles, and ventilation shafts. A novel feature was a forward conning tower just ahead of the foremast, a location which kept it clear of smoke but which could not be fitted with a wheel.

The machinery was old-fashioned for the late 1870s—a single set of Penn trunk engines and eight boilers operating at only 32-lb pressure.

Channel Fleet to Coastguard

Neptune served first with the Channel Fleet for two years, then in the Mediterranean. In 1886 it underwent a refit, with the removal of the mainmast and rigging, and the placing of military tops very high up, but its subsequent career was spent as coastguard ship at Holyhead, Wales, May 1887–November 1893, then ten years in reserve. Sold for £18,000 in September 1903, it hit and almost sank HMS *Victory*, and collided with HMS *Hero* while being towed out of Portsmouth. It was broken up in 1904.

SPECIFICATIONS

DISPLACEMENT: 9,130 tons (9,276.5 tonnes)

DIMENSIONS: 300 ft x 63 ft x 25 ft (91.44 m x 19.2 m x 7.62 m)

PROPULSION: one shaft, two-cylinder Penn horizontal trunk engine, eight rectangular boilers, 7,993 ihp (5,960 kW)

ARMAMENT: Four 12-in (305 mm) MLR, two 9-in (228 mm) MLR, six 20-pounder BL guns; two 14-in (356 mm) torpedo tubes

ARMOR: Belt 12 in–9 in (305–228 mm), citadel 10 in (254 mm), turrets 13 in–11 in (330–229 mm), decks 3 in–2 in (76–50 mm)

SPEED: 14.22 knots (16.4 mph; 26.3 km/h)

CREW: 541

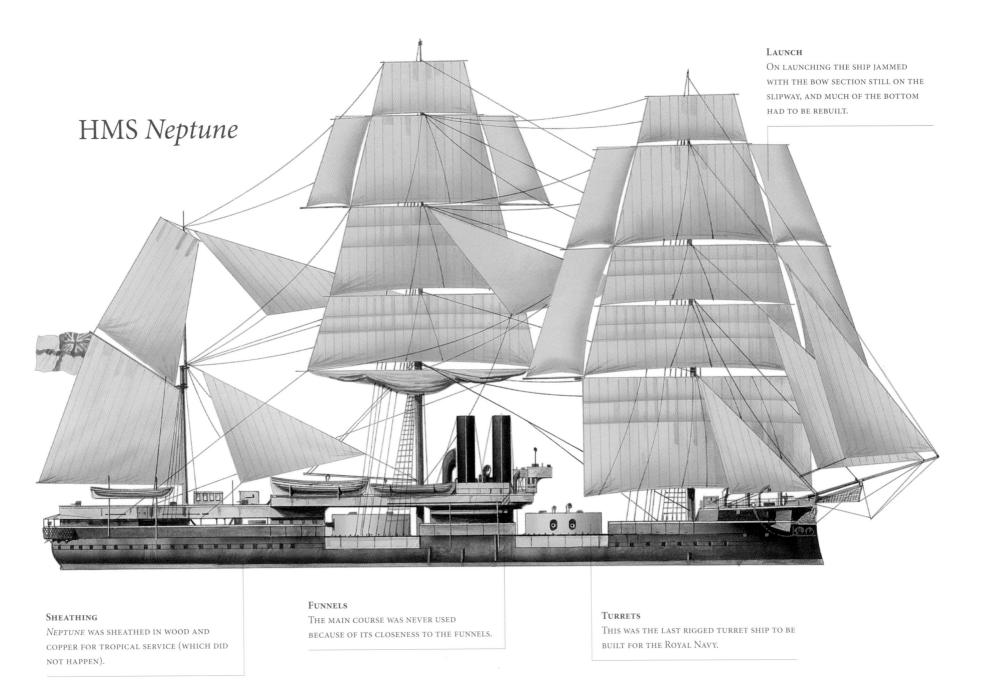

HMS *Neptune*

LAUNCH
ON LAUNCHING THE SHIP JAMMED
WITH THE BOW SECTION STILL ON THE
SLIPWAY, AND MUCH OF THE BOTTOM
HAD TO BE REBUILT.

SHEATHING
NEPTUNE WAS SHEATHED IN WOOD AND
COPPER FOR TROPICAL SERVICE (WHICH DID
NOT HAPPEN).

FUNNELS
THE MAIN COURSE WAS NEVER USED
BECAUSE OF ITS CLOSENESS TO THE FUNNELS.

TURRETS
THIS WAS THE LAST RIGGED TURRET SHIP TO BE
BUILT FOR THE ROYAL NAVY.

HMS *Inflexible* (1881)

HMS *INFLEXIBLE* WAS INTENDED TO SURPASS THE ITALIAN SHIPS *CAIO DUILIO* AND *DANDOLO*, THE MOST HEAVILY ARMORED AND FASTEST WARSHIPS OF THEIR TIME. LAID DOWN AT PORTSMOUTH ON FEBRUARY 24, 1874, *INFLEXIBLE* WAS LAUNCHED ON APRIL 27, 1876 BUT NOT COMPLETED UNTIL OCTOBER 18, 1881, AT A COST OF £812,485.

Its weakest aspect was the guns. Muzzle loaders of 16-in (406 mm) caliber, they fired a 1,684-lb (764 kg) shell capable of piercing armor 23 in (584 mm) thick at a distance of 1,000 yards (914 m). Within a few years they were outclassed by lighter, faster-firing, longer-range breech-loaders. The arrangement, modeled on *Duilio*'s, had two large twin central turrets in echelon formation, the port one set ahead of the starboard one, at opposite corners of a citadel of unprecedented armored strength, 24 in (609 mm) at the maximum.

A 3 in (76 mm) armored deck ran the length of the ship, beneath the main deck and below waterline level, in place of vertical armor along the waterline. The ship was the broadest in relation to length yet built, in order to ensure stability and give the gun turrets the maximum possible arc of fire. The forward and stern sections were not armored but subdivided into many watertight compartments with coal bunkers on each side and inner walls thickly lined with cork. This was also the first armored ship to mount underwater torpedo tubes, with two placed experimentally in the bows. Other technical advances incorporated were compound expansion engines, and dynamos for electric lighting (the first warship so fitted). In important ways, notably the full-length armored lower deck, *Inflexible* established standards which later battleships would follow, though the debt to Brin should not be forgotten.

Action in Alexandria

Perhaps as a gesture to the Italians, it was dispatched to join the Mediterranean Fleet in October 1881. At Alexandria in July 1882, it helped suppress an Egyptian uprising against the British-backed Khedive, and took a few hits from shore forts. It remained in the Mediterranean until 1885, and after refitting and a few years spent largely in reserve, returned there in 1890–93. From 1893 to 1897 it served as guard ship at Portsmouth, then went to Fleet Reserve in 1897, Dockyard Reserve in 1901, and was sold for scrapping in September 1903.

SPECIFICATIONS

DISPLACEMENT: 11,880 tons (12,071 tonnes)

DIMENSIONS: 320 ft x 75 ft x 26 ft 6 in (97.5 m x 22.9 m x 8.08 m)

PROPULSION: Twin shafts, 12 boilers, two Elder 3-cylinder compound engines, 8,407 ihp (6,269 kW)

ARMAMENT: Four 16-in (406-mm) 80-ton (81.3 tonne) MLR, six 20-pounder guns; four 14 in (356 mm) (two submerged torpedo tubes, two torpedo carriages)

ARMOR: Citadel 24–16 in (610–406 mm), bulkheads 22–14 in (559–356 mm), turrets 17–16 in (432–406 mm), deck 3 in (76.2 mm)

SPEED: 14.75 knots (17 mph; 27.3 km/h)

HMS *Inflexible*

SAILS
SAIL AREA WAS 18,500 SQ FT (1,719 SQ M). IN AN 1885 REFIT, THE RIGGED MASTS WERE ABANDONED FOR TWO POLES.

TORPEDO BOATS
AT THE STERN, TWO SINGLE-TUBE TORPEDO BOATS WERE CARRIED, LAUNCHED BY A DERRICK FROM THE AFTERMAST.

TURRETS
THE TURRETS WERE OF 33 FT 10 IN (10.3 M) DIAMETER AND WEIGHED 750 TONS (762 TONNES) APIECE; IT TOOK A FULL MINUTE FOR THEM TO MAKE A ROTATION.

ARMOR
THE ARMOR ANTICIPATED THE LATER AMERICAN "ALL OR NOTHING" SYSTEM, WITH VERY HEAVY PROTECTION ROUND THE CENTRAL CITADEL (A THIRD OF THE HULL LENGTH) PROTECTING MAGAZINES AND MACHINERY, WHILE THE ENDS OF THE SHIP WERE UN-ARMORED.

Ting Yuen (1883)

WITH ITS SISTER SHIP *CHEN YUAN*, THE DELIVERY OF THIS CENTRAL-CITADEL TURRET SHIP
MARKED A PHASE OF REORGANIZATION AND MODERNIZATION OF THE CHINESE NAVY IN THE
EARLY 1880S. IT WAS SUNK IN THE BATTLE OF WEI-HAI-WEI IN 1894.

Laid down at the Vulcan Yard in Stettin (now Szczecin, Poland), in March 1881, launched on December 28 the same year, *Ting Yuen* ("Eternal Peace") was completed by May 1883. Vulcan had just completed the central citadel ironclad *Württemberg*, of the *Sachsen* class, but in its gun arrangement the Chinese ship more closely resembled the British *Inflexible*.

Designed with "soft ends" on the form derived from the Italian *Duilio*, *Ting Yuen* had a steel hull, with two turrets mounted in echelon forward of the center, between the foremast and the leading funnel. Krupp 12-in (305 mm) BL guns were mounted. A conning tower was placed between the turrets. Secondary armament consisted of two 5.9-in (150 mm) guns mounted at the bow and stern, and three 14-in (356 mm) torpedo tubes were fitted, two forward of the citadel, one in the stern. In addition the ship carried two 16-ton (16.25 tonne) torpedo boats, though these were taken off in Chinese service.

Flagship at Battle of Yalu River

Delayed by Germany because of war between China and France, it was July 3, 1885, before the two ships left for China, joining the Peiyang (Northern) Fleet in late October, with *Ting Yuen* as flagship. In 1894 the Japanese and Chinese empires went to war over control of Korea. At the Battle of the Yalu River, *Ting Yuen* was the flagship of Admiral Ting Ju-Chang, and was hit nearly 200 times, but its unarmored bow and stern were not destroyed. Fourteen men were killed and 25 wounded. Emergency repairs were made at Port Arthur, and the fleet then moved to Wei-Hai-Wei. A final fleet sortie was made, without result, in November. *Ting Yuen*'s guns were in action in the early stages of the Japanese assault on Wei-Hai-Wei from January 20, 1895, but on February 4–5, 1895, a Japanese torpedo from TB-23 struck the stern. The ship was run ashore and possibly disabled by its crew to prevent its use by the Japanese. Later the wreck was scrapped. In 2005 a full-size replica of the ship was inaugurated at Wei-Hai-Wei.

SPECIFICATIONS

DISPLACEMENT: 7,220 tons (7,336 tonnes), 7,670 tons (7,793 tonnes) full load

DIMENSIONS: 308 ft x 59 ft x 20 ft (93.88 m x 17.98 m x 6.1 m)

RIG: Two masts, square rig on foremast

PROPULSION: Twin shafts, horizontal compound reciprocating engines, eight cylindrical boilers, 7,500 ihp (5,592.75 kW)

ARMAMENT: Four 12-in (305 mm)/20-caliber, two 5.9-in (150 mm) guns; three 14-in (356 mm) torpedo tubes

ARMOR: Belt 14 in (356 mm); barbettes 14 in–12 in (356–305 mm), casemates and conning tower 8 in (203 mm)

SPEED: Not known

CREW: 350

Ting Yuen

DECKS
DESPITE THE WIDE BEAM, THE DECKS
HAD TO BE EXTENDED OUTWARDS ROUND
THE TURRET AREA.

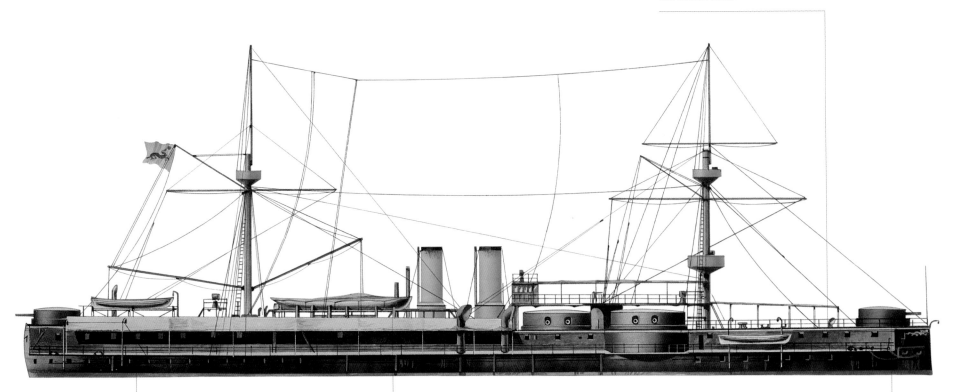

COAL BUNKERS
LATERAL COAL BUNKERS WERE ALSO INTENDED
AS PART OF THE PROTECTIVE SYSTEM.

TORPEDO BOATS
THE TORPEDO BOATS (STEAM POWERED) WERE
CARRIED AFT OF THE FUNNELS.

GUNS
THE EXTREME LOCATIONS OF THE BOW AND
STERN GUNS WAS UNUSUAL.

Aquidaban (1885)

TWO NEW BATTLESHIPS BUILT FOR THE BRAZILIAN NAVY IN THE 1880S HELPED TO MAKE IT THE STRONGEST FLEET IN AMERICAN WATERS UNTIL THE US NAVY BEGAN BUILDING CAPITAL SHIPS. BUT A NAVAL REVOLT MADE THE FLEET ITS OWN WORST ENEMY.

Samuda Brothers of London built numerous ships for foreign navies, and they followed Brazil's battleship *Riachuelo* of 1883 with *Aquidaban*, laid down on June 18, 1883, and launched on January 17, 1885. *Aquidaban* was shorter but of the same beam as *Riachuelo*, and carried the same armament, four 9.2-in (234 mm) guns mounted in two turrets, set in echelon with the forward one offset to port and the after one to starboard. It was three-masted with a full ship rig including a bowsprit—an almost obsolete feature in a ship otherwise technically up to date. Mechanical power came from two inverted compound engines; with eight boilers compared to *Riachuelo*'s ten, it was the slower ship of the two, though still faster than most.

The Armada's Revolt

Aquidaban reached Rio de Janeiro on January 29, 1886. It was involved in the vicissitudes of internal politics, with two naval revolts, 1891 and 1893–94. Between these it made a visit to the United States for the International Naval Review of 1893. In the Revolta da Armada, led by Admiral Custodio de Mello against President Floriano Peixoto, it came under attack on April 16, 1894, from torpedo boats, was hit twice, and sank in shallow water. This exploit did much to speed up anti-torpedo boat defense systems in other navies.

Refloated in June 1894, the battleship was twice renamed, as *Dezesseis de Abril*, then *Vinte Quatro de Mayo*. Between 1897 and 1898 it was extensively refitted at Stettin (Szczecin) and Newcastle, England, with the sailing rig replaced by two hollow pole masts. The original name was restored in 1900. In a further refit in 1904 the massive masts were removed and replaced by lighter masts; after this it was used primarily as a training ship. Its career ended in disaster on January 21, 1906 when the powder magazine exploded at Jacuecanga Bay, near Rio de Janeiro. Within three minutes *Aquidaban* sank. Of those on board, 212 were killed and 36 injured, with 98 survivors.

SPECIFICATIONS

DISPLACEMENT: 4,921 tons (5,000 tonnes)

DIMENSIONS: 280 ft x 52 ft x 18 ft 4 in (85.34 m x 15.85 m x 5.59 m)

RIG: Three masts, square rig

PROPULSION: Twin shafts, inverted compound engines, eight cylindrical boilers; 6,500 ihp (4,847 kW)

ARMAMENT: Four 9.2-in (234 mm), four 5.5-in (140 mm), thirteen 1-pounder guns; five 14-in (356 mm) torpedo tubes

ARMOR: Belt 11 in–7in (279–178 mm), turrets and conning tower 10 in (254 mm)

SPEED: 15.8 knots (18 mph; 29 km/h)

CREW: 277

Aquidaban

DECK
APART FROM THE FORECASTLE AND
STERN, BUILT UP AS GUN POSITIONS, THE
SHIP WAS FLUSH-DECKED.

SAILS
SAILING RIG WAS ABANDONED AROUND
THE END OF THE 1880S.

VENTILATORS
INTENDED FOR USE IN EQUATORIAL WATERS, THE
SHIP WAS WELL PROVIDED WITH VENTILATORS,
THOUGH BOILER-ROOM CONDITIONS MUST HAVE
BEEN CLOSE TO INTOLERABLE.

TORPEDO TUBES
THREE OF THE TORPEDO TUBES WERE
MOUNTED ON THE DECK, TWO IN THE HULL.

HMS *Conqueror* (1886)

CLASSIFIED AS A TURRET RAM, *CONQUEROR* WAS THE CLASSIC EXAMPLE OF THE "SHIP AS PROJECTILE." NEVER CALLED UPON TO RAM IN EARNEST, IT EARNED ITS KEEP AS AN EXPENSIVE GUNNERY TENDER. RAMMING AN ENEMY HAD ALWAYS BEEN A CAPTAIN'S LAST RESORT IN BATTLE, SO THE VICTORIAN FASHION FOR SHIPS BUILT SPECIFICALLY AS RAMS SEEMS A STRANGE ONE.

Although other weapons could be tested in safety, when the whole ship was to be considered a weapon, this was impossible. Consequently debates about the efficacy of the purpose-built ram were inconclusive. *Conqueror* was laid down at Chatham on April 28, 1879, floated on September 8, 1881, and completed in March 1886, at a cost of £401,991. A single two-gun turret pointed forward, ahead of a superstructure that extended right to the stern. A conning tower was placed—for the first time—at the front end of the superstructure, with a charthouse and bridge above it, in what would become a standard layout. Boats, including a second-class steam torpedo boat with dismountable funnel, were carried on the top deck.

Apart from the two 12-in (305 mm) BL guns, torpedoes were the main armament, with six 14-in (356 mm) above-water tubes. These were intended for use in the event of a failure to ram. Twin screws powered by inverted compound engines gave a respectable speed of 14 knots (16 mph; 26 km/h). *Conqueror* was well-armored, with the turret-base and engines enclosed in an octagonal redoubt and belt armor extending from the ram to a point 27 ft (8.2 m) from the stern.

Unseaworthy in Heavy Weather

Commissioned at Chatham on July 5, 1887, *Conqueror* took part in Queen Victoria's Jubilee Review, then went to Devonport on reserve. In 1889 it became tender to the gunnery school HMS *Cambridge*. Though taking part regularly in maneuvers up to 1894, it was never regarded as a suitable addition to the seagoing fleet because of its tendency to roll violently and the difficulty of firing its main guns because of waves coming over the bow. In good conditions it was said to handle well and to respond quickly to the wheel, essential attributes for a ram. But *Conqueror* never rammed anything.

SPECIFICATIONS

DISPLACEMENT: 6,200 tons (6,299.5 tonnes)

DIMENSIONS: 288 ft x 58 ft x 22 ft (87.8 m x 18 m x 6.7 m)

PROPULSION: Twin shafts, Humphreys & Tennant inverted compound engines, 4,500 ihp (3355.6 kW)

ARMAMENT: Two 12-in (305 mm) BL, four 6-in (152 mm) BL, seven 6-pounder QF guns; six torpedo tubes

ARMOR: Belt 12–8 in (305–203 mm), bulkhead 11 in (279 mm), citadel 12–10.5 in (305–266 mm), turret face 14 in (356 mm), conning tower 12–6 in (305–152 mm), deck 2.5–1.5 in (63–37 mm)

SPEED: 14 knots (16.1 mph; 26 km/h)

CREW: 330

HMS *Conqueror*

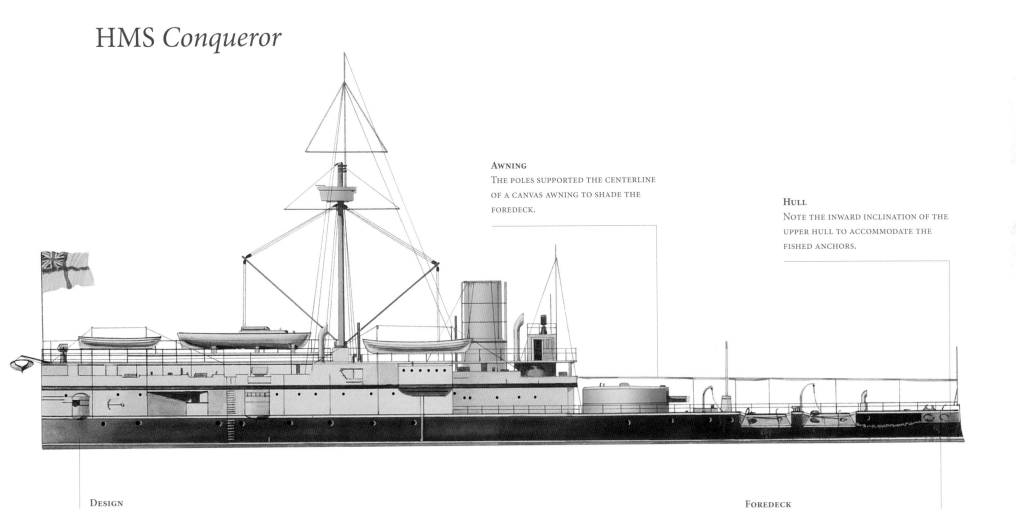

Awning
The poles supported the centerline of a canvas awning to shade the foredeck.

Hull
Note the inward inclination of the upper hull to accommodate the fished anchors.

Design
The built-up superstructure aft gives the ship a back-heavy look, but the weight of the turret and citadel more than compensated.

Foredeck
Even in a moderate sea the foredeck was likely to be awash.

HMS *Collingwood* (1887)

BIG GUNS MOUNTED HIGHER THAN EVER BEFORE IN A BRITISH SHIP, BREECH-LOADING AND MOUNTED IN BARBETTES FORE AND AFT, WITH SECONDARY GUNS GROUPED IN LATERAL BATTERIES, MADE *COLLINGWOOD* THE PATTERN FOR A GENERATION OF BATTLESHIPS.

Collingwood, Britain's first "barbette battleship," was laid down at Pembroke Dock on July 12, 1880, launched on November 22, 1882, and completed in July 1887. The cost was £636,996. The Royal Navy had finally opted for breech-loading, and four 45-ton (45.7 tonne) BL guns were set in barbettes raised above the open deck fore and aft of the superstructure, 28 ft (8.5 m) above the waterline, keeping drier in a sea, and better placed for plunging fire. Protection was less than in a turret, but many gun crews disliked the restricted space and foul air of a turret, and the open position improved sighting and laying. A substantial anti-torpedo boat armament was installed, and spotting platforms were built on the mast. Side armor was concentrated in short amidships lines extending 5 ft (1.5 m) below the waterline and 2.5 ft (0.75 m) above, linked by transverse bulkheads. The sides were lined with coal bunkers. The 6 in (152 mm) guns were set in a group, firing through gun ports. Four of the 6-pounders were placed at the corners of this battery section, with eight on the boat deck above. Ammunition was stored beneath the armored deck, with a heavily protected ammunition trunk, 10 ft (3 m) wide, passing through that deck and through the armored floor of the barbette. The gun breeches were positioned above this trunk.

Lightly Armored Design

Criticism of the design focused on its lack of armor, with the narrow waterline belt seen as inadequate. But the unarmored ends were designed to be riddled with shot and yet only flood to a limited extent, without impairing the ship's fighting ability. In addition, *Collingwood*'s guns could fire nine rounds a minute, greatly increasing its chances of disabling an enemy vessel before incurring serious damage itself.

In fact its career gave it no chance to prove its qualities in battle. Briefly commissioned for the Queen's Jubilee Review in July 1887, it was immediately put in reserve. Its longest stint of duty was nine years with the Mediterranean Fleet from November 1889 to March 1897, including a refit at the Malta dockyard in 1896. It was guard ship at Bantry from March 1897 to June 1903, then returned to reserve until March 11, 1909, when it was sold for scrap.

SPECIFICATIONS

DISPLACEMENT: 9,500 tons (9,652 tonnes)

DIMENSIONS: 325 ft x 68 ft x 26 ft 4 in (99.06 m x 20.7 m x 8.03 m)

PROPULSION: Twin shafts, 12 boilers, two sets Humphreys inverted compound 3-cylinder triple expansion engines; 7,000 ihp (5,200 kW)

ARMAMENT: Four 12-in (305 mm) BL, six 6-in (152 mm) BL guns; twelve 6-pounder, 14 small QF guns; four 14-in (356 mm) torpedo tubes

ARMOR: Belt 18–8 in (457–203 mm), barbettes 11.5–10 in (292–250 mm), conning tower 12–2 in (304–50 mm), deck 3–2 in (76–50 mm)

SPEED: 16.8 knots (19.3 mph; 31km/h)

CREW: 498

HMS *Collingwood*

COMBUSTION

THIS WAS THE FIRST RN SHIP TO EMPLOY FORCED DRAFT: INJECTING AIR INTO THE 36 FURNACES AT ABOVE ATMOSPHERIC PRESSURE, TO INCREASE COMBUSTION AND STEAM PRODUCTION. OUTPUT WAS RAISED TO 9,573 IHP (7,139 kW) BUT ADDED ONLY 0.24 KNOTS (0.28 MPH; 0.4KM/H) TO THE SPEED.

UNARMORED SECTIONS

AS AN EXPERIMENT, THE UNARMORED FORE AND AFT SECTIONS WERE FLOODED, WITH A LOSS IN SPEED OF ONLY HALF A KNOT.

GUNS

SMALL SPONSONS EXTENDED FROM THE AFTERDECK FOR LIGHT QUICK-FIRING GUNS, AND OTHERS WERE PLACED IN THE FIGHTING-TOP AND ON THE SUPERSTRUCTURE.

ARMOR

THOUGH IT WAS TERMED A "CITADEL SHIP," THE ARMORED AREA IN FACT WAS A BELT 140 FT (42.7 M) LONG AND 7 FT 6 IN (2.3 M) HIGH PROTECTING THE BARBETTES AND MACHINERY.

Terrible (1887)

FIRST OF A CLASS OF FOUR, *TERRIBLE* CONFIRMED THE FRENCH NAVY'S MOVE FROM CENTRAL BATTERY TO BARBETTE WARSHIPS. HOWEVER, ITS FIGHTING ABILITY WAS COMPROMISED BY SLOW-FIRING GUNS.

By the 1880s the concept of the central battery ship no longer met the requirements of modern navies. Guns were larger, heavier, and the French Navy had already built a barbette ship, in *Amiral Duperré* (1883) and the *Terrible* class was first of several before the (improved) turret system was restored. It was laid down at Brest, France, in December 1877, launched in 1881 and completed in January 1887—a lengthy gap typical of French naval building at the time.

With a profile formed by a breastwork between the two barbettes, a pair of massive double funnels set alongside each other, and a bipod foremast placed ahead of the superstructure and navigation bridge, the ships had a distinctive appearance. At least one of the class, *Caïman*, had three masts, though un-rigged. Also notable were the two barbette-mounted guns, each a single massive 75-ton (76.2 tonne)16.5-in (418 mm) cannon. Those of *Terrible* had to be reduced in caliber from 22 to 19.3 (see glossary) because of firing problems. In any case these were slow-firing and of less destructive power than the British 16.25-in (412 mm) gun, though the general design of the class had a strong influence on the planning of HMS *Collingwood*. *Terrible* carried steel armor, while the others in the class had the new, more effective compound armor. All had ram bows.

Coastal Defense

They were classified as first-class battleships, for coastal defense: not intended for long-range action, though a contemporary British observer noted that they could be compared to HMS *Devastation*, and were capable of a wider range of duties than coastal defense. It was suggested that with their relatively shallow draft they were intended for deployment in a Baltic offensive in any future war with Germany. *Terrible* was rearmed with two 13.4-in (340 mm)/35-caliber M1893 guns in 1898 and two of its four torpedo tubes were taken out. Although the other ships of the class survived into the 1920s, *Terrible* was stricken in 1911 and disposed of for scrap.

SPECIFICATIONS

DISPLACEMENT: 7,519 tons (7,640 tonnes)

DIMENSIONS: 278 ft 10 in x 59 ft x 24 ft 6 in (85 m x 18 m x 7.5 m)

PROPULSION: Twin shaft, triple-expansion engines

ARMAMENT: Two 16.5-in (418 mm), six 3.9-in (100 mm) guns; four torpedo tubes

ARMOR: Belt 19.7 in (500 mm), turret 9.8 in (250 mm), deck 3.1 in (80 mm)

SPEED: 15 knots (17.2 mph; 27.8 km/h)

CREW: 396

Terrible

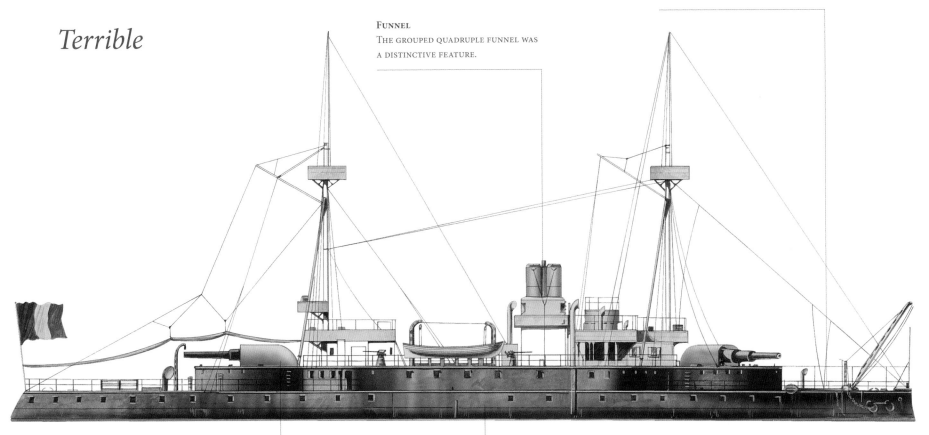

DESIGN
BY NOW FRANCE WAS NO LONGER
BUILDING RIGGED WARSHIPS.

FUNNEL
THE GROUPED QUADRUPLE FUNNEL WAS
A DISTINCTIVE FEATURE.

TURRETS
THE TURRETS, OF NOVEL SHAPE, WERE
MOUNTED ON THE CENTERLINE, AND
REVOLVED USING STEAM POWER.

ARMOR
WITH A BELT 19.7 IN (500 MM) THICK, THE CLASS
WAS AMONG THE MOST HEAVILY ARMORED OF
THE TIME.

Formidable (1888)

WITH ITS SISTER SHIP *AMIRAL BAUDIN*, THIS BARBETTE SHIP INITIATED A NEW PHASE IN FRENCH NAVAL DESIGN, COMBINING A HIGH FREEBOARD AND "TUMBLEHOME" SIDES. *FORMIDABLE* WAS LAID DOWN AT LORIENT IN SEPTEMBER 1879, LAUNCHED ON APRIL 16, 1885, AND COMMISSIONED ON DECEMBER 29, 1888.

Viewed head-on, the hull was shaped like a pear with the top sliced off: the beam at the waterline considerably wider than on the open deck. The profile was dominated by a huge single funnel and two tall masts, with a pronounced ram below. A hexagonal flying deck enclosed both the foremast and the funnel.

Three big 75.1-ton (75.3 tonne) guns, of St. Chamond manufacture (M1875), were mounted in barbettes on the centerline, with one placed midships between the funnel and the mainmast, giving lateral fire only. Light protective shields were fitted over the guns some time after completion. A solid belt of St. Etienne steel protected the hull from about 1 ft (.3 m) above the waterline to 6 ft (1.8 m) below. The upper sides were not armored, though the cellular internal arrangement was intended to localize the effects of any strike. Six to eight boats were carried, slung from davits outside and below the deck but above the tumblehome. Forced draft could be employed on the vertical compound engines. The ship carried 790 tons (802.7 tonnes) of coal fuel.

Mediterranean Flagship and Presidential Transport

On commissioning, the ship joined the Mediterranean Squadron at Toulon, as flagship. In 1890 it was used to conduct tests of captive balloons, for reconnaissance and signaling purposes. On two occasions it carried President Sadi Carnot, during maneuvers in 1890 and on a visit to Corsica in April 1891. Later in 1891 it was transferred to the Atlantic Squadron, based at Brest. Numerous modifications were made during the later 1890s. A small navigation control house was mounted on the flying deck forward of the foremast, and multiple fighting tops were placed on both masts. The central barbette was removed in 1896–98 and an armored redoubt was installed with four 6.4-in (162 mm) guns. *Formidable* was decommissioned on February 9, 1909, and stricken in December 1911.

SPECIFICATIONS

DISPLACEMENT: 11,013 tons (11,910 tonnes)

DIMENSIONS: 331 ft 4 in x 68 ft 11 in x 27 ft 10 in (101 m x 21 m x 8.5 m)

PROPULSION: Twin shafts, 12 boilers, two vertical compound engines, 9,700 ihp (7,233 kW)

ARMAMENT: Three 14.5-in (370 mm), twelve 5.4-in (138 mm) guns; six 17.7-in (450 mm) torpedo tubes

ARMOR: Belt 21.6 in (550 mm), magazine 22 in (560 mm), deck 3.9 in (100 mm)

SPEED: 16 knots (18.4 mph; 29.6 km/h)

CREW: 650

Formidable

TOPMAST

THE TOPMAST ON THE MAINMAST WAS REMOVED FOR BALLOON-FLYING TESTS: THIS WAS FOR SIGNALING PURPOSES.

FUNNEL

FUNNEL-CAPS, TO STOP FLYING LUMPS OF CLINKER AND BURNING COAL, WERE ESSENTIAL, PARTICULARLY WHEN FORCED DRAFT WAS EMPLOYED.

DESIGN

LARGE-DIAMETER POLE MASTS WOULD BE A STANDARD FEATURE OF FRENCH BATTLESHIP DESIGN.

ANCHOR

THE FISHED ANCHOR IS SUPPORTED ON BRACKETS RATHER THAN IN AN EMBRASURE.

Pelayo (1888)

A SHIP OF HANDSOME AND BALANCED PROPORTIONS, DESPITE BEING SPAIN'S ONLY UP-TO-DATE BATTLESHIP AT THE TIME OF THE SPANISH–AMERICAN WAR, *PELAYO* WAS NEVER INVOLVED IN A FLEET ACTION.

French-built, at the Compagnie des Forges et Chantiers de la Méditerranée, La Seyne, *Pelayo* was laid down in April 1885, launched on February 2, 1887, and completed in mid-1888. It was contemporary with the French *Marceau*, built in the same yard to the plans of Amable Lagane, and shared its basic features, including the bulgy tumblehome hull, the armored masts (its original design specified pole masts with yards and sails), and the diamond arrangement of guns, with two barbettes in forward and stern positions and two more to port and starboard amidships—these being sponsored out, in theory to give a wider arc of fire, though blast effects limited this in practice. In addition to external armor, the ship had a double bottom, and thirteen transverse bulkheads. *Pelayo* was longer and slightly wider than *Marceau*, but of lesser draft, so that it could traverse the Suez Canal—the shortest route to Spain's colony of the Philippines.

It had two widely-spaced funnels, with the bridge set between them. Though it extended to the sides, it was far from an ideal position for navigation. A feature, found also on many battleships when the freeboard was high enough, was an "admiral's walk" round the stern. The guns were made at the Hontoria works, near Oviedo, Spain, and the barbettes were of French Canet type, which allowed for loading in any position.

Too Late to Defend the Philippines

Pelayo spent most of its active service on ceremonial duties, making visits to Piraeus, Greece, in 1891, Genoa, Italy, in 1892, and Kiel, Germany, for the inauguration of the Kaiser-Wilhelm Canal in 1895. In 1897 the original 12 return boilers were replaced at La Seyne by 16 Niclausse boilers and the refit was barely complete when the Spanish–American War broke out in 1898. With a small squadron *Pelayo* was dispatched to hold Manila, in the Philippines, on June 16, 1898, but was recalled from Suez as Manila had already fallen. Its only use in hostilities was to fire at shore positions in the Spanish–Moroccan war of 1909. In 1912 it grounded near Mahón, Minorca, and after repairs was used only as a training ship. Decommissioned in 1923, it was scrapped in 1925.

SPECIFICATIONS

DISPLACEMENT: 9,745 tons (9,901 tonnes)

DIMENSIONS: 393 ft 7 in x 66 ft 3 in x 24 ft 11 in (120 m x 20.2 m x 7.58 m)

RIG: Two masts, schooner-type rig

PROPULSION: Twin shafts, 12 return boilers, two 2-cylinder compound engines, 9,600 ihp (7,159 kW)

ARMAMENT: Two 12.6-in (320 mm) BL, two 11-in (280 mm) BL, three 2.2-in (57 mm) QF, thirteen 1.4-in (37 mm) QF guns; 7 torpedo tubes

ARMOR: Belt 17.7–11.8 in (450–300 mm), barbettes 15.75–11.8 in (400–300 mm), conning tower 6.1 in (155 mm), deck 2.75–1.9 in (70–50 mm)

SPEED: 16.7 knots (19.2 mph; 31 km/h)

CREW: 520

Pelayo

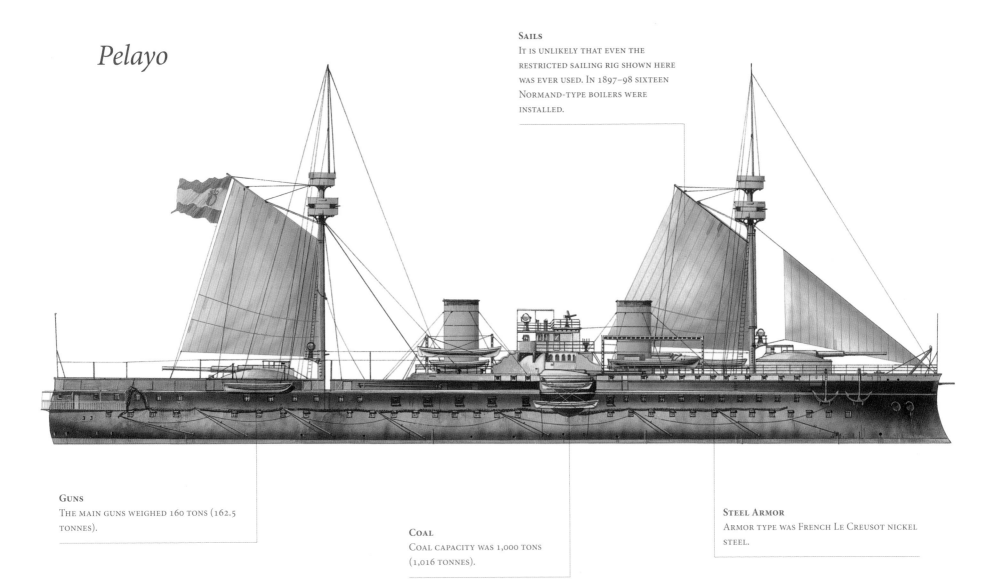

SAILS
IT IS UNLIKELY THAT EVEN THE
RESTRICTED SAILING RIG SHOWN HERE
WAS EVER USED. IN 1897–98 SIXTEEN
NORMAND-TYPE BOILERS WERE
INSTALLED.

GUNS
THE MAIN GUNS WEIGHED 160 TONS (162.5
TONNES).

COAL
COAL CAPACITY WAS 1,000 TONS
(1,016 TONNES).

STEEL ARMOR
ARMOR TYPE WAS FRENCH LE CREUSOT NICKEL
STEEL.

HMS *Camperdown* (1889)

MODELED ON HMS *COLLINGWOOD*, BUT WITH HEAVIER GUNS AND ARMOR, AND MORE POWERFUL ENGINES, THIS WAS ONE OF THREE "ADMIRAL"-CLASS SHIPS COMPLETED WITHIN THREE MONTHS OF ONE ANOTHER IN 1889.

Camperdown was laid down at Portsmouth Naval Dockyard on April 24, 1883, launched on February 17, 1886, and completed in May 1889 as the second of four ships (*Rodney* was completed in June 1888). The unusually long fitting-out period was caused by delays in constructing the new guns. Though of very similar dimensions to *Collingwood*, and of similar appearance, there were numerous differences. Barbette armor was strengthened, the belt was 10 ft longer, and the funnels were more substantial.

The main guns were 67-ton (68 tonne) 13.5-in (343 mm) BL, there was a more extensive secondary armament, and five torpedo tubes were fitted. Though the gun mountings were some 6 ft (2 m) above the weather deck, partially protected from waves by the barbettes, *Camperdown* and the other "Admirals" had the same low freeboard as *Collingwood*, which made them officially regarded as unsuitable for general fleet service as like all low-freeboard ships, they lost speed against a head sea. *Camperdown* was reported as shipping "hundreds of tons" of water when steaming into a gale.

From Flagship to Guard Ship

On July 18, 1889, the ship was commissioned and joined Home Fleet maneuvers, then after a brief spell in reserve was flagship first of the Mediterranean, then of the Channel Fleet. In late 1892 it was back in the Mediterranean and during maneuvers on June 22, 1892, through a disastrous order by the admiral in command, rammed and sank the new turret ship HMS *Victoria*; *Camperdown* came very close to capsizing. The damage was repaired by September. A large-scale refit in 1896–97 provided a second mast for signaling purposes. Further spells in reserve were followed by recommissioning in July 1900 as guard ship at Lough Swilly, Ireland, until May 1903. Its final service was as a berthing ship for submarines at Harwich, England, from October 1908 to July 11, 1911, when it was sold for breaking, for £28,000

SPECIFICATIONS

DISPLACEMENT: 10,600 tons (10,800 tonnes)

DIMENSIONS: 330 ft x 68 ft 6 in x 27 ft 3 in (100 m x 20.88 m x 8.3 m)

PROPULSION: Twin shafts, two Maudslay compound inverted engines, 11,500 ihp (8,575 kW)

ARMAMENT: Four 13.5 in (340 mm) BL guns; four 6 in (152 mm) guns; twelve 6-pounder QF guns; ten 3-pounder QF guns; five torpedo tubes

ARMOR: Belt 18–8 in (457–203 mm), bulkheads 16–7 in (406–178 mm), barbettes 11.5–10 in (291–254 mm), conning tower 12–2 in (305–50 mm)

SPEED: 17.1 knots (19.7 mph; 31.7 km/h)

CREW: 530

HMS *Camperdown*

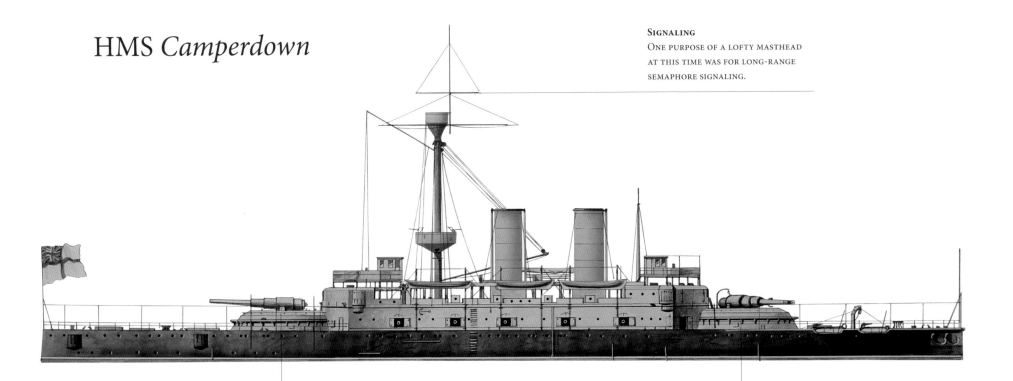

SIGNALING
ONE PURPOSE OF A LOFTY MASTHEAD AT THIS TIME WAS FOR LONG-RANGE SEMAPHORE SIGNALING.

GUNS
THE 13.5-IN (343 MM) MK II GUNS WERE 36 FT 1 IN (11 M) LONG (30 CALIBER) AND FIRED A SHELL WEIGHING 1,250 LB (567 KG) CAPABLE OF PENETRATING IRON 28 IN (712 MM) THICK AT 1,000 YARDS (914 M).

BARBETTES
BY CONTRAST WITH THE FRENCH *TERRIBLE*, THE MAIN GUNS WERE UNPROTECTED, IN OPEN BARBETTES.

Hoche (1890)

CONTEMPORARY WITH *FORMIDABLE* AND BUILT IN THE SAME YARD, ORIGINALLY CONCEIVED AS A MEMBER OF THE SAME CLASS, *HOCHE* EMERGED WITH A VERY DIFFERENT APPEARANCE. IN THE COURSE OF NINE YEARS THE DESIGN OF *HOCHE* WAS ALTERED MANY TIMES, AND IT WAS THE FIRST OF SEVERAL ONE-OFF SHIPS, KNOWN AS THE "FLEET OF TRY-OUTS."

Construction of French capital ships, never rapid because of limited resources, was further disrupted during the 1880s and 1890s by a controversy among naval designers not only as to the best form of a battleship, but whether battleships, in the age of the torpedo boat, were any longer worth their huge expense to build and maintain.

Laid down at Lorient in June 1881, launched in September 1886, it was completed in 1890 as a ship of low freeboard with a high superstructure, of four levels, a large almost-rectangular funnel, and two armored pole masts, both rising through the superstructure.

Two single guns of 13.4-in (340-mm)/28 caliber were mounted in fore and aft turrets, with decking extended over each. Two 10.8-in (274 mm) 28-caliber guns were mounted in barbettes, sponsoned out amidships on each side. Of M1881 type, its big guns were more effective than the larger guns of *Formidable*.

Unwieldy and Accident-Prone

Incident-prone, *Hoche* rammed a steamer, *Maréchal Canrobert*, off Marseilles in 1892, and grounded twice, once in the Teignouse Passage, Quiberon Bay, in 1898, and once on a shoal off Porquerolles in 1905. The high deck housing made it top-heavy and it was not permitted to travel at its maximum speed of 16.5 knots. In a refit from September 1894 to April 1895 its 5.5-in (140 mm) guns were replaced by 12 QF guns of the same caliber and the mainmast was replaced by a pole without fighting tops.

Between 1899 and 1902 a new engine and boilers were installed, the massive funnel was replaced by two oval stacks, side by side, and the superstructure was reduced. In this form *Hoche* remained in service, mostly with the Atlantic squadron, until removed from the list in May 1911. Used as a target ship, it was sunk by *Jauréguiberry* and *Pothuau* on November 25, 1913.

SPECIFICATIONS

DISPLACEMENT: 10,877 tons (11,052 tonnes)

DIMENSIONS: 337 ft 11 in x 65 ft 5 in x 27 ft 3 in (103 m x 20 m x 8.3 m)

PROPULSION: Twin shafts, two vertical compound engines, 8,120 ihp (6,055 kW)

ARMAMENT: Two 13.4-in (340 mm), two 10.8-in (274 mm), eighteen 5.5-in (140 mm) guns; 5 torpedo tubes

ARMOR: Belt 17.7 in (450 mm), barbettes 15.75 in (400 mm), deck 3.1 in (80 mm)

SPEED: 16.5 knots (19 mph; 30.5 km/h)

CREW: 650

Hoche

SUPERSTRUCTURE
THE HIGH SUPERSTRUCTURE
GAINED *HOCHE* THE NICKNAME
OF "GRAND HOTEL."

MAST
THE POLE MAST IS ARMORED: NOTE
THE OPENING FOR SIGHTING AND GUN
TRAINING.

BATTERY GUNS
FOURTEEN 5.5-IN (140 MM) GUNS WERE DISPOSED
IN BATTERY FORMATION AT THE BASE OF THE
SUPERSTRUCTURE, WITH FOUR MORE LOCATED
TWO DECKS UP.

GUN MOUNTINGS
THIS WAS THE ONLY BATTLESHIP TO COMBINE
BOTH TURRET AND RAISED BARBETTE GUN
MOUNTINGS.

HMS *Victoria* (1890)

WITH ITS SISTER SHIP HMS *SANS PAREIL*, *VICTORIA* MARKED THE BRITISH ADMIRALTY'S RETURN TO THE TURRET-SHIP CONCEPT. THE FIRST BATTLESHIP TO HAVE TRIPLE-EXPANSION ENGINES, IT HAD A SHORT CAREER ENDING IN DISASTER WHILE ON MANEUVERS.

Comparison of this ship with the French *Hoche* and *Marceau* is interesting, as they were designed with the envisaged possibility of fighting each other. Although some features were common to both, the British ships had differently shaped hulls, longer forecastles, and a different gun arrangement. *Victoria* was laid down at Elswick, England, on the Tyne, on April 23, 1885, launched on April 9, 1887, and completed in March 1890. Its main guns, two 16.25 in (413 mm) weighing 110 tons (111.7 tonnes) apiece, were mounted in a single forward turret and a single 10-in (254 mm) gun was mounted at the stern.

Lateral twin funnels were placed just behind the foremast and the navigation house, and the superstructure, with boats on top, extended to the stern, placing the rear gun higher than the main turret. Triple-expansion engines, fitted for the first time, proved very effective, but

Victoria's funnels had to be heightened by 17 ft (5.2 m) in August 1890 to improve the draft. The side armor covered 152 ft (46.3 m) and was 18 in (457 mm) thick, with a bulkhead of 16 in (406 mm) at each end. In all, *Victoria* carried 2,950 tons (2,997 tonnes) of armor. With coal capacity for a maximum of 1,000 tons (1,016 tonnes), the ship was intended for long-range work, with an operational radius of some 7,000 miles (11,265 km) at 10 knots (11.5 mph; 19.5 km/h).

Flagship's Disastrous Maneuver

Victoria was flagship of Sir George Tryon, commander-in-chief of the Mediterranean Fleet, which was steaming in two columns and approaching Tripoli on June 22, 1893, when Tryon gave the inexplicable order for the first division to alter course 16 points to starboard, and the second 16 points to port, while "preserving the order of the fleet." As a result the lead ships

converged, and *Camperdown* rammed *Victoria* behind the bow, penetrating 9 ft at a depth of 12 ft below the waterline. Watertight doors could not be secured in time, and despite an attempt to reach shallow water, the ship capsized and sank with the loss of 359 crew, including Tryon.

SPECIFICATIONS

DISPLACEMENT: 11,020 tons (11,200 tonnes)

DIMENSIONS: 340 ft x 70 ft x 26 ft 9 in (11 m x 21 m 8.15 m)

PROPULSION: Twin shafts, two Humphreys & Tennant triple-expansion engines, 8,000 ihp (6,000 kW)

ARMAMENT: Two 16.25-in (413 mm) BL, one 10-in (250 mm) BL, twelve 6-in (152 mm) BL guns; six 14-in (360mm) torpedo tubes

ARMOR: Belt 18 in (457 mm), bulkheads 16 in (406 mm), turrets 17 in (429 mm), conning tower 14–2 in (356–50 mm), deck 3 in (76 mm)

SPEED: 16 knots (18 mph; 30 km/h)

CREW: 430

HMS *Victoria*

TURRET
VICTORIA AND *SANS PAREIL* WERE THE
LAST BATTLESHIPS OF THE ROYAL NAVY
TO MOUNT ONLY A SINGLE HEAVY-GUN
TURRET.

QUARTERS
WARDROOMS AND OFFICERS'
ACCOMMODATION WERE AT THE STERN,
MEN FORWARD; OPERATING AS A FLAGSHIP,
VICTORIA PACKED IN 583 CREW.

COAL BUNKER
LATERAL COAL BUNKERS WERE ALSO PART OF
THE PROTECTION SYSTEM.

TORPEDO TUBES
THE BELOW-WATERLINE TORPEDO TUBES
COULD BE TRAINED TO FIRE ABEAM.

Marceau (1891)

THE *MARCEAU* WAS A MORE HEAVILY GUNNED VERSION OF *HOCHE*, BUT WITH A LOWER PROFILE. ORIGINALLY INTENDED TO HAVE TURRET AND BARBETTE-MOUNTED GUNS, IT WAS FINALLY COMPLETED AS AN ALL-BARBETTE SHIP.

Although the announcement in 1880 of four new French battleships to be built caused some excitement among other naval powers, long delay in construction ensured that by the time they appeared, they were in many respects obsolescent.

Marceau is often considered as a class leader, with *Neptune* and *Magenta* following. All were of very much the same tonnage and dimensions, similarly armored and armed, with the typical diamond arrangement of big guns, and with the same shape of outward-bulging hull. All three were completed between 1891 and 1893: *Marceau* was laid down at La Seyne in 1881, but the French Navy's controversy over the necessity for battleship construction delayed building; it was launched on May 24, 1887, and completed on March 14, 1891.

Unlike the other two, it had a relatively low superstructure (in the case of *Neptune* the funnel rose only a short distance above the armored deckhouse). All had "military" masts but *Marceau's* were less massive than on the others. A lattice launching frame straddled the boats while the later two had conventional davits. Some images of *Marceau* show it with a hat-like funnel cap. The ship carried two 13.4-in (340 mm) guns of M1881 and two of M1884 design.

Service in the Mediterranean

Commissioned on April 18, 1891, *Marceau* joined a squadron that made visits to Portsmouth in England and Kronstadt in Russia between May and August, and on return was deployed to the Mediterranean squadron at Toulon. The rest of its career was spent in the Mediterranean, serving with the fleet until 1900, when it underwent a substantial refit that lasted into 1902. The military masts were trimmed down considerably, and

16 Niclausse type replaced the original eight Admiralty boilers. It then went into reserve, emerging in 1906 for use as a torpedo-training school. During the 1914–18 war it was adapted and equipped as a submarine tender, based at Malta and Corfu, Greece. Decommissioned in 1920, it was sold for scrap, but broke away on tow to Toulon and was wrecked on the African coast near Bizerta.

SPECIFICATIONS

DISPLACEMENT: 10,680 tons (10,850 tonnes) full load

DIMENSIONS: 333 ft 4 in x 66 ft 4 in x 27 ft 3 in (101.6 m x 20.2 m x 8.3 m)

PROPULSION: Twin shafts, vertical triple-expansion engines, 11,169 ihp (8,215 kW)

ARMAMENT: Four 13.4-in (340 mm), sixteen 5.5-in (140 mm), seven 2.6-in (65 mm) guns; twelve 1.9-in (47 mm), eight Hotchkiss 5-barrel revolver machine guns; five 17.7-in (450 mm) torpedo tubes

ARMOR: Belt 17.7–9.1 in (450–230 mm), barbettes 17.7 in (450 mm), deck 3.1 in (80 mm)

SPEED: 16.2 knots (18.6 mph; 30 km/h)

CREW: 651

Marceau

TOPS
THE ARRANGEMENT OF SPOTTING TOPS AND
FIGHTING TOPS WENT THROUGH SEVERAL CHANGES
DURING THE LIFE OF THE SHIP.

MASTS
THE ORIGINAL PLANS SHOWED THREE POLE MASTS
WITH FORE AND AFT RIG, BUT BY THE LATE 1880S
THIS WAS DISCARDED.

DESIGN
BY COMPARISON WITH *HOCHE*, THOUGH THE
OVERALL PROFILE IS LOWER, *MARCEAU* HAS
A MUCH HIGHER FREEBOARD, MAKING IT A
MORE SEAWORTHY VESSEL.

ARC OF FIRE
THE DANGER OF BLAST DAMAGE TO THE
SUPERSTRUCTURE LIMITED THE ARC OF FIRE
OF THE END GUNS TO AROUND 180° AND
THAT OF THE MIDSHIPS GUNS TO SLIGHTLY
OVER 90°.

Imperator Alexander II (1891)

INTENDED TO ASSERT RUSSIAN DOMINATION OF THE BALTIC SEA, ITS DESIGN REFLECTED THE ONGOING DEBATE ABOUT WHETHER BIG GUNS SHOULD BE PLACED IN BARBETTES OR TURRETS. THE SHIP WAS LAID DOWN AT THE NEW ADMIRALTY YARDS, ST. PETERSBURG, IN NOVEMBER 1885 AND LAUNCHED IN JULY 1887. COMPLETION WAS NOT UNTIL JUNE 1891.

As with some French warships of the period, only a single turret, mounted forward, carried heavy guns, thus 4,750 tons (4,826 tonnes) of ship supported each 12-in (305 mm) gun; this may be compared with HMS *Collingwood*, of the same displacement, but with 2,375 tons (2,413 tonnes) per 12-in gun, though it should be added that the Russian ship's secondary armament was considerably greater than *Collingwood's*.

Designed in Russia, the ship shows less French influence than the *Borodino* class, with a long forecastle and relatively straight sides. The forecastle was inclined gently towards the bow, to enable forward fire at an enemy's hull: this was in line with the concept of ramming. In this ship the 12-in (305 mm) guns were placed in a barbette, while in its sister ship *Imperator Nikolai I*, they were turret-mounted, the different designs reflecting the ongoing uncertainty, common to all navies,

about the advantages and disadvantages of each method. The main guns were Model 1877, made at the Obukhov State Works, St. Petersburg, to a Krupp design, firing 731.3-lb (331.7 kg) shells with a maximum range of 5,570 yards (5,090 m) at an elevation of 6^0. Five torpedo tubes were carried, two in the bows, two midships, and one in the stern. The hull was of steel and the armor was up-to-date compound-type with a full-length belt. Its engines were made at the Baltic Works, St. Petersburg.

Russia's Flagship in the Baltic

Imperator Alexander II was extensively refitted at La Seyne, France, around 1900, with the secondary battery wholly replaced by five 8-in (203 mm)/45-caliber and eight 6-in (152 mm)/45-caliber guns, supplemented by ten 3-pounders. The torpedo tubes were removed. Further work, including the fitting of new boilers,

was done in Russia. It was not part of the ill-fated fleet dispatched to fight the Japanese in 1904–5 and remained as flagship in the Baltic. In 1917 it was renamed *Zarya Svobodii* ("Freedom's Dawn"). It was sold for scrapping in Germany, on August 22, 1922.

SPECIFICATIONS

DISPLACEMENT: 9,224 tons (9,392 tonnes)

DIMENSIONS: 346 ft 6 in x 66 ft 11 in x 25 ft 9 in (105.6 m x 20.4 m x 7.85 m)

PROPULSION: Twin shafts, vertical compound engines, 12 cylindrical boilers, 8,289 ihp (6,181 kW)

ARMAMENT: Two 12-in (305 mm), four 9-in (229 mm), eight 6-in (152 mm) guns; ten 1.9-in (47 mm), ten 1.5-in (37 mm) Hotchkiss revolving guns; five 15-in (381 mm) torpedo tubes

ARMOR: Belt 14–4 in (356–102 mm), bulkheads 6 in (152 mm), barbettes 10 in (254 mm), conning tower 8 in (203 mm), deck 2.5 in (64 mm)

SPEED: 15.3 knots (17.6 mph; 28.3 km/h)

CREW: 616

Imperator Alexander II

DESIGN
A TWO-LEVEL WHEEL AND CHARTHOUSE STRUCTURE IS CANTILEVERED OUT FROM THE SUPERSTRUCTURE.

BRIDGE
THE AFTER FLYING BRIDGE EXTENDS THE FULL WIDTH OF THE SHIP.

TURRET
THE "TURRET" IS REALLY A LIGHTLY ARMORED SHELTER WHICH TURNS WITH THE GUNS.

HMS *Royal Sovereign* (1892)

LEAD SHIP OF A CLASS OF SEVEN, *ROYAL SOVEREIGN* WAS THE FIRST BRITISH BATTLESHIP
TO EXCEED 12,000 TONS (12,192 TONNES) DISPLACEMENT, AND THE FIRST TO HAVE
STEEL-PLATE ARMOR.

Britain's Naval Defense Act of 1889 provided for the construction of eight large battleships of 14,150 tons (14,377 tonnes) and one of 10,500 tons (10,668 tonnes). At the time, Britain possessed 22 first-class battleships and 15 second-class; France had 14 and 7 respectively, and Russia had 7 and one. Germany, watching developments with interest, was about to expand its battleship strength. *Royal Sovereign* was laid down at Portsmouth on September 30, 1889, launched on February 26, 1891, and completed in March 1892, at a cost of £913,986.

It was a barbette rather than a turret ship and the consequent reduction in weight enabled it to ride higher in the water and to achieve a greater speed. Like some preceding capital ships, including HMS *Trafalgar*, it had two funnels side by side, placed above the division between the two boiler rooms which were set in line, with the engine room aft. As was by now standard, twin screws were fitted. The barbettes, housing four 13.5-in (343 mm) BL guns, were of similar shape and design to those of *Collingwood*, of 6-in (152 mm) armored steel, though the armored walls extended down to belt level. The secondary armament was placed in armored casemates 6 in (152 mm) thick on the main deck level, and behind gun shields on the upper deck (altered to casemates on refit in 1903). Six-pounder guns were distributed along both decks and 3-pounders were placed on the shelter deck and in fighting tops of both masts. Seven 14-in (356 mm) torpedo tubes were incorporated, but this was altered to four 18 in (456 mm) in a 1903–04 refit.

Channel Fleet to Portsmouth Guard

Initially assigned to the Channel Fleet, *Royal Sovereign* was part of the British squadron at the opening of the Kiel Canal in June 1895. From June 1897 to August 1902 it served in the Mediterranean (one of the 6-in [152 mm] guns exploded in November 1901, killing six men) and was then guard ship at Portsmouth until 1905. On reserve at Devonport from May 1905 to February 1907, it was subsequently put on "Special Service" with a skeleton crew. From April 1909 to 1913 it was in the 4th Division of the Home Fleet. In October 1913 it was sold off.

SPECIFICATIONS

DISPLACEMENT: 15,585 tons (15,835 tonnes) full load

DIMENSIONS: 380 ft x 75 ft x 28 ft (115.8 m x 22.86 m x 8.5 m)

PROPULSION: Twin shafts, eight cylindrical single-ended boilers, two 3-cylinder vertical triple-expansion engines, 9,000 ihp (6,711 kW)

ARMAMENT: Four 13.5-in (343 mm), ten 6-in (152 mm) QF, sixteen 6-pounder QF and twelve 3-pounder QF guns; seven 14-in (356 mm) torpedo tubes

ARMOR: Belt 18–14 in (457–356 mm), bulkheads 16–14 in (406–356 mm), barbettes 17–11 in (432–279 mm), casemates 6 in (152 mm), conning tower (forward) 14 in (356 mm), aft 3 in (76 mm), deck 3–2.5 in (76–63 mm)

SPEED: 18 knots (20.7 mph; 33.3 km/h)

CREW: 712

HMS *Royal Sovereign*

GUNS
THE 6-IN (152 MM) QUICK-
FIRING GUNS WERE MOUNTED IN
CASEMATES, FOR THE FIRST TIME
IN A BRITISH CAPITAL SHIP.

KEEL
BILGE KEELS HAD TO BE FITTED TO ALL THE
ROYAL SOVEREIGN CLASS TO CURE THEIR
TENDENCY TO EXCESSIVE ROLLING.

ARMOR
ROYAL SOVEREIGN'S BELT AND BARBETTE
ARMOR WAS OF COMPOUND TYPE, BUT THE
HULL PARTS BEYOND THE BELT WERE OF
NEW 5-IN (125 MM) "HARVEYISED" STEEL,
BACKED BY THE COAL BUNKERS.

ANCHORS
DOUBLE ANCHORS WERE ON THE STARBOARD
ONLY, NOT YET SECURED IN THE HAWSE-HOLES
BUT WITH EMBRASURES AT DECK LEVEL TO FISH
THEM.

SMS *Wörth* (1893)

IMPERIAL GERMANY'S NAVAL EXPANSION REALLY GOT UNDER WAY WITH THE FOUR BATTLESHIPS OF THE *BRANDENBURG* CLASS, ALL FOUR LAID DOWN IN 1890. *WÖRTH* WAS THE FIRST OF THE "BRANDENBURGS" TO BE COMPLETED, ON OCTOBER 31, 1893, HAVING BEEN LAID DOWN AT THE GERMANIAWERFT, KIEL, IN 1890 AND LAUNCHED ON AUGUST 6, 1892.

Battleships of the 1890s came to be called "pre-Dreadnoughts" though of course their designers were unaware of what was to come. Following a complete reorganization of the German Admiralty in the late 1880s, a new fleet was planned, including ships of long-range capacity able to protect, or preserve, Germany's new colonies.

Wörth was planned by Alfred Dietrich, chief designer of the Imperial Navy, and his aim was to provide modern battleships on a par with those of other navies, especially Britain's. It was armed with six 11-in (280 mm) guns, mounted in three rounded turrets; the fore and aft guns were of 40 caliber, in the central turret they were 35 caliber, the shorter barrels being necessary to let the turret to fully revolve. A hurricane deck over this turret connected the two parts of the superstructure. Lateral hull extensions on each side of the forward turret carried forward-firing 3.4-in (86 mm) guns, a feature not incorporated in subsequent German ships. Abaft of these the forward superstructure sloped inwards in an armored face protecting the secondary guns, and its after end was angled to improve the central turret's arc of fire. Two pole masts were fitted, each with long cargo booms reaching to the fighting tops.

A Show of Force in China

In February 1899 an edict of the Imperial Cabinet altered the status of the Brandenburgs from *Panzerschiff* ("armored ship") to *Linienschiff* ("ship of the battle line"). In 1900–01 all four were sent to China in a show of force at the time of the "Boxer Rising." During the 1900s *Wörth* acquired two additional 4.1-in (105 mm) guns and one of the six torpedo tubes was taken out. By 1914 the ship was obsolete and though assigned to the Fifth Squadron of the High Seas Fleet it played no part in World War I. In 1915 it was reclassed as a coastal defense ship, then disarmed in 1915 and used as an accommodation ship (as was *Brandenburg*), in Danzig (now Gdansk, Poland). It was broken up in 1919.

SPECIFICATIONS

DISPLACEMENT: 10,500 tons (10,670 tonnes)

DIMENSIONS: 379 ft 7 in x 64 ft x 24 ft 11 in (115.7 m x 19.5 m x 7.6 m)

PROPULSION: Twin shafts, triple expansion engines, 10,000 ihp (7,457 kW)

ARMAMENT: Four 11-in (280 mm)/40-caliber, two 11-in (280 mm)/35-caliber, eight 4.1-in (105 mm), eight 3.4-in (86 mm) guns; six 17.7 in (450 mm) torpedo tubes

ARMOR: Belt 16–12 in (406–305 mm), turrets 9 in (230 mm), deck 3 in (76 mm)

SPEED: 17 knots (20 mph; 31 km/h)

CREW: 568

SMS *Wörth*

RADIO
Wörth AND ITS SISTER SHIPS WERE
THE FIRST GERMAN WARSHIPS TO BE
FITTED WITH RADIO APPARATUS.

TURRETS
THE TURRETS, THOUGH IMPOSING,
WERE RELATIVELY LIGHTLY ARMORED.
THEY COULD BE RE-LOADED ONLY IN
FORE-AND-AFT (OR STRAIGHT LATERAL)
POSITION.

WHITE SHIP
THE SHIP WAS INITIALLY PAINTED WHITE,
WITH GRAY UPPER WORKS.

ARMOR
THE ARMOR WAS COMPOUND-TYPE; SISTER SHIPS
WEISSENBURG AND *KURFÜRST FRIEDRICH WILHELM*
HAD SUPERIOR KRUPP CEMENTED ARMOR.

Re Umberto (1893)

ITALY'S FIRST ALL-STEEL BATTLESHIP, *RE UMBERTO* INCORPORATED MANY IDEAS OF BENEDETTO BRIN IN A DESIGN THAT WAS A SUBSTANTIAL ADVANCE ON ITS PREDECESSORS OF THE *ITALIA* AND *RUGGIERO DI LAURIA* CLASSES.

Among the largest warships of the time, *Re Umberto* was laid down at Castellammare Navy Yard, Naples, on July 10, 1884, launched on October 17, 1888, and completed on February 16, 1893. It was a barbette ship, resembling the British "Admiral" class, with big guns placed in two barbettes, fore and aft, built up from a low-freeboard hull. The secondary guns were placed in a slope-sided redoubt amidships. It had triple funnels, the front two abreast of each other, the third placed well to the stern, with a single tall pole mast equidistant between them.

The 13.5-in (343 mm)/30-caliber Mk IV guns were manufactured by Armstrongs in England, based on those supplied for the "Admirals." Brin had planned for limited armoring over vital parts, as with *Italia* and *Duilio*, based partly on the ship's ability to make 18.5 knots (21.3 mph; 34.3 km/h), but the increasing use of medium-caliber QF guns in other navies, firing explosive armor-piercing shells, compelled a rethink and the installation of 4-in (102 mm) side armor, a very limited safeguard. Gun shields were also mounted on the barbettes, giving the appearance of turrets though again of only 4 in (102 mm) thickness. It was classified as a first-class battleship, and completion of the third in the class, Sardegna, in 1895 gave Italy ten ships designated "first class," compared with four German, five Russian, ten French, and 19 British.

A Diplomatic Mission

Re Umberto's service consisted primarily of fleet maneuvers and diplomatic visits. It was on active service in the Italian–Turkish war of 1911–12 which resulted in Italy's acquisition of Libya, but in October 1912 it was laid up at Genoa and used as a depot ship there and at La Spezia, Italy. Decommissioned in 1914, it was recommissioned on December 9, 1915, and converted to a floating battery first at Brindisi, then at Valona (Vlorë, Albania). A 1918 project to use it as an assault ship on Pola (Pula, Croatia), Austria's main naval base, was abandoned with the end of the war in November. It was finally stricken on July 4, 1920, and broken up.

SPECIFICATIONS

DISPLACEMENT: 13,673 tons (13,892 tonnes); 15,454 tons (15,702 tonnes) full load

DIMENSIONS: 418 ft 7 in x 76 ft 10 in x 30 ft 6 in (127.6 m x 23.4 m x 9.3 m)

PROPULSION: Twin shafts, vertical compound engines, 18 cylindrical boilers, 19,500 ihp (14,541 kW)

ARMAMENT: Four 13.5-in (343 mm)/30-caliber, eight 6-in (152 mm)/40-caliber, sixteen 4.7-in (120 mm), sixteen 2.2-in (57 mm), ten 1.5-in (37 mm) guns; five 17.7-in (450 mm) torpedo tubes

ARMOR: Belt and casemate 4 in (102 mm), barbettes 13.75 in (349 mm), conning tower 11.9 in (302 mm), deck 3 in (76 mm)

SPEED: 18.5 knots (21.3 mph; 34.3 km/h)

CREW: 733

Re Umberto

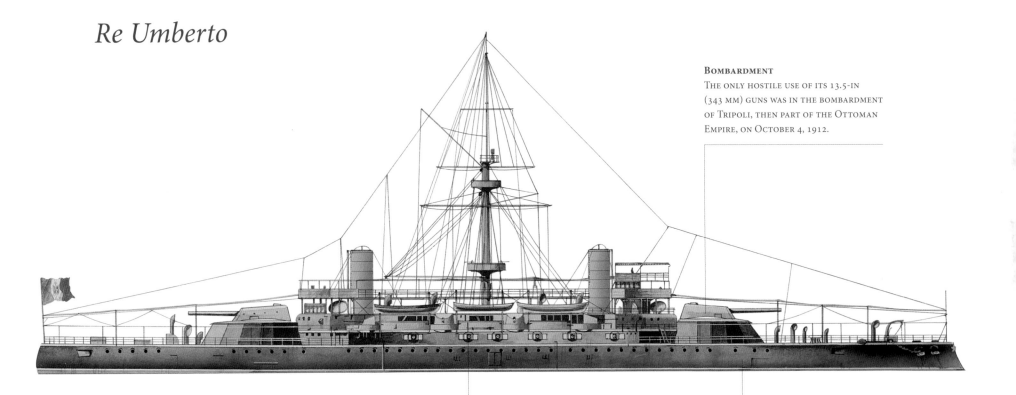

BOMBARDMENT
THE ONLY HOSTILE USE OF ITS 13.5-IN
(343 MM) GUNS WAS IN THE BOMBARDMENT
OF TRIPOLI, THEN PART OF THE OTTOMAN
EMPIRE, ON OCTOBER 4, 1912.

GUNS
FORTY-TWO GUNS OF FOUR DIFFERENT
CALIBERS WAS AN UNUSUALLY LARGE
SECONDARY ARMAMENT.

ARMOR
THE STEEL SIDE ARMOR WAS MADE
IN FRANCE BY SCHNEIDERS.

USS *Maine* (1895)

DISPATCHED TO HAVANA, CUBA, AT A TIME OF HIGH INTERNATIONAL TENSION TO "SHOW THE FLAG" AND PROTECT US INTERESTS, *MAINE* BLEW UP IN AN EXPLOSION WHOSE CAUSE WOULD REMAIN A SUBJECT OF CONTROVERSY FOR MORE THAN THREE QUARTERS OF A CENTURY.

Laid down in the New York Navy Yard as an armored cruiser on October 17, 1888, *Maine* was redesignated as a second-class battleship. Launched on November 18, 1890, it was not commissioned until September 17, 1895. Construction cost was $4,677,788. Battleships were a relatively new thing in the US Navy and those of the 1890s were officially designated as coastal, emphasizing a defensive role. Brazil had recently acquired *Riachuelo* and *Aquidabā* and the United States government felt it was essential to match these developments.

Maine's turrets were set in an elongated echelon formation, extending on sponsons, with the starboard one set well forward in front of the superstructure. The guns, set to maximum elevation of 15⁰, had a range of 20,000 yards (18,000 m). The turrets revolved on hydraulic power and could be loaded at any angle of train. The secondary armament of six 6-in (152 mm) guns was set in casemates on each side. Six-pounder guns, intended as anti-torpedo boat defense, were placed higher on the superstructure and one was installed in each fighting top. Four 18-in (457 mm) torpedo tubes were fitted, all on the main deck. The original design also provided for two single-tube torpedo boats to be carried, but these were not mounted.

Sinking of USS *Maine*

Cuba in 1897 was still a Spanish colony but an independence struggle was under way, and *Maine* was dispatched to Havana as a deliberate show of force against Spain, arriving on January 25, 1898. On February 15 at 21:40, a massive explosion in the forward part of the hull left the ship a half-submerged wreck, with 252 crew dead or missing. An attack could not be ruled out and a US court of inquiry decided that *Maine* had been blown up by a mine. Further inquiries and many theories have explored the disaster. In 1975 Admiral Hyman Rickover's report concluded that the explosion was an internal one, most probably caused by a fire in the coal bunker adjoining the reserve magazine, and that remains the likeliest explanation. The remains were raised and sunk in the open sea with full naval honors on March 12, 1914.

SPECIFICATIONS

DISPLACEMENT: 6,682 tons (6,789 tonnes)

DIMENSIONS: 324 ft 4 in x 57 ft x 21 ft 5 in (98.9 m x 17.4 m x 6.5 m)

PROPULSION: Twin shafts, eight boilers, two Palmer inverted vertical triple-expansion engines, 9,293 ihp (6,930 kW)

ARMAMENT: Four 10-in (254 mm) guns, six 6-in (152 mm) guns, seven 6-pounder, and eight 1-pounder guns; four 18-in (457 mm) torpedo tubes

ARMOR: Belt 12 in (305 mm), turrets 8 in (203 mm), conning tower 10 in (254 mm), deck 4 in (102 mm)

SPEED: 16.45 knots (19 mph; 30.47 km/h)

CREW: 374

MASTS

THE ENGINES WERE TO HAVE BEEN SUPPLEMENTED
BY SAILS ON THREE MASTS WITH A BARQUE RIG, BUT
BETWEEN LAUNCH AND COMPLETION THE THIRD MAST
WAS REMOVED AND THE OTHERS FITTED AS "MILITARY"
MASTS WITH FIGHTING TOPS AND SIGNAL YARDS.

FIGHTING TOP

EACH FIGHTING TOP HELD
A 1-POUNDER GUN, PART OF
THE ANTI-TORPEDO BOAT
DEFENSES (NOTE ALSO THE
SEARCHLIGHTS). THESE GUNS
FIRED 1.1-LB (0.5 KG) SHELLS
TO A RANGE OF APPROXIMATELY
3,500 YARDS (3,200 M).

USS *Maine*

DESIGN

WITHIN THE HULL THERE WERE 214
WATERTIGHT COMPARTMENTS. A
WATERTIGHT BULKHEAD RUNNING
LENGTHWISE SEPARATED THE TWO ENGINE
COMPARTMENTS, AND A DOUBLE BOTTOM
UNDERLAY THE CENTRAL ARMORED BOX.

TURRETS

THE TWO MAIN TURRETS WERE NOT
COUNTERBALANCED, AND IF BOTH WERE
TRAINED IN ONE DIRECTION THE SHIP HEELED.
AFTER *MAINE* AND USS *TEXAS* THE *EN ECHELON*
FORMATION WAS DROPPED.

USS *Oregon* *(1896)*

THE US NAVY'S BATTLESHIP NO. 3 MADE AN HISTORIC VOYAGE TO ENGAGE SPANISH SHIPS IN THE SPANISH-AMERICAN WAR OF 1898, AND HAD A LONG AND EVENTFUL CAREER. *OREGON* WAS LAID DOWN NOVEMBER 19, 1891, BY UNION IRON WORKS, SAN FRANCISCO, LAUNCHED ON OCTOBER 26, 1893, AND COMMISSIONED ON JULY 15, 1896, THEN FITTED OUT FOR DUTY ON THE PACIFIC STATION.

As tensions with Spain grew, on March 12, 1898, it was ordered to the East Coast. *Oregon* left San Francisco on March 19 for Callao, Peru, on May 24 it anchored off Jupiter Inlet, Florida, having had sailed over 14,000 miles (22,531 km) in 66 days. From June 1 it was with Admiral William Sampson's fleet off Santiago, Cuba, shelling military installations and helping in the destruction of Admiral Pasqual Cervera's fleet on July 3. *Oregon* then went to the New York Navy Yard for a refit, and in October sailed for the Asiatic station.

Long Service in the Pacific

Future service was all to be in the Pacific Ocean, in the Philippines, Japan, China, and the US West Coast, until decommissioning at the Puget Sound Navy Yard on April 27, 1906. Recommissioned on August 29, 1911, the ship was in and out of reserve over the

next nine years, and on July 17, 1920, was redesignated BB–3. In 1921 a movement was begun to preserve it as an object of historic and sentimental interest. From January 4, 1924, it was retained on the Navy List as a relic "unclassified." In June 1925 it was loaned to the State of Oregon, restored, and moored at Portland as a floating monument. Its naval use was not over, however.

On February 17, 1941, *Oregon* was redesignated IX–22. Struck from the Navy List on November 2, 1942, sold on December 7, it was returned to the Navy to be used as a storage hulk in connection with the reconquest of Guam, and by July 1944 it had been loaded with ammunition and towed to that island, where its hulk remained for several years.

During a typhoon on November 14–15, 1948, it broke loose and drifted to sea, located on December 8 some 500 miles (805 km) southeast of Guam and towed

back. It was sold on March 15, 1956, resold again, finally towed to Kawasaki, Japan, and scrapped.

SPECIFICATIONS

DISPLACEMENT: 11,688 tons (11,875 tonnes)

DIMENSIONS: 351 ft 2 in x 69 ft 3 in x 24 ft (107 m x 21.1 m x 7.3 m)

PROPULSION: Twin shafts, vertical inverted triple-expansion engines, four double-ended Scotch boilers, 11,111 ihp (8,285 kW)

ARMAMENT: Four 13-in (330 mm)/35-caliber, eight 8-in (203 mm)/35-caliber, four 6-in (152 mm)/40-caliber, twenty 6-pounder, six 1-pounder guns; six 18-in (457 mm) torpedo tubes

ARMOR: Belt 18–8 in (460–203 mm), main turrets 15 in (380mm), conning tower 10 in (254 mm), deck 4.5 in (110 mm)

SPEED: 16.8 knots (19.3 mph; 31.1 km/h)

CREW: 473

USS *Oregon*

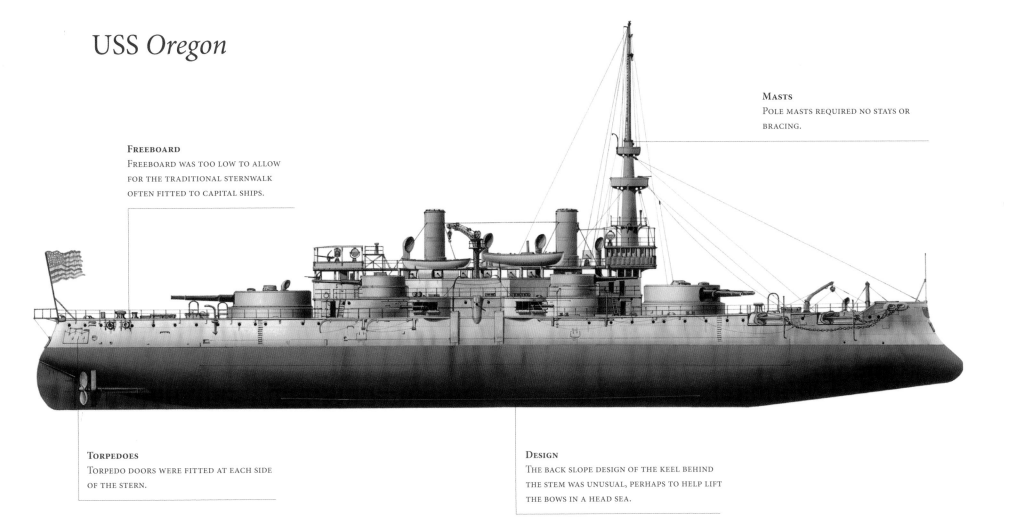

MASTS
POLE MASTS REQUIRED NO STAYS OR
BRACING.

FREEBOARD
FREEBOARD WAS TOO LOW TO ALLOW
FOR THE TRADITIONAL STERNWALK
OFTEN FITTED TO CAPITAL SHIPS.

TORPEDOES
TORPEDO DOORS WERE FITTED AT EACH SIDE
OF THE STERN.

DESIGN
THE BACK SLOPE DESIGN OF THE KEEL BEHIND
THE STEM WAS UNUSUAL, PERHAPS TO HELP LIFT
THE BOWS IN A HEAD SEA.

Jauréguiberry *(1896)*

NAMED FOR A FAMOUS NAVAL COMMANDER, *JAUREGUIBERRY* WAS OFFICIALLY CLASSIFIED AS A *CUIRASSÉ D'ESCADRES* (FLEET ARMORED SHIP) AND WAS ONE OF THE FIRST FRENCH BATTLESHIPS TO HAVE GUNS MOUNTED IN TURRETS.

Designed by the naval architect Amable Lagane, laid down at La Seyne-sur-Mer on April 23, 1891, launched on October 27, 1893, it entered service on January 30, 1896. The main guns were placed at extreme positions fore and aft. Its maximum beam was 75 ft 6 in (23 m) but the bulging tumblehome construction of the hull meant that the main deck was relatively narrow. Two massive sponsons just aft of the after funnel supported two 10.8 in (274 mm) guns. Solid Le Creusot nickel steel armor was applied in a waterline belt with a upper belt above. Positioning of the big guns gave a field of fire in all directions, with up to three able to fire a "broadside." Secondary armament was installed with anti-torpedo defense in mind, and consisted of eight 5.4-in (138 mm) guns in twin turrets placed at the four corners of the superstructure. Two vast columnar masts with fighting tops and lookout posts rose above.

Mediterranean Service

Jauréguiberry became the flagship of the Mediterranean Fleet in May 1897. In February 1904 it was transferred to Brest and the Northern Squadron, and was damaged after hitting a rock off Brest. On a visit to Portsmouth in 1905 it collided with an English steamer and in the same year suffered damage to its propellers from a torpedo accidentally fired from the *Sagaie*. During repairs in 1906 the torpedo tubes were removed. In 1907 it was based at Toulon and placed in the reserve division of the Mediterranean Squadron until April 1908. From then it remained in service alternately at Brest and Toulon, and in October 1913 became flagship of the training division. In World War I, the oldest French battleship still on the active list, it went on service in the Mediterranean, initially as a troop carrier and escort, and from March to August 1915 was French flagship in the Gallipoli campaign; then was based at Port Said, Egypt, to defend the Suez Canal, until decommissioned in 1917. On March 6, 1919, it returned to Toulon for disarming, and was struck from the list on June 20, 1920. It was used as an accommodation hulk for engineers at Toulon until 1932. In July 1934 it was sold for scrap.

SPECIFICATIONS

DISPLACEMENT: 12,036 tons (12,229 tonnes) full load

DIMENSIONS: 377 ft 4 in x 72 ft 6 in x 27 ft 9 in (112.6 m x 22.15 m x 8.45 m)

PROPULSION: Twin shafts, 24 Lagrafel d'Allest watertube boilers, two vertical inverted triple-expansion engines, 14,441 ihp (10,769 kW)

ARMAMENT: Two 12-in (305 mm), two 10.8-in (274 mm), eight 5.4-in (138 mm) guns; eight 3.9-in (100 mm) and sixteen 3-pounder guns; four 18-in (457 mm) torpedo tubes

ARMOR: Belt 15.7–6.3 in (400–160 mm), upper belt 6.7–4.7 in (170–120 mm), deck 3.5 in (90mm), main turrets 15–11 in (370–280 mm), conning tower 9.8 in (250 mm)

SPEED: 17.07 knots (19.6 mph; 32.8km/h)

CREW: 597

Jaureguiberry

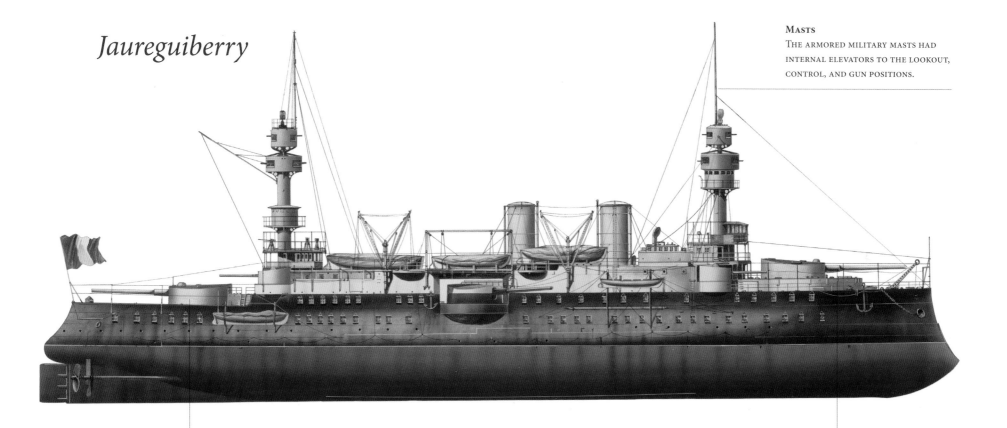

MASTS
THE ARMORED MILITARY MASTS HAD
INTERNAL ELEVATORS TO THE LOOKOUT,
CONTROL, AND GUN POSITIONS.

TURRETS
THE MAIN TURRETS EACH HELD A SINGLE GUN;
THE FRENCH NAVY WAS LAST TO MOVE TO
MULTIPLE BIG-GUN TURRETS. THE 5.4-IN
(138 MM) GUNS WERE IN TWIN TURRETS.

RANGE
THE FIRING ARC OF THE 12-IN (304-MM) GUNS WAS 250°, AND
AT MAXIMUM ELEVATION OF 15° COULD SEND A 750-LB (340
KG) SHELL 13,000 YARDS (12,000 M), WHICH WAS RATHER MORE
THAN THE MAXIMUM RANGE ANTICIPATED FOR SHIP-TO-SHIP
FIGHTING IN THE YEARS BEFORE 1910.

HMS *Renown* (1897)

THOUGH A HANDSOME SHIP, *RENOWN*'S MAIN GUNS WERE OF MODEST CALIBER COMPARED WITH ITS RIVALS. IN TERMS OF SECONDARY ARMAMENT AND ARMOR PROTECTION, HOWEVER, IT WAS WELL ENDOWED.

Renown was laid down at Pembroke Dock in February 1893, launched on May 8, 1895, and completed in January 1897, at a cost, including guns, of £751,206. It was originally intended to be given 12-in (305 mm) guns as the first of a new class, but suitable guns had not been developed by the time of fitting out, and it received 10-in (254 mm) guns, the same as its immediate predecessors, HMS *Centurion* and *Barfleur*. This lack of heavy gun power limited the ship's potential usefulness. Its design was well-balanced, with two funnels placed laterally, slightly forward of midships, two tall pole masts, and an elegant hull with a pronounced sheer both fore and aft.

Innovative Armored Design

In terms of armor it was an innovative ship. Previous warships had a level protective deck inside the hull, but here the protective deck sloped downwards at the sides to meet the lower edge of the armored belt. This aspect of design, intended to deflect incoming shells and minimize flooding, became standard both in the British and other navies. All the armor was of nickel steel.

A fast ship, capable of 19.75 knots (22.7 mph; 36.5 km/h) with forced draft applied to its triple expansion engines, and a good sea boat, *Renown* was flagship at the 1897 Jubilee Review, and on the West Indies and North America station from 1897 to 1899, and of the Mediterranean Fleet from 1899 to 1902. In the latter year the main deck 6-in (152 mm) guns were removed for a ceremonial visit by the Duke and Duchess of Connaught to India and those on the upper deck taken out during a refit in 1904 preparatory to another royal visit to India.

Its steadiness and good steaming qualities made it particularly suitable for such non-military purposes. In reserve between 1902–04 and 1906–07, when it was assigned to the 4th Division of the Home Fleet, the ship's final role was as a stokers' training vessel at Portsmouth, from 1909 to 1913. It was sold for breaking in 1914.

SPECIFICATIONS

DISPLACEMENT: 12,865 tons (13,071 tonnes) full load

DIMENSIONS: 412 ft 3 in x 72 ft 4 in x 27 ft 3 in (125.7 m x 22 m x 8.3 m)

PROPULSION: Twin shafts, vertical triple-expansion engines, eight boilers, 10,000 ihp (7,457 kW)

ARMAMENT: Four 10-in (254 mm) BL, ten 6-in (152 mm) QF, twelve 12-pounder QF, twelve 3-pounder QF guns; five 18-in (457 mm) torpedo tubes

ARMOR: Belt 8–6 in (203–152 mm), bulkheads 10–6 in (254–152 mm), barbettes 10 in (254 mm), turrets 6–3 in (152–76 mm), conning tower 9–3 in (229–76mm), deck 3–2 in (76–50 mm)

SPEED: 19 knots (22 mph; 35 km/h)

CREW: 674

HMS *Renown*

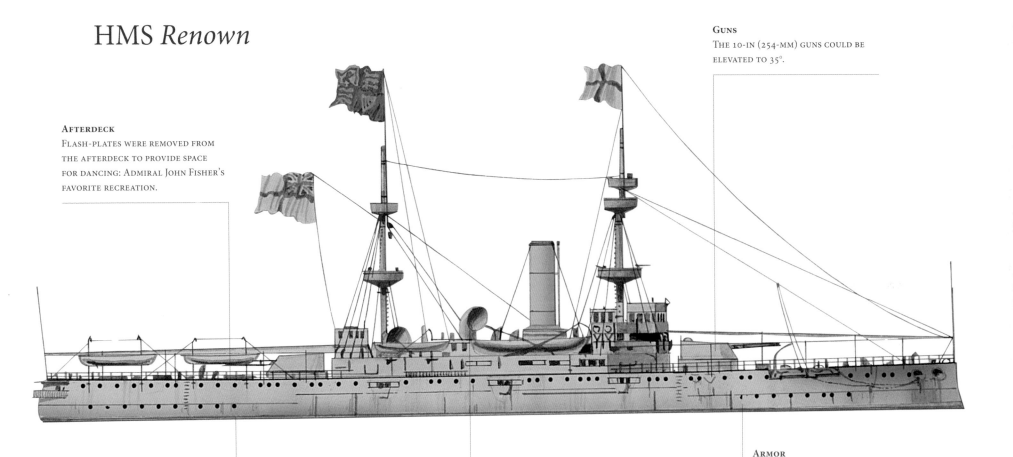

GUNS
THE 10-IN (254-MM) GUNS COULD BE
ELEVATED TO 35°.

AFTERDECK
FLASH-PLATES WERE REMOVED FROM
THE AFTERDECK TO PROVIDE SPACE
FOR DANCING: ADMIRAL JOHN FISHER'S
FAVORITE RECREATION.

ARMOR
THE INCREASING AMOUNT OF SUPERSTRUCTURE
ON BATTLESHIPS PRESENTED A BIGGER TARGET.
RENOWN WAS DESIGNED TO HAVE A WIDE
SPREAD OF ARMOR, OF THINNER BUT TOUGHER
"HARVEYISED" NICKEL STEEL.

COPPER BOTTOM
THE SHIP'S BOTTOM WAS COPPERED TO
MINIMIZE FOULING IN TROPICAL WATERS.

VENTILATOR
THE AFT VENTILATOR COWLS WERE
REPLACED BY WIND VANES DURING REFIT.

Charles Martel (1897)

FIRST OF A SERIES OF FIVE SHIPS OF BROADLY SIMILAR DISPLACEMENT AND FORM, ALL ARMED WITH TWO 12-IN (305 MM) MAIN GUNS, DIFFERING GREATLY IN DETAILS, THE *CHARLES MARTEL* WAS UNMISTAKABLY OF FRENCH DESIGN.

Charles Martel was ordered in 1882 but building was suspended until April 1891. Launched at Brest (to a new design) on August 29, 1893, it was completed in June 1897. With a ram bow and a high forecastle deck carrying the main forward turret, and with a single 12-in (305 mm) gun, it had an almost pagoda-like five-tiered foremast. Midships the sides were drawn up in a high tumblehome formation covering the central battery and topped by a flying deck through which the two funnels and tall ventilators rose, and which stretched back to make a platform round the mainmast.

The ship was armed with a considerable (perhaps too great) array of guns of different sizes. 10.8-in (274 mm) guns were mounted on sponsons flanking the after end of this castle, in the diamond arrangement, and there was a second pole mast with three platform fighting tops. A second main turret was placed just abaft

of it. The fortress-like superstructure was in fact unarmored. Protection was of nickel steel, concentrated at the waterline belt and on the gun turrets. The internal armored deck was of 2.7-in (68 mm) steel on two layers of 0.4-in (10 mm) plating at the maximum, arching up from the upper edge of the main belt and sloping towards the bow. In British opinion, though impressive in appearance, its stability in a seaway was dubious.

With the Mediterranean Squadron

The ship's service was almost entirely in the Mediterranean Squadron, either active or in reserve, apart from one joint exercise in the English Channel with the Northern Squadron in 1900. In 1900 it was flagship of the 2nd Division. In fleet maneuvers of 1901 it was struck by a dummy torpedo fired from the submarine *Gymnote*. By August 1914 *Charles Martel* had been laid

up at the Brest naval base for some years. During 1914–18 it was used as a floating barracks, and was formally taken off the Navy list in 1922. It was sold that year and towed to Holland for breaking up.

SPECIFICATIONS

DISPLACEMENT: 11,693 tons (11,880 tonnes)

DIMENSIONS: 378 ft 11 in x 71 ft x 27 ft 6 in (115.49 m x 21.64 m x 8.38 m)

PROPULSION: Two shafts, vertical triple-expansion engines, 24 Lagrafel d'Allest boilers, 14,900 ihp (11,100 kW)

ARMAMENT: Two 12-in (305 mm)/45-caliber, two 10.8-in (274 mm)/45-caliber, eight 5.5-in (137 mm)/45-caliber QF guns; four 9-pounder, twelve 3-pounder, eight 1-pounder revolvers; two 18-in (457 mm) torpedo tubes

ARMOR: Belt 18 in–10 in (457–254 mm), upper belt 4 in (102 mm), main turrets 15 in (375 mm), conning tower 9 in (228 mm)

SPEED: 18 knots (21 mph; 33 km/h)

CREW: 644

Charles Martel

DECKS
THE AFTERDECK IS AT THE HEIGHT OF
THE INTERNAL MAIN DECK.

MASTS
SUCCESSIVE CAPTAINS COMPLAINED,
WITHOUT RESULT, ABOUT THE SHIP'S
INSTABILITY CAUSED BY THE WEIGHT OF
THE ARMORED MASTS.

ARMOR
THIS WAS THE FIRST FRENCH BATTLESHIP
TO HAVE NICKEL STEEL ARMOR, MADE BY
SCHNEIDERS OF LE CREUSOT.

COMPARTMENTS
THE HULL WAS DIVIDED BY 14 TRANSVERSE
BULKHEADS INTO 209 COMPARTMENTS, OF WHICH
138 WERE WATERTIGHT.

USS *Iowa* (1897)

THE UNITED STATES' FOURTH "MODERN" BATTLESHIP, *IOWA* WAS A ONE-OFF DESIGN, BUILDING ON THE EXPERIENCE GAINED WITH THE USS *OREGON* AND OTHER TWO SHIPS OF THE PIONEERING *INDIANA* CLASS.

Known as "Battleship No. 4" until the "BB" classification of 1921, *Iowa* was laid down at William Cramp's yard, Philadelphia, on August 5, 1893, launched on March 28, 1896, and commissioned on June 16, 1897, the four years indicating that capital ship building in the United States was still a new business, though Cramp had built both USS *Indiana* and *Massachusetts*. It had a very long forecastle deck reaching almost to the after gun turret. Its four 12-in (305 mm) guns were in two main turrets. The superstructure was low, with a single military mast rising from a narrow conning tower, and bridge wings on each side. Two tall thin funnels dominated the profile. Large sponsons on each side supported the 8-in (203 mm) turrets.

Almost exactly half the length was protected by the 186-ft (56.7 m) armored belt. Powered by vertical triple-expansion engines, the ship could make 17.09 knots (19.7 mph; 31.6 km/h) with forced draft. In 1909 a cage or "basket" mainmast was added in the course of a refit in which four 4-in (102mm) guns replaced all but a couple of the 6-pounder guns.

Taking Fire at Santiago

From May 28, 1898, the ship was on blockade duty off Santiago de Cuba, with the Atlantic Fleet under Rear-Admiral William Sampson. On July 3 it participated in the battle when a squadron of six Spanish warships came out from Santiago harbor. *Iowa* was hit at least twice by Spanish shells, and fire broke out on board but was rapidly put out. Conflicting accounts of the battle were published but the most authoritative suggest that *Iowa* and the armored cruiser USS *Brooklyn* (commissioned December 1896) played major parts in the destruction of the Spanish squadron. On October 12, 1898, it was dispatched to the Pacific, and served for two years on the West Coast before duty with the South Atlantic (1902–03) and North Atlantic (1903–07) Squadrons. From May 2, 1910, to May 27, 1914, it was a seagoing training ship. On March 29, 1919, it was re-designated Coast Battleship No. 4, and on March 23, 1923, was sunk as a target ship in the Gulf of Panama.

SPECIFICATIONS

DISPLACEMENT: 11,346 tons (11,528 tonnes)

DIMENSIONS: 360 ft x 72 ft 1 in x 24 ft (110 m x 22 m x 7.3 m)

PROPULSION: Twin shafts, Cramp vertical triple-expansion engines, 12 boilers, 11,000 ihp (8,203 kW)

ARMAMENT: Four 12-in (305 mm)/35-caliber, eight 8-in (203 mm)/35-caliber, six 4-in (102 mm)/40-caliber guns; twenty 6-pounder, four 1-pounder guns; four 14-in (360 mm) torpedo tubes

ARMOR: Belt 14–4 in (356–102 mm), barbettes 15–12.5 in (381–318 mm), main turrets 17–15 in (432–381 mm), secondary 8–4 in (203–102 mm), conning tower 10 in (254 mm)

SPEED: 17.9 knots (19 mph; 31 km/h)

CREW: 727

USS *Iowa*

FUNNELS
US BATTLESHIPS OF THE PERIOD HAD NOTABLY TALL, THIN FUNNELS, INTENDED TO INCREASE DRAFT THROUGH THE FURNACES.

TURRETS
THE 12-IN (305 MM) GUN TURRETS WERE HYDRAULICALLY POWERED.

TARGET SHIP
FROM 1919, AS COAST BATTLESHIP NO. 4, IT WAS THE FIRST RADIO-CONTROLLED TARGET SHIP TO BE USED IN FLEET EXERCISES.

TRAGIC GUN EXPLOSION
ON APRIL 9, 1903, THE FORWARD PORT 12-IN (305 MM) GUN BURST DURING TARGET PRACTICE, KILLING THREE CREW MEMBERS.

Fuji *(1897)*

THE FIFTH WARSHIP OF IMPERIAL JAPAN'S NEW NAVY TO BE BUILT AT A BRITISH YARD, *FUJI* WAS BY FAR JAPAN'S LARGEST WARSHIP WHEN COMMISSIONED, THOUGH SOON OVERTAKEN IN SIZE BY THE *SHIKISHIMA* CLASS.

Fuji was built by Thames Ironworks at Poplar, London, laid down on August 1, 1894, launched on March 31, 1896, and completed on August 17, 1897. A sister ship, *Yashima*, was completed at Elswick on the Tyne a month later. HMS *Royal Sovereign* was the design model, though Japanese engineers incorporated many points of their own. The 12-in (305 mm) guns were mounted in barbettes fore and aft, with light armor protection; and four 6-in (152 mm) guns were in sponsons placed amidships, with the others on the upper deck, protected by shields. Two pole masts with broad yards were fitted, with fighting tops in which four 3-pounder guns were placed. The other sixteen 3-pounders were removed in the course of a 1901 refit and replaced by sixteen 12-pounders. Four underwater torpedo tubes were fitted, two on each broadside, and one above the waterline in the bow.

Fuji was powered by twin-shaft vertical triple-expansion engines, fired by ten single-ended cylindrical boilers. With a bunker coal capacity of 1,200 tons (1,219 tonnes) it had an operational radius of 4,000 nautical miles at a speed of 10 knots (11.5 mph; 18.5 km/h). Harvey-type nickel-steel armor was fitted.

Heavy Action in the Russo–Japanese War

Fuji and *Yashima* were both in action with Admiral Togo Heihachiro's fleet in the Russo–Japanese War of 1904–05. In the Battle of Tsushima, May 27, 1905, *Fuji* was hit twelve times and one of its main guns in the after barbette was put out of action. The other continued to be fired, and sank the Russian battleship *Borodino* in the closing phase of the battle. A major refit was done in Japan in 1910, with Japanese-made 12-in (305 mm) guns replacing the original Armstrong guns;

and new machinery powered by Miyabara water-tube boilers. As a pre-dreadnought, the vessel was downgraded to the status of coastal defense ship. But by then Japan had a new battle fleet. From 1923 it was disarmed and used as a training ship. It remained afloat until 1945, when it capsized in harbor, and was scrapped at Sasebo, Japan, in 1948.

SPECIFICATIONS

DISPLACEMENT: 12,533 tons (12,734 tonnes)

DIMENSIONS: 412 ft x 73 ft x 26 ft 6 in (125.5 m x 22.4 m x 8.07 m)

PROPULSION: Twin shafts, reciprocating vertical triple-expansion engines, 14,000 ihp (10,440 kW)

ARMAMENT: Four 12-in (305 mm); ten 6-in (152 mm); twenty 3-pounder, four 2.6-pounder guns; five 18-in (457 mm) torpedo tubes

ARMOR: Belt 18–14 in (457–356 mm), barbettes 14 in–9 in (356–228 mm), casemates 6 in–2 in (152–50 mm), conning tower 14 in (356 mm), deck 2.5 in (63 mm)

SPEED: 18 knots (20.7 mph; 33.3 km/h)

CREW: 637

Fuji

GUNS
THE 12-IN (305 MM) GUNS WERE OF SMALLER CALIBER THAN THOSE OF HMS *ROYAL SOVEREIGN*, BUT MORE POWERFUL.

HOODS
THE MAIN GUNS WERE PROTECTED BY LIGHTLY ARMORED HOODS, WHICH PROVED VULNERABLE AT TSUSHIMA.

ELEVATION
SIX OF THE 6-IN (152 MM) GUNS WERE MOUNTED AT OR ABOVE MAIN DECK LEVEL, GIVING MORE EFFECTIVE FIRING POSITIONS.

TORPEDO NETS
THE JAPANESE PRACTICED STEAMING WITH TORPEDO NETS EXTENDED, BUT DID NOT DO SO DURING THE WAR WITH RUSSIA.

SMS *Kaiser Friedrich III* (1898)

LEAD SHIP OF THE "KAISER" CLASS, IT HAD RELATIVELY LIGHT MAIN GUNS BUT A HEAVY SECONDARY ARMAMENT. FOLLOWING THE COMMISSIONING OF HMS *DREADNOUGHT*, "KAISER"-CLASS SHIPS UNDERWENT CONSIDERABLE MODIFICATION.

Laid down at the new German North Sea base of Wilhelmshaven in 1895, the ship was launched on July 31, 1896 and completed on October 7, 1898, the same day as *Kaiser Wilhelm II*, which had been launched a year later at the same yard. With their two sister ships they were products of the naval rivalry between Britain and Germany that saw both countries enlarging their battle fleets at colossal expense in the 1900s.

The "Kaisers" originally had a high and vulnerable superstructure, though on all of them it was substantially cut back between 1907 and 1910. At the same time the funnels were heightened to improve draft in the boilers and the heavy masts reduced. The main guns were four new-type Krupp 9.4-in (238 mm) guns in circular turrets firing high-velocity shells, forming a lightweight armament, though the secondary armament was unusually extensive. The forward turret

was mounted on a raised deck, 30 ft (9 m) above the waterline, and above a gun house with two 5.9-in (150 mm) guns. In a 1908 modernization four of the 5.9-in (150 mm) guns were removed, along with the stern torpedo tube, and two 8.8-in (223 mm) guns were added. Radio communication was installed.

Flagship of the *Heimatsflotte*

The ship was assigned to the 1st Squadron of the *Heimatsflotte*, precursor of the High Seas Fleet, as flagship. On January 2, 1901, it was holed by a submerged obstacle on the eastern approach to Kiel, fire broke out and the magazines and engine rooms were flooded. Repairs were made in Wilhelmshaven. In 1910 the ship was put into reserve, but recommissioned in August 1914, when the "Kaisers" formed the 5th Battle Squadron, operating in the Baltic Sea until February 1915 when they went again into reserve, being too

lightly armed and slow. In 1916 *Friedrich III* with the others was disarmed and hulked, serving first as a prison ship at Kiel, later as an accommodation ship first at Flensburg, then Swinemünde (Świnoujście, Poland). Removed from the navy list on December 6, 1919, it was broken up at Kiel in 1920.

SPECIFICATIONS

DISPLACEMENT: 10,974 tons (11,150 tonnes); 11,416 tons (11,599 tonnes) full load

DIMENSIONS: 411 ft x 67 ft x 25 ft 11 in (125.3 m x 20.4 m x 7.9 m)

PROPULSION: Triple shafts, vertical triple expansion engines, 13,000 ihp (9,694 kW)

ARMAMENT: Four 9.4-in (238 mm)/ 40-caliber, eighteen 5.9-in (150 mm), twelve 3.5-in (88 mm), twelve 1-pounder guns; six 18-in (457 mm) torpedo tubes

ARMOR: Belt 12–5.9 in (305–150 mm), turrets 9.8 in (250 mm), casemates 5.9 in (150 mm), conning tower 10 in (254 mm), deck 2.6 in (65 mm)

SPEED: 18 knots (20.7 mph; 33.3 km/h)

CREW: 687

SMS *Kaiser Friedrich III*

MAST
THE HOLLOW TOWER MAST WAS ONE
OF A NUMBER OF FEATURES BORROWED
FROM FRENCH PRACTICE.

GUNS
THE DESIGN ALLOWED FOR END-ON FIRE
FROM AS MANY GUNS AS POSSIBLE.

PROPULSION
THE CLASS INTRODUCED TRIPLE-SHAFT
PROPULSION WHICH BECAME STANDARD ON
GERMAN BATTLESHIPS.

FUEL
THIS WAS THE FIRST HEAVY GERMAN
WARSHIP TO USE OIL FUEL AS A SUPPLEMENT
TO COAL, TO HELP IN QUICK STEAM-RAISING.

HMS *Canopus* (1899)

DESIGNED FOR LONG-RANGE CRUISING, THE *CANOPUS* CLASS WERE THE ROYAL NAVY'S FIRST BATTLESHIPS TO HAVE WATER-TUBE BOILERS AND KRUPP ARMOR. THE CLASS WERE PRIMARILY USED IN THE FAR EAST TO COUNTER RISING JAPANESE POWER.

The rapid expansion of the Imperial Japanese Navy prompted the British Admiralty to introduce a new battleship class intended for the China Station, based at Hong Kong, in order to maintain British sea power at a high level. *Canopus*, first of six ships all placed in service between December 1899 and April 1902, was laid down at Portsmouth Dockyard on January 4, 1897, launched on October 12 in the same year and completed in December 1899.

An essential aspect of the design was a draft able to negotiate the Suez Canal, and a saving in weight, along with other advantages, was obtained by the use, for the first time in a British battleship, of water-tube boilers. Pioneered in France, these worked at higher pressure and were more economical on fuel than the established cylindrical boilers. Another Continental borrowing was the Krupp cemented armor in the belt and barbettes;

its thickness of 5.75 in (146 mm) equated to 7.5 in (190 mm) of American "Harveyised" armor and to 12 in (305 mm) of compound armor. The casemates on the main deck were extended out into sponsons at each end to allow end-on fire by the 6-in (152 mm) guns. A fire-control position was mounted on the foremast in 1907. In 1916, at the end of its effective career, the main-deck 12-pounder guns were replaced by two 6-in (152 mm) guns.

The Falklands and the Dardanelles Campaign

Despite being designed for the Pacific, *Canopus* never joined the China Station, serving at first in the Mediterranean, from December 1899 to April 1903, when it returned to Britain for a refit, May 1903–June 1904, then went into reserve until May 1905. It then joined first the Atlantic, then the Channel Fleet. It remained based at Portsmouth, was refitted again 1907–08

and returned to the Mediterranean from April 1908 to June 1909, when it again joined the Home Fleet. Sent as guard ship to the Falkland Islands in October 1914, it was briefly in action against von Spee's German squadron in December 1914. From January to May 1915 it served in the Dardanelles campaign. From 1916 it was used as an accommodation ship at Chatham Naval Dockyard. *Canopus* was sold in 1920.

SPECIFICATIONS

DISPLACEMENT: 13,150 tons (13,360 tonnes)

DIMENSIONS: 421 ft 6 in x 74 ft x 26 ft (128 m x 23 m x 8 m)

PROPULSION: Twin shafts, triple-expansion engines, 20 Belleville boilers, 15,400 ihp (11,484 kW)

ARMAMENT: Four 12-in (305 mm)/35-caliber, twelve 6-in (152 mm)/40-caliber QF, ten 12-pounder QF guns; four 18-in (457 mm) torpedo tubes

ARMOR: Belt 5.75 in (146 mm), barbettes 12 in (305 mm), conning tower 12 in (305 mm), deck 2 in (50 mm)

SPEED: 18.3 knots (21 mph; 34 km/h)

CREW: 682

HMS *Canopus*

WIRELESS
MARCONI WIRELESS TELEGRAPHY EQUIPMENT
WAS FITTED ON *CANOPUS* IN 1901.

MASTS
THE BROAD YARDS ON BOTH MASTS WERE
REMOVED BY 1914.

FIRING PLATFORM
THOUGH PART OF REAR-ADMIRAL CHRISTOPHER CRADOCK'S
FORCE, *CANOPUS* WAS NOT PRESENT AT THE BRITISH DEFEAT OF
CORONEL ON NOVEMBER 1, 1914 AND WAS A STATIONARY FIRING
PLATFORM AT THE FALKLAND ISLANDS ON DECEMBER 8.

RAM
IN THE ROYAL NAVY ONLY THE RAM-SHIP
HMS *POLYPHEMUS* (1875) HAD A MORE
PROMINENT RAM THAN THE *CANOPUS* CLASS,
WHICH HAD CAST-STEEL RAMS.

Charlemagne (1899)

FIRST OF A CLASS OF THREE, WITH *CHARLEMAGNE* THE FRENCH NAVY ADOPTED THE TWIN-GUN TURRETS ALREADY IN WIDE USE BY OTHER FLEETS. *CHARLEMAGNE* WAS LAID DOWN AT BREST ARSENAL ON JULY 14, 1894, LAUNCHED ON OCTOBER 17, 1895, AND COMPLETED IN DECEMBER 1899.

With its two-gun turrets it marked a step forward, though its 12-in (305 mm) M1893 guns were of 40 caliber compared to 45 caliber in the preceding, larger *Bouvet* class (1898). The turrets were turned by electric power and, unusually, were armored to a thickness greater than the bore diameter of the guns. Limitations on its displacement prevented the class from carrying 10.8-in (274 mm) guns and the secondary armament was ten 5.5-in (139 mm)/45-caliber QF.

In typical French style the sides had a pronounced tumblehome, and the central part of the 5.5-in (139 mm) battery was sponsoned out to support the gun positions. Even for the time the ship had an exceptionally bulbous bow, and the forward position of the turret made it extremely wet in even a moderate head sea. Harveyised nickel steel armor was fitted, but though the waterline belt ran the full length of the hull, it was relatively narrow, and there was no armor protection between its upper level and the battery, though internally there was a splinter-deck. Of the four torpedo tubes, the two mounted above water were removed in 1912–13, as were most of the 3-pounder guns.

Action in World War I

The ship served with both the Northern and Mediterranean Squadrons during the 1900s and was flagship in the Mediterranean from 1901, passing into reserve in October 1912 but recommissioned as a training ship in August 1913. In World War I it acted as a convoy escort in the Mediterranean and participated in the Dardanelles campaign between November 1914 and April 1915, bombarding Turkish shore forts and suffering some damage from return fire, then undergoing repairs at the Bizerta base. It remained in the Eastern Mediterranean until 1917, when it returned to Toulon and was disarmed. In 1920 it was sold for breaking.

SPECIFICATIONS

DISPLACEMENT: 11,100 tons (11,278 tonnes)

DIMENSIONS: 374 ft x 56 ft 5 in x 27 ft 6 in (114 m x 20.24 m x 8.38 m)

PROPULSION: Triple shafts, vertical triple-expansion engines, 20 Belleville boilers; 15,000 ihp (11,185.5 kW)

ARMAMENT: Four 12-in (305 mm)/40-caliber, ten 5.5-in (139 mm)/45-caliber QF, eight 3.9-in (101 mm), twenty 3-pounder, four 1-pounder guns; four 18-in (457 mm) torpedo tubes

ARMOR: Belt 14.5 in–8 in (368–203 mm), upper belt 4 in (102 mm), battery 3 in (76 mm), turrets 15 in (375 mm), conning tower 13 in (330 mm)

SPEED: 18 knots (20.7 mph; 33.3 km/h)

CREW: 694

Charlemagne

DESIGN
DESPITE THE SHIP'S MASSIVE
APPEARANCE, THE AMOUNT OF
SUPERSTRUCTURE WAS ACTUALLY
QUITE SMALL.

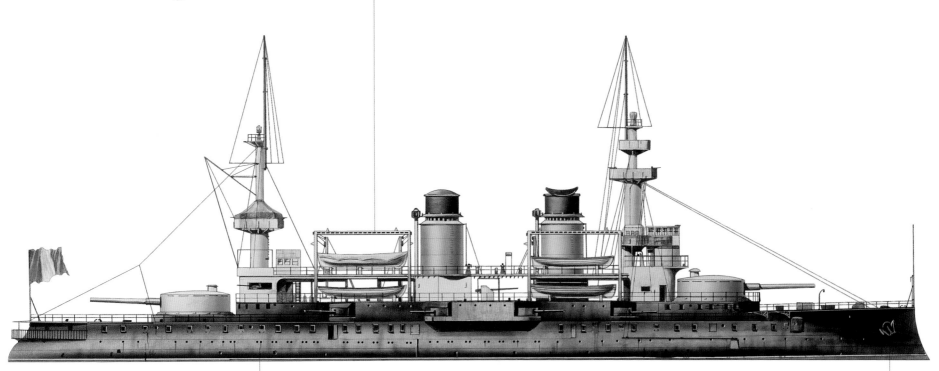

ARMOR
A COMPLETE WATERLINE BELT OF HARVEYISED
ARMOR WAS FITTED, WITH A HEIGHT OF 10 FT 8
IN (3.26 M), ITS THICKNESS TAPERING TOWARDS
THE SHIP'S EXTREMITIES.

ANCHORS
CHARLEMAGNE WAS AMONG THE FIRST
CAPITAL SHIPS TO BE FITTED WITH
STOCKLESS ANCHORS WHICH COULD BE
DRAWN UP TO THE HAWSE HOLE.

Shikishima (1900)

THE ORDERING OF *SHIKISHIMA* AND ITS SISTER SHIP *HATSUSE* MADE VERY CLEAR THAT THE JAPANESE EMPIRE WAS SET ON BECOMING A SIGNIFICANT, PERHAPS EVEN THE MOST SIGNIFICANT, NAVAL POWER IN THE WESTERN PACIFIC.

Japan's buildup of its naval strength began as a counter to the Imperial Chinese fleet, but continued after its defeat of China in 1895, to rival Russia as a power in the western Pacific. Its construction, and that of three other battleships, was paid for out of Chinese war indemnities. Though larger than the two *Fuji*-class ships, *Shikishima* and *Hatsuse* had the same main armament but a heavier battery of secondary guns.

Triple-funneled, with broad yards on both masts, they had a distinctly British look, hardly surprising as they were built in England and modeled on the British *Majestic* class turned out in 1895–98. *Shikishima* followed *Fuji* at the Thames Ironworks, London, laid down on March 29, 1897, launched on November 1, 1898, and completed on January 26, 1900. Construction was on the bracket frame system, which provided lateral spaces used for extra coal bunkers which also

served as shock absorbers against shell strikes. The ship had a double bottom and the new type of armored deck designed for HMS *Renown*, sloping up from the base of the protective belt. Internally there were 261 watertight compartments. The engines, slightly more powerful than *Fuji*'s, were of the same Humphreys Tennant type, and bunker capacity of 1,722 tons (1,750 tonnes) gave it an operational radius of 5,000 nautical miles (5,754 miles; 9,260 km) at 10 knots (11.5 mph; 18.5 km/h).

Bombardment of Port Arthur

As part of the 1st Division of the 1st Fleet, *Shikishima* joined in the bombardment of Port Arthur, on the Chinese coast, in April 1904, and the blockade of the port, and participated in the Battle of the Yellow Sea and Tsushima against the Russian fleet. In 1921 it was classed as a coast defense ship, and under the terms of the Washington

Naval Treaty was disarmed and its propellers were removed. From 1923 it was used as a floating training school, and survived until 1947, when it was scrapped at Sasebo.

SPECIFICATIONS

DISPLACEMENT: 14,850 tons (15,088 tonnes); 15,453 tons (15,701 tonnes) full load

DIMENSIONS: 438 ft x 75 ft 6 in x 27 ft 6 in (133.5 m x 23 m x 8.29 m)

PROPULSION: Twin shafts, vertical triple-expansion engines, 14,500 ihp (10,812.6 kW)

ARMAMENT: Four 12-in (305 mm), fourteen 6-in (152 mm), twenty 12-pounder QF, six 3-pounder, six 2.5-pounder guns; five 18-in (457 mm) torpedo tubes

ARMOR: Main belt 9 in–4 in (228–102 mm), upper belt 6 in (152 mm), barbettes 14 in–8 in (356–203 mm), casemates 6 in–2 in (152–50 mm), conning tower 14 in–3 in (356–76 mm), deck 4 in–2.5 in (102–63 mm)

SPEED: 18 knots (20.7 mph; 33.3 km/h)

CREW: 836

Shikishima

EXPLOSION

PREMATURE EXPLOSION OF A SHELL
IN THE BREECH WRECKED ONE OF THE
FORWARD 12-IN (305 MM) GUNS IN THE
BATTLE OF THE YELLOW SEA, AUGUST
1904; THE SAME THING HAPPENED IN
THE BATTLE OF TSUSHIMA, APRIL 1905.

BARBETTE

THE FORM OF THE BARBETTE STRUCTURE
AND SERVICE TUBE IS SHOWN IN THE
CUTAWAY.

MAGAZINES

THE MAGAZINES WERE LOW IN THE HULL,
PROTECTED BY THE BELT'S MAXIMUM
THICKNESS.

GUNS

THE 6-IN (152 MM) GUNS WERE ALL IN SINGLE
CASEMATES.

USS *Kearsarge* (1900)

BEARING AN ALREADY FAMOUS NAME, *KEARSARGE*, THE ONLY US BATTLESHIP NOT NAMED
AFTER A STATE OF THE UNION, BECAME ONE OF THE BEST-KNOWN OF AMERICAN WARSHIPS.
BUT IT ALSO HAD A VALUABLE LATER INCARNATION.

The second *Kearsarge* was laid down on June 30, 1896, at Newport News Shipbuilding Company, launched on March 24, 1898, and completed on February 20, 1900. It cost $1,849,380.

Among its innovations was 4-in (102 mm) bow armor. Another was the mounting of a powerful secondary armament, consisting of four 8-in (203 mm) guns, their turrets placed directly on top of the main turrets. The advantages were a shared barbette and hoisting trunk, and control of both turrets by a single officer. But the disadvantages included heavy weight on the main turret bearings and the likelihood of all forward guns being put out of action by one hit. Though light guns would often be placed on heavy turrets in the future, the experiment of double-deck heavy and semi-heavy guns was not repeated.

Warship of the "Great White Fleet"

Kearsarge was deployed as flagship of the North Atlantic Squadron. In the summer of 1903 it served as flagship of a special squadron on a goodwill visit to European countries. On December 1 it left New York for Guantanamo, Cuba, for the formal handover of the US base there. Further goodwill visits were to Spain and Greece in June–July 1904. *Kearsarge* was also a member of the "Great White Fleet" which showed the American flag around the world between December 16, 1907, and February 22, 1909. In September 1909 a long modernization process was begun at the Philadelphia Navy Yard and it was not back in commission until June 23, 1915, landing marines at Vera Cruz, Mexico, between September 28, 1915, and January 5, 1916. On reserve from February 4 until April 1917, it then served as a training ship while

also patrolling the East Coast between Massachusetts and Florida.

On May 10, 1920, *Kearsarge* was decommissioned and work began on converting it into a crane ship, its superstructure replaced by a giant 250-ton (254 tonne) crane for dockyard work and salvage. It raised the sunken submarine *Squalus* off the New Hampshire coast on May 23, 1939, and as Crane Ship No. 1 continued to serve after 1945, first at San Francisco, then at Boston, where it was finally stricken on June 22, 1955, and sold for scrap on August 9 that year.

SPECIFICATIONS

DISPLACEMENT: 11,540 tons (11,725 tonnes)

DIMENSIONS: 375 ft 4 in x 72 ft 3 in x 23 ft 6 in (114.4 m x 22.02 m x 7.16 m)

PROPULSION: Twin shafts, two vertical triple-expansion engines, 10,000 ihp (7,457 kW)

ARMAMENT: Four 13-in (330 mm), four 8-in (203 mm), four 5-in (152 mm), twenty 6-pounder, and eight 1-pounder guns; four 18-in (457 mm) torpedo tubes

ARMOR: Belt 16.5–5 in (419–127 mm), barbettes 15–12.5 in (381–318 mm), main turrets 17–15 in (432–381 mm), upper 11–6 in (279–15 mm), conning tower 10 in (254 mm)

SPEED: 16 knots (18.4 mph; 30 km/h)

USS *Kearsarge*

MASTS
THE LOFTY POLE MASTS WERE REPLACED
BY BASKET MASTS DURING THE 1909
REFIT.

HULL
THE WIDE HULL, WITH A RATIO TO THE SHIP'S
LENGTH OF MORE THAN 20 PERCENT, WOULD
MAKE IT VERY SUITABLE FOR CONVERSION TO A
FLOATING CRANE.

CASEMATES
THE SEVEN-A-SIDE CASEMATES
WERE A DISTINCTIVE FEATURE.
SPLINTER PROTECTION WAS
PROVIDED BETWEEN THE GUN
COMPARTMENTS.

DRAFT
IT WAS TO MAKE OPERATIONS IN SHALLOW WATERS OFF
MEXICO POSSIBLE THAT *KEARSARGE*'S DRAFT WAS LIMITED TO
23 FT 6 IN (7.16 M); FULLY LOADED, INCLUDING COAL TO ITS
MAXIMUM CAPACITY OF 1,590 TONS (1,615 TONNES), THE SHIP
WOULD UNDOUBTEDLY HAVE EXCEEDED THAT.

Peresviet *(1901)*

RUSSIA'S FIRST THREE-FUNNELED BATTLESHIP, THIS SHIP HAD THE UNIQUE FATE OF BEING SUNK TWICE, IN SUCCESSIVE WARS, BY ENEMY ACTION. FIRST OF A CLASS OF THREE, *PERESVIET* WAS LAID DOWN AT THE BALTIC WORKS, ST. PETERSBURG, ON NOVEMBER 21, 1895, LAUNCHED ON MAY 19, 1898, AND COMPLETED IN JULY 1901.

Ironically, through exaggerated intelligence reports, the *Peresviet* class, more akin to heavy cruisers though without the speed, prompted the British Admiralty to build the 12-in (305 mm) gunned *Duncan* class of first-class battleships as a response. Exceptionally high freeboard gave the ship a massive look, though the superstructure was relatively low. Two tubular French-type masts were fitted, with pole topmasts.

Four 10-in (254 mm) guns were carried in twin turrets, fore and aft. The turrets were electrically powered and the ship carried much up-to-date equipment including stadiametric rangefinders, optical gunsights developed at the Obhukov Works, and Geisler electro-mechanical transmission between fire control and guns. Vertical armor was largely of Harveyised nickel steel though Krupp cemented armor was used for the turrets and barbettes. When fully loaded,

packed in all available spaces with 2,060 tons (2,090 tonnes) of coal, *Peresviet*'s armored belt, of 7 ft 9 in (2.4 m) height, was below the waterline. Ten transverse bulkheads divided the hull into watertight compartments and a partial centerline bulkhead separated the two forward engine rooms. Though it made its design speed of 18.5 knots (21.3 mph; 34.3 km/h) on trials, its best sea speed was around 16 knots.

Sunk in Shallow Waters

On completion the ship joined the Pacific Squadron at Port Arthur as flagship of the second-in-command. In the Battle of the Yellow Sea, August 10, 1904, *Peresviet* was hit 39 times but made a safe return to Port Arthur. Eventually the Japanese established land firing positions from which to shell the Russian ships, and after taking many hits, the ship was scuttled in shallow water on December 10. Repaired

at Yokosuka Navy Yard in 1905–08, and fitted with Armstrong-type guns and Miyabara boilers, it was commissioned as *Sagami* in April 1908. Returned to Russia in 1916, it was renamed *Peresviet*. On January 4, 1917, on the way from Vladivostok to join the Arctic Squadron, it hit a mine off Port Said, planted by the German *U-73*, and sank, with the loss of 116 of its crew.

SPECIFICATIONS

DISPLACEMENT: 13,320 tons (13,534 tonnes); 14,408 tons (14,639 tonnes) full load

DIMENSIONS: 434 ft 5 in x 71 ft 6 in x 26 ft (132.4 m x 21.8 m x 7.9 m)

PROPULSION: Triple shafts, vertical triple-expansion engines, 30 Belleville boilers, 14,500 ihp (10,813 kW)

ARMAMENT: Four 10-in (254 mm), eleven 6-in (152 mm), twenty 3-in (76 mm), eight 1.5-in (37 mm) guns; five 15-in (381 mm) torpedo tubes; 45 mines

ARMOR: Belt 9–7 in (229–178 mm), turrets 9 in (229 mm), deck 3–2 in (76–51 mm)

SPEED: 16 knots (18.4 mph; 29.6 km/h)

CREW: 771

Peresviet

MAST
THE YARDS AND GAFF ON THE MAINMAST
WERE FOR SIGNALING PURPOSES, NO RIG
WAS EVER CARRIED.

FIGHTING TOPS
FIGHTING TOPS WERE REMOVED IN THE
JAPANESE RECONSTRUCTION OF 1905–08.

CONNING TOWERS
CONNING TOWERS IN RUSSIAN WARSHIPS
WERE QUITE ROOMY STRUCTURES BUT
OFFICERS PREFERRED TO REMAIN IN THE
OPEN, EVEN IN BATTLE.

HULL
THE HULL WAS SHEATHED WITH WOOD AND
COPPER TO MINIMIZE UNDERWATER FOULING.

Retvizan (1901)

RETVIZAN WAS THE ONLY RUSSIAN BATTLESHIP TO BE BUILT IN THE UNITED STATES.
SUNK BY THE JAPANESE IN 1904, IT WAS RAISED, REPAIRED, AND COMMISSIONED AS
HIZEN IN THE JAPANESE NAVY.

Laid down in William Cramp's yard, Philadelphia, in May 1898, launched in October 1900, *Retvizan* ("Justice," named for a Swedish ship captured in 1790) was completed in December 1901, two years earlier than *Kniaz Potemkin Tavricheskii*, launched in the same month at Nicolaiev, and which it closely resembled, as the design was essentially a Russian one, not by Cramp. Total construction cost was $4,360,000. It presented a long, broad, high side, with a two-level battery, topped by two pole masts, with the distinctive funnels between, their casing narrowing at around two-thirds of their height. Krupp cemented armor was used. The 12-in (305 mm) guns were made at the Obhukov Works in St. Petersburg and shipped to Philadelphia for installation. Four of the six torpedo tubes were above water, two below, mounted forward. Like some other Russian battleships, it could carry two light torpedo boats. The ship also carried 45 mines. Cramps went on to build the second USS *Maine*, with more than a superficial resemblance to *Retvizan*.

From the Russian to the Japanese Navy

Retvizan was stationed with the 1st Pacific Squadron at Port Arthur from 1902. In the Japanese attack on the Russian base on February 9, 1904, it was hit by a torpedo, shipping some 2,100 tons of water, and sustained further damage in the Battle of the Yellow Sea, on August 10, from shell fire. During the siege of Port Arthur in November–December 1904 it took thirteen hits from 11-in (279 mm) howitzer shells, and sank on December 6. After the war it was raised by the Japanese and despite extensive damage, was repaired and commissioned into the Japanese Navy as *Hizen* in 1908. Although engaged in long Pacific patrols in World War I, it saw no hostile action. Re-rated as a coastal defense ship, first-class, in September 1921, disarmed in 1922 and stricken in 1923, it was finally sunk as a target ship during exercises in the Bungo Straits, in July 1924.

SPECIFICATIONS

DISPLACEMENT: 12,900 tons (13,107 tonnes)

DIMENSIONS: 386 ft 8 in x 72 ft 2 in x 26 ft (117.8 m x 22 m x 7.92 m)

PROPULSION: Twin shafts, vertical triple-expansion engines, 24 Niclausse boilers, 17,000 ihp (12,677 kW)

ARMAMENT: Four 12-in (305 mm)/ 40-caliber, twelve 6-in (152 mm)/ 45-caliber, twenty 11-pounder, twenty-four 2-pounder, eight 1-pounder guns; six 15-in (375 mm) torpedo tubes, 45 mines

ARMOR: Belt 9 in–5 in (228–125 mm), turrets 9 in–8 in (228–203 mm), battery and casemates 5 in (125 mm), conning tower 10 in (254 mm)

SPEED: 18 knots (20.7 mph; 33.3 km/h)

CREW: 738

Retvizan

TURRETS
THE TURRETS WERE OF FRENCH TYPE,
ELECTRICALLY OPERATED. ELEVATION
WAS FROM −5° TO 15°.

GUNS
FOUR 5-BARREL 1.4-IN (37 MM)
HOTCHKISS MACHINE GUNS WERE
MOUNTED IN EACH OF THE ARMORED
FIGHTING TOPS.

TORPEDO BOATS
RETVIZAN WAS DESIGNED TO CARRY TWO LIGHT
TORPEDO BOATS, EACH WITH A SINGLE TUBE AND
LIGHTWEIGHT QF GUN.

TORPEDOES
THE FORWARD BROADSIDE-MOUNTED
TORPEDO TUBES WERE BELOW THE
WATERLINE.

Mikasa *(1902)*

ADMIRAL TOGO'S FLAGSHIP, MIKASA WAS INVOLVED IN TWO FIERCE BATTLES, IN THE
YELLOW SEA AND AT TSUSHIMA. LATER SUNK, AND RAISED, IT IS THE ONLY SURVIVING
BATTLESHIP OF THE PRE-DREADNOUGHT ERA.

Laid down at the Vickers yard at Barrow-in-Furness, England, on January 24, 1899, launched on November 8, 1900, and commissioned on March 1, 1902, *Mikasa* cost £880,000. The design was an enlarged version of the Royal Navy's HMS *Majestic*, whose plans were drawn up in 1897–98. A slightly raised forecastle topped a ram bow, and its four 12-in (305 mm) gun turrets were mounted in barbettes at each end of a casemate which housed ten 6-in (152 mm) guns, with an upper level armed with a further four 6-in (152 mm) and twenty 12-pounder guns, four of them mounted on the 6-in casemates. *Mikasa* had two pole masts fitted with derricks and radio aerials.

Battle Hardened

Mikasa's capacities were heavily tested in the Russo–Japanese war of 1904–05. In the fast-moving Battle of the Yellow Sea, August 10, 1904, it sustained around 20 shell strikes. The aft main turret was put out of action, but its machinery was undamaged. Nine months later, the Battle of Tsushima was fought in the waters between Japan and Korea on May 27–28, 1905, with *Mikasa* again as Togo's flagship. Although the Japanese had only four battleships against the Russians' eight, they had many more cruisers, destroyers, and torpedo boats—altogether 89 vessels against the Russians' 28. The result was a Nelsonian-scale victory for Togo, with 7 Russian battleships and 14 other enemy vessels sunk, for the loss of three torpedo boats. Though *Mikasa* took some forty strikes, no major damage was done. Only a few weeks later, at the Sasebo base, after a fire and internal explosion, *Mikasa* sank in relatively shallow water on September 11, killing 339 of the crew.

Refloated on August 8, 1906, it was repaired at Maizuru Naval Arsenal and restored to active service in 1908, with new 12-in (305 mm) guns. By September 1921 it was rated as "coastal defense ship, first class." Shortly after that, it grounded off the Russian coast while supporting forces intervening in Russia's post-revolutionary civil war. Though repaired, that marked the end of its active service. Decommissioned late in 1921, since 1925 it has been a museum display ship at Yokosuka (restored 1958–61).

SPECIFICATIONS

DISPLACEMENT: 15,200 tons (15,444 tonnes)

DIMENSIONS: 432 ft x 75 ft 6 in x 27 ft 6 in (131.7 m x 23.2 m x 8.28 m)

PROPULSION: Twin shafts, two vertical triple-expansion engines, 25 Belleville boilers, 15,000 ihp (11,185 kW)

ARMAMENT: Four 12-in (305 mm), fourteen 6-in (152 mm), twenty 12-pounder, eight 3-pounder, four 2.5-pounder guns; four 18-in (457 mm) torpedo tubes

ARMOR: Belt 9–4 in (229–102 mm), bulkheads 12 in (305 mm), deck 3 in (76 mm), barbettes 14–10 in (356–254 mm), main turrets 10–8 in (254–203 mm), lower deck redoubt and battery 6 in (152 mm)

SPEED: 18 knots (20.7 mph; 33.3 km/h)

CREW: 830

Mikasa

FUNNELS
Mikasa AS PRESERVED IS PAINTED IN "BATTLESHIP GRAY" BUT THIS PAINT FINISH, WITH THE TRIPLE-STRIPE FUNNELS, WAS ORDERED FOR ITS ORIGINAL COMPLETION.

TURRETS
FOUR BARR & STROUD FA3 COINCIDENCE RANGEFINDERS, EFFECTIVE UP TO 8,000 YARDS (7,315 M) WERE FITTED, AND THE TURRETS HAD 24-POWER MAGNIFICATION GUNSIGHTS.

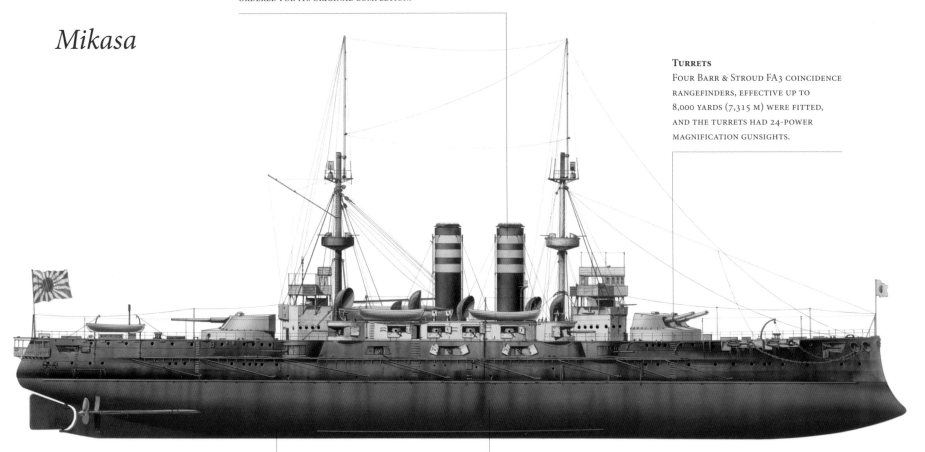

ARMOR
KRUPP CEMENTED ARMOR, WHICH HAD REPLACED NICKEL STEEL AS THE MOST SHELL-RESISTANT PROTECTION, WAS FITTED TO THE STEEL PLATES.

BATTLE OF TSUSHIMA
AN ADMIRER OF NELSON, ADMIRAL TOGO HAD THIS SIGNAL HOISTED AT TSUSHIMA: "THE FATE OF THE EMPIRE DEPENDS ON THIS BATTLE. LET EVERY MAN DO HIS UTMOST."

HMS *London* (1902)

LONDON WAS AMONG THE FIRST CAPITAL SHIPS TO BE ADAPTED FOR NAVAL AVIATION.
CONVERTED TO A MINELAYER IN WORLD WAR I, IT SERVED MOSTLY IN THE
MEDITERRANEAN THEATER.

By 1900 Britain's new battleships, now of 14,000 tons (14,225 tonnes) plus, were costing more than a million pounds. A naval arms race with Germany was under way, and between September 1901 and October 1904, 14 first-class battleships were completed for the Royal Navy. *London* was first of its class to be laid down, at Portsmouth on December 8, 1898, and launched on October 18, 1899, but HMS *Bulwark* was completed three months sooner, in March 1902.

They were very similar to the preceding *Formidable* class, carrying the same armament but with some variations in armor, losing a forward bulkhead in order to strengthen the forward belt. Long-range fire from high-angle guns had made decks more vulnerable and the *London*'s had three armored decks, of 2 in (50 mm) on the main deck over the citadel, and a maximum of 2.5 in (63 mm) on the lower deck. The main guns could pierce a 12-in (305 mm) steel plate at a range of 4,800 yards (4,390 m).

Both classes were powered by 20 Belleville water-tube boilers, and a notable feature of both was the row of ventilator cowls amidships. In 1912 a sloping steel trestle was mounted from the forward turret to the bow, to launch seaplanes, and a loading boom was fitted to the foremast to lift the aircraft from the water.

At the Coronation Review

In June 1902 *London* was flagship at King Edward VII's Coronation Review, then was deployed with the Mediterranean Fleet until 1907. After a refit at Chatham in 1908 it served with the Atlantic Fleet as flagship. In 1912 it was used for seaplane experiments with the 5th Squadron of the 2nd Fleet, at the Nore. From August 1914 to March 1915 it was with the Channel Fleet, then sent first to the Mediterranean and later into the Adriatic, in support of the Italian fleet. In 1918, it joined the 1st Minelaying Squadron in the North Sea. Placed in reserve in 1919, it was sold for breaking in 1920.

SPECIFICATIONS

DISPLACEMENT: 15,000 tons (15,241 tonnes)

DIMENSIONS: 431 ft 9 in x 75 ft x 27 ft 5 in (131 m x 23 m x (8.3 m)

PROPULSION: Twin shafts, vertical triple-expansion engines, 15,500 ihp (11,558 kW)

ARMAMENT: Four 12-in (305 mm)/40-caliber, twelve 6-in (152 mm)/45-caliber, sixteen 12-pounder QF, six 3-pounder QF guns; four 18-in (450 mm) torpedo tubes (submerged)

ARMOR: Belt 9 in (229 mm), bulkheads 12–9 in (305–229 mm), barbettes 12 in (305 mm), turrets 10–8 in (254–203 mm), casemates 6 in (152 mm), conning tower 14 in (356 mm), deck 2.5–1 in (64–25mm)

SPEED: 18 knots (20.7 mph; 33.3 km/h)

CREW: 760

HMS *London*

GUNS
THE 12-IN (305 MM) GUNS WEIGHED
50 TONS (50.8 TONNES), FIRING SHELLS
OF 850-LB (385.5 KG). THEY COULD
BE LOADED AT ANY POSITION AND
ELEVATION.

ARMOR
THE ARMOR BELT EXTENDED ALL THE
WAY TO THE STERN, WHICH WAS PERHAPS
A FACTOR IN SELECTING *LONDON* FOR A
MINELAYING ROLE.

MINELAYER
AS A MINELAYER, THE SHIP'S MAIN GUNS WERE
TAKEN OUT AND STORAGE SPACE AND LAUNCHING
RAILS FOR 240 MINES WERE INSTALLED, IN
FEBRUARY–APRIL 1918.

Tsesarevich (1903)

TSESAREVICH WAS BUILT IN FRANCE AND CLOSELY RESEMBLED FRENCH BATTLESHIPS OF THE TIME. IT SURVIVED THE END OF THE TSARIST ERA TO RECEIVE THE NAME "CITIZEN" UNDER THE SOVIET REGIME.

*T*sesarevich ("Crown Prince") was laid down on August 7, 1899, at La Seyne-sur-Mer, France, launched on February 23, 1901, and commissioned on September 3, 1903. It was very like *Jauréguiberry*, though larger, with the main and secondary guns mounted in twin turrets. A longitudinal bulkhead divided the armored deck for anti-torpedo protection. The guns were manufactured by Schneiders of Le Creusot to the design of Gustave Canet, the leading gun designer of the time. Two pole masts were fitted, the aftermast having a derrick attached.

Ordered for the Pacific fleet, *Tsesarevich* was immediately deployed to Port Arthur as flagship. In the unannounced attack on Port Arthur (February 8, 1904) that preceded Japan's declaration of war against Russia, it was struck by a torpedo and remained out of action for several weeks. On August 10 it led the fleet out to break the Japanese blockade of the port in the day-long battle of the Yellow Sea. At 18:00 a shell splinter killed Admiral Vitgeft on the *Tsesarevich*'s bridge and a further hits virtually wrecked the bridge and jammed the steering wheel, sending the ship into a sharp turn. Mistaking this for a planned movement, other ships followed, breaking the Russian line and creating confusion among the captains. *Tsesarevich*, escorted by three destroyers, was able to make the Chinese port of Tsingtao (Qingdao), then an enclave of German control (from 1898 to 1914), where it was interned until the war ended.

"Crown Prince" Renamed "Citizen"

In 1905 *Tsesarevich* was transferred to the Baltic Fleet. A courtesy visit was made to Portsmouth, England, in 1913. In World War I it was engaged on Baltic patrols. With the end of the Tsarist regime in 1917, renamed *Grazhdanin*, "Citizen," it was with the Gulf of Riga Squadron along with the *Borodino*-class battleship *Slava* and a force of cruisers and destroyers. On October 17, 1917, they were attacked in Moon Sound, off the Estonian coast, by German ships including the dreadnought-type *König* and *Kronprinz Wilhelm*. *Slava*, heavily damaged, was scuttled by its crew, but *Grazhdanin* survived. In 1918 it was hulked, and sold to Germany for scrapping in 1924.

SPECIFICATIONS

DISPLACEMENT: 12,915 tons (13,122 tonnes)

DIMENSIONS: 388 ft 9 in x 76 ft 1 in x 27 ft 11 in (118.5 m x 23.2 m x 8.5 m)

PROPULSION: Twin shafts, 2 vertical triple-expansion engines, 20 Belleville boilers, 16,300 ihp (12,155 kW)

ARMAMENT: Four 12-in (305 mm), twelve 6-in (152 mm), sixteen 3-in (76 mm), four 1.9-in (47 mm) 3-pounder guns; six 18-in (457 mm) torpedo tubes

ARMOR: Belt 9–5 in (230–150 mm), main turrets 10 in (250 mm), secondary turrets 5.9 in (150 mm), conning tower 10 in (250 mm), deck 2.25 in (57 mm)

SPEED: 18 knots (20.7 mph; 33.3 km/h)

CREW: 779

Tsesarevich

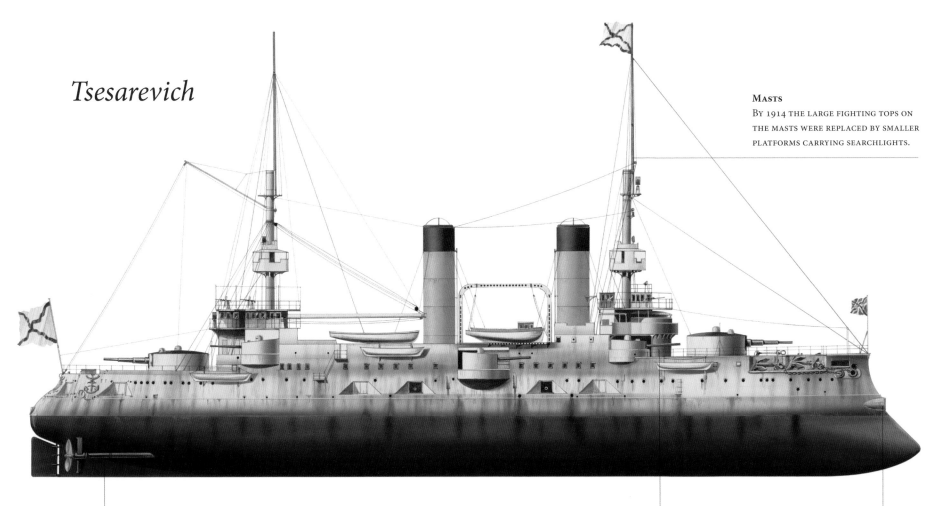

MASTS
BY 1914 THE LARGE FIGHTING TOPS ON THE MASTS WERE REPLACED BY SMALLER PLATFORMS CARRYING SEARCHLIGHTS.

ARMOR
KRUPP-TYPE CEMENTED ARMOR WAS FITTED, THE REDUCED THICKNESS COMPARED WITH EARLIER SHIPS DEMONSTRATING ITS RESISTANCE POWER.

DIRECT HIT
A 12-IN (305 MM) SHELL HIT BETWEEN THE UPPER AND LOWER BRIDGES, FOLLOWED BY A SECOND, WHICH EXPLODED AGAINST THE CONNING TOWER: FRAGMENTS ENTERING THROUGH THE OBSERVATION SLIT KILLED OR WOUNDED THOSE INSIDE.

TORPEDOES
ONE OF THE FOUR TORPEDO TUBES WAS POSITIONED ABOVE THE RAM, JUST ABOVE THE WATERLINE.

Kniaz Potemkin (1903)

ITS CREW STAGED A MUTINY IN 1905 AND THE SHIP WAS RENAMED BUT REMAINS FAMOUS DUE TO THE FILM *BATTLESHIP POTEMKIN*. ITS ENTIRE CAREER WAS SPENT WITH THE BLACK SEA FLEET, WITH MUCH ACTION AGAINST OTTOMAN FORCES DURING WORLD WAR I.

The ship was laid down at the Black Sea Nicolaiev shipyard in February 1898, launched in October 1900, and completed in November 1903. Of similar displacement and design to *Peresviet*, it had 12-in (305 mm) main guns mounted in small French-type turrets, but presented the same large extent of unarmored superstructure. It carried sixteen 6-in (152 mm) guns, twelve in the main deck battery and four in upper deck casemates. On June 27, 1905, the crew mutinied against bad food and conditions, and in the fighting the captain and most of the officers were killed. Hoping in vain to start a general mutiny, the crew took the ship to Constanta, Romania, from where it was handed back to Russia.

On August 9 it was renamed *Panteleimon* and carried that name until February 1917 when *Potemkin* was restored briefly, then *Borets za Svobodu*

("Freedom Fighter"). The Russian fleet dominated the Black Sea until the outbreak of war in August 1914, and the arrival of the German battlecruiser *Goeben*, under the Turkish flag. *Goeben* could have taken on more than one of Russia's five pre-dreadnoughts of the Black Sea Battle Squadron, but the Russians ensured that all five operated as a combined force. *Goeben/Yavuz Sultan Selim* could not combat them all, and withdrew from an encounter on November 18, 1914. But Russian action was confined to minelaying and raids on the Turkish coast.

Service on the Black Sea

In April 1918 German forces entered Sebastopol and the German imperial flag was briefly hoisted over the ship. During the civil war following the Russian Revolution British forces entered the Black Sea in support of the anti-

Bolsheviks, and the ship's machinery was destroyed by British sailors from the cruiser HMS *Calypso* on April 25, 1919, but it was recaptured by the Red Army in November 1920. By the time Sergei Eisenstein was making his celebrated film, the ship was at the breakers', and other surviving pre-dreadnoughts of the Black Seas Fleet were used as stand-ins.

SPECIFICATIONS

DISPLACEMENT: 12,582 tons (12,784 tonnes)

DIMENSIONS: 378 ft 6 in x 73 ft x 27 ft (115.3 m x 22.25 m x 8.2 m)

PROPULSION: Twin shafts, vertical triple-expansion engines, 22 Belleville boilers, 11,300 ihp (8,426 kW)

ARMAMENT: Four 12-in (305 mm)/40-caliber, sixteen 6-in (152 mm)/45-caliber, fourteen 3-in (76 mm), six 3-pounder QF guns; five 18-in (456 mm) torpedo tubes (submerged)

ARMOR: Belt 9–6 in (229–152 mm), turrets 10 in (254 mm), casemates 6–5 in (152–125 mm), conning tower 9 in (229 mm), deck 3–2.5 in (76–63 mm)

SPEED: 16 knots (18.4 mph; 29.6 km/h)

CREW: 741

Kniaz Potemkin

TURRETS
THE MAIN TURRETS WERE OPERATED ELECTRICALLY. RATE OF FIRE WAS ONE ROUND EVERY FOUR MINUTES, FIRING A 745-LB (338 KG) SHELL WITH A RANGE OF 13,000 YARDS (12,000 M) AT AN ELEVATION OF 10°.

GUNS
THE SECONDARY BATTERY OF SIXTEEN 6-IN (152 MM)/45-CALIBER GUNS WAS UNUSUALLY EXTENSIVE.

BURNERS
A COMBINATION OF COAL AND OIL FIRING WAS USED AT FIRST, WITH EIGHT OIL-BURNING AND 14 COAL-BURNING BOILERS; IN 1904 THE OIL BURNERS WERE CONVERTED TO COAL.

HMS *Dominion* (1903)

ONE OF EIGHT SHIPS OF THE *KING EDWARD VII* CLASS, THE FIRST BRITISH BATTLESHIPS TO CARRY 9.2-IN (232 MM) GUNS AS AN "INTERMEDIATE" CALIBER. *DOMINION* WAS LAID DOWN AT THE VICKERS YARD AT BARROW-IN-FURNESS ON MAY 23, 1902, LAUNCHED ON AUGUST 25, 1903, AND COMPLETED IN JULY 1905, AT A COST OF £1,364,318.

The *King Edward*'s were handsome and well-proportioned ships but even as pre-dreadnoughts they were outclassed while still under construction by the design of the *Lord Nelson* class. As originally planned, the masts were without fighting tops, but fire-control tops on both masts were added prior to completion. The inclusion of 9.2-in (232 mm) guns to supplement the main armament reflected developments in other navies as well as the general increase in attackable superstructure surface. They were mounted on the upper deck, on each side of the fore and main masts, in single turrets, and necessitated an increase in displacement of over 1,000 tons (1,016 tonnes). The ten 6-in (152 mm) guns were mounted on the deck below in a central box battery.

A full-width bridge forward of the foremast, with a larger charthouse, made docking maneuvers easier as well as providing a more effective navigation deck. A balanced rudder was fitted, the first British battleships to have this since the 1870s. *Dominion* and *Commonwealth* were the only two ships in the class to be fully powered by water-tube boilers (Babcock & Wilcox): the others had a combination of water-tube and cylindrical. *Dominion* also had oil-sprayers fitted when re-boilered in 1911, to supplement the coal fuel.

Service During World War I

Dominion was commissioned into the Atlantic Fleet on August 5, 1905. It grounded at Chaleur Bay, in the Gulf of St. Lawrence, on August 16 and remained under repair at Bermuda and Chatham until June 1907. In April 1909 it was assigned to the 2nd Division of the Home Fleet, then to the 2nd Battle Squadron of the First Fleet from May 1912, then from October 1913 to the 3rd Battle Squadron in the Mediterranean. From August 1914 it was part of the 3rd Battle Squadron of the Grand Fleet, serving as flagship August–September 1915. Refitted at Devonport, England, in the winter of 1915–16, it was used as a depot ship for raids on Zeebrugge and Ostend on the Belgian coast in 1917–18. Sold on May 9, 1921, it was scrapped in 1924.

SPECIFICATIONS

DISPLACEMENT: 16,350 tons (16,612 tonnes); 17,500 tons (17,781 tonnes) full load

DIMENSIONS: 453 ft 8 in x 78 ft x 25 ft 6 in (138.3 m x 24 m x 7.7 m)

PROPULSION: Twin shafts, vertical triple expansion engines, 16 Babcock & Wilcox boilers, 18,000 ihp (13,423 kW)

ARMAMENT: Four 12-in (305 mm)/40-caliber, four 9.2-in (234 mm)/47-caliber, ten 6-in (152 mm)/45-caliber, fourteen 12-pounder QF, fourteen 3-pounder QF guns; five 18-in (457 mm) torpedo tubes (submerged)

ARMOR: Belt 9–8 in (229–203 mm), bulkheads, barbettes and conning tower 12 in (305 mm), main turrets 12–8 in (305–203 mm), deck 2.5–1 in (63–25 mm)

SPEED: 18.5 knots (21.3 mph; 34.3 km/h)

CREW: 777

HMS *Dominion*

GUNS
THREE-POUNDER GUNS WERE MOUNTED
ON THE MAIN TURRETS AT TIMES.

MAST
FROM 1914 THE MAIN TOPMAST WAS
REPLACED BY A SHORTER LIGHT POLE.

RUDDER
THE BALANCED RUDDER MADE THE SHIP EASILY
MANEUVERABLE BUT THE CLASS WAS NOTORIOUS
FOR ITS DIFFICULTY IN MAINTAINING A STRAIGHT
COURSE.

ARMOR
TOTAL ARMOR WEIGHT WAS 4,175 TONS
(4,242 TONNES).

BRIDGE
THE OPEN STRUCTURE OF THE FORWARD BRIDGE
AREA CAN BE COMPARED TO THE ARMORED
TOWER-FORM OF *SCHWABEN*.

SMS *Schwaben* (1904)

SCHWABEN WAS LAST OF FOUR *WITTELSBACH* CLASS SHIPS, THE FIRST BATTLESHIPS ORDERED UNDER TIRPITZ'S NAVY LAW OF 1898. MODELED VERY MUCH ON THE PRECEDING *KAISER* CLASS, THEY HAD SHORT CAREERS IN ACTIVE SERVICE.

Schwaben was laid down at Wilhelmshaven in 1900, launched on November 9, 1901, and completed on April 13, 1904, as the last ship of the class to go into commission, 18 months after the class leader. In appearance they resembled the *Kaiser Friedrich III* class, with the same built-up superstructure and twin funnels, and two wide-diameter pole masts, topped by tall narrow extensions. But they were flush-decked. Internally, the hull, of steel plates riveted to steel frames, was divided into 14 watertight compartments, and a double bottom was fitted between the main gun turrets.

The limitations of their main armament of four 9.4-in (240 mm) guns was almost immediately apparent and it was clear that they could be employed only on secondary duties, but there were few of these for second-class battleships in the German Navy.

As a Training Ship

On commissioning, the ship was used for torpedo training. In May 1904 it hit a reef near Fehmarn Island in the Baltic Sea and was under repair until late in the year. From January 1905 it was used as a gunnery school ship and took part in many exercises. From August 1910 until September 1912 it was partly with the 3rd Squadron of the High Seas Fleet and partly in reserve.

From August 1914 until November 10, 1915, it was involved in naval operations in the Baltic Sea but with the other *Wittelsbach*'s was considered unfit for combat duties against the more heavily armed Russian *Gangut* class, and was transferred to Wilhelmshaven for engineering training, and partially disarmed from early 1916, losing its main guns and with the secondary armament reduced to six 5.9-in (150-mm) and four 3.5-in (88 mm) guns. In 1919 *Schwaben* underwent conversion as a depot ship for twelve minesweeping FM motor boats, operating in the Baltic from August 1, 1919, to June 19, 1920. It was stricken on March 8, 1921, and sold in the same year for scrapping at Kiel.

SPECIFICATIONS

DISPLACEMENT: 12,596 tons (12,798 tonnes)

DIMENSIONS: 416 ft x 74 ft 9 in x 26 ft 4 in (126.8 m x 22.8 m x 8.04 m)

PROPULSION: Triple shafts, triple expansion engines; 15,000 ihp (11,185.5 kW)

ARMAMENT: Four 9.4-in (240 mm), eighteen 5.9-in (150 mm), twelve 3.5-in (88 mm) guns; 12 machine guns; six 17.7 in (450 mm) torpedo tubes

ARMOR: Belt 12 in (305 mm); deck 2.5 in (55 mm)

SPEED: 17.5 knots (20.1 mph; 32.4 km/h)

CREW: 683

SMS *Schwaben*

GUNS
THE *WITTELSBACH* CLASS MOUNTED
A SUBSTANTIAL FORWARD-FIRING
ARMAMENT.

HULL
INSIDE THE HULL WERE 14 WATERTIGHT
COMPARTMENTS, AND 70 PERCENT OF THE
LENGTH WAS PROTECTED BY A DOUBLE
BOTTOM.

RANGE
MAXIMUM COAL CAPACITY WAS 1,772 TONS
(1,800 TONNES), ENABLING A RANGE OF 5,000
NAUTICAL MILES (5,754 MILES; 9,260 KM) AT 10
KNOTS (11.5 MPH; 19.5 KM/H)

HMS *Dreadnought* (1906)

A NEW ERA OF FAST, BIG-GUN BATTLESHIPS WAS INAUGURATED BY THE APPEARANCE OF HMS *DREADNOUGHT*. SIMILAR SHIPS WERE ALREADY BEING PLANNED OR CONSIDERED BY OTHER NAVIES AND THE EFFECT, INSTEAD OF ASSURING BRITISH DOMINANCE, WAS TO INTENSIFY THE NAVAL ARMS RACE.

Dreadnought was laid down at Portsmouth, England, on October 2, 1905, launched on February 10, 1906, and completed in December 1906. The cost was £1,783,883. Speed of construction was made possible by preassembly of the materials. The main deck had 19 ft (5.8 m) freeboard, with a forecastle deck raised to 28 ft (8.5 m). The main turrets were disposed in symmetrical array, three on the centerline and one each to port and starboard just abaft of the main deckhouse and leading funnel. Five thousand tons (5,080 tonnes) of armor was applied, with armor plating of diminishing thickness along the entire sides. The aim was to let the ship safely sustain two torpedo strikes. Magazines were located centrally, well away from the sides.

The most revolutionary aspect of the ship was its turbine engines, never fitted in a battleship before. The decision proved a triumphant success. Within the hull a system of fully watertight compartments was rigorously applied, with no doors or openings and each compartment having independent ventilation, pumps (electrically driven) and drainage. Lifts gave access between the machinery compartments. Dreadnought was faster than any other battleship, mechanically more reliable, and more economical on fuel. Its engine space was more compact, sat lower in the hull, and gave substantially more power per ton of weight. A reverse turbine was placed on each of the four shafts, one high- and one low-pressure on each side.

Most Powerful Warship Afloat

Dreadnought was assigned to the Home Fleet, and from January–March 1907 went on a shakedown cruise to the Mediterranean, then across to Trinidad. Its return journey of 7,000 miles (11,265 km) was accomplished with no mechanical hold-ups and at an average speed of 17.5 knots (20.1 mph; 32.4 km/h). No previous warship had been capable of this.

From April 1907 to May 1912 it was flagship of the Home Fleet, then of the 4th Battleship Squadron until May 1916. It sank *U-29* by ramming, in the North Sea on February 18, 1915: an ironic exploit considering that a ram bow had been deliberately omitted from its design as not required in a modern battleship. From July 1916 it was flagship of the 3rd Battleship Squadron at Sheerness, but briefly rejoined the Grand Fleet between March and August 1918. In February 1919 it was placed on reserve at Rosyth, Scotland, and stricken on March 31, 1920. In May 1921 it was sold for scrapping.

SPECIFICATIONS

DISPLACEMENT: 17,900 tons (18,186 tonnes); 21,845 tons (22,195 tonnes) full load

DIMENSIONS: 527 ft x 82 ft x 26 ft 6 in (160.4 m x 25 m x 8.1 m)

PROPULSION: Quadruple shafts, four Parsons turbines, 18 Babcock & Wilcox boilers, 26,350 shp (19,649 kW)

ARMAMENT: Ten 12 in (305 mm) guns, twenty-seven 12-pounder guns; five 18 in (457 mm) torpedo tubes (submerged)

ARMOR: Belt 11–4 in (279–102 mm), bulkhead 8 in (203 mm), barbettes 11–4 in (279–102 mm), turrets 11 in (279 mm), conning tower 11–8 in (279–203 mm)

SPEED: 21.6 knots (24.8 mph; 40k m/h)

CREW: 773

HMS *Dreadnought*

GUNS
WHEN THE EIGHT-GUN 12-IN (305 MM) SALVO WAS FIRST FIRED, AN EXPERT OBSERVER NOTICED NO MORE THAN "A MUFFLED ROAR AND A BIT OF A KICK ON THE SHIP."

RUDDERS
TWO PARALLEL RUDDERS WERE FITTED, CENTER-MOUNTED, ABAFT OF THE INNER SCREWS, CONTRIBUTING TO THE SHIP'S EXCELLENT HANDLING QUALITIES.

FUEL
1,120 TONS (1,138 TONNES) OF OIL FUEL WAS CARRIED IN THE BOTTOM UNDER THE MACHINERY SPACES. A MAXIMUM 2,900 TONS (2,946 TONNES) OF COAL COULD BE CARRIED IN THE BUNKERS.

HULL
THE HULL SHAPE WAS CAREFULLY WORKED OUT TO ENSURE THAT THE REQUIRED SPEED OF 21 KNOTS (24.2 MPH; 38.9 KM/H) COULD BE ACHIEVED ON THE LEAST HORSEPOWER: SEVEN SUCCESSIVE MODELS WERE TESTED IN AN EXPERIMENTAL TANK.

Republique (1906)

THE LARGEST WARSHIP YET BUILT IN A FRENCH YARD, *RÉPUBLIQUE* WAS A PRE-DREADNOUGHT STYLE BATTLESHIP THAT MARKED A NEW EFFORT TO PROVIDE THE NAVY WITH BATTLESHIPS OF A STANDARDIZED CLASS. THE LEAD SHIP OF HER CLASS, SHE HAD ONLY ONE SISTER SHIP: *PATRIE*.

Designed by Louis-Émile Bertin, director of naval construction, it was laid down at the Brest Naval Arsenal on December 2, 1901, launched on September 4, 1902, and completed on June 12, 1906. Bertin had been a member of the Jeune École ("young school") group that viewed battleships as out of date, but since other navies continued to build them, the French felt compelled to follow suit.

In appearance the ship was less idiosyncratic than its predecessors. The high freeboard of the forecastle deck was continued to abaft the mainmast, with the second main turret on a lower quarterdeck. Projected length had been 439 ft (133.8 m) cut back to 434 ft 7 in (132.4 m), even so the notably large distance between the second and aft funnels gave it a lengthy appearance. A tubular foremast was fitted with two armored control stations, with a pole topmast above; and a pole mainmast. Caps and clinker screens were fitted to the funnels. A respectful article in a British naval journal considered it as almost equal to the *King Edward VII* class: it also noticed the increasing tendency of the battleships of different navies to resemble one another. In the event *République* was an effective design, though the aim at standardization was compromised when later ships of the class, after *Patrie,* were given 7.6 in (194 mm) secondary guns rather than the class leader's 6.4 in (164 mm).

France's Mediterranean Battleship

Republique's service career was wholly in the Mediterranean Sea. It suffered minor damage when accidentally hit by a torpedo from *Patrie* on February 18, 1910, and when the *Liberté*, anchored close by, blew up on September 25, 1911.

In World War I it patrolled the Otranto Straits between the Mediterranean and Adriatic seas in 1914–15, then with *Patrie* was assigned to the Salonica Division in support of land units fighting against Bulgaria. It fired shots into the city of Athens during fighting between Allied sailors and pro-German elements in the Greek army on December 1, 1916. On July 1, 1918, it was placed on reserve, then recommissioned on September 15, 1919, as a gunnery training ship based at Toulon, France, with its main turrets removed. It was struck from the navy list on May 18, 1921, and sold for breaking in 1922.

SPECIFICATIONS

DISPLACEMENT: 14,374 tons (14,605 tonnes)

DIMENSIONS: 439 ft x 79 ft 7 in x 27 ft 7 in (133.8 m x 24.26 m x 8.41 m)

PROPULSION: Triple shafts, three triple-expansion engines; 18,000 ihp (13,422.6 kW)

ARMAMENT: Four 12-in (305 mm) BL, eighteen 6.4-in (164 mm) QF guns; five 17.7-in (450 mm) torpedo tubes, two submerged

ARMOR: Belt 11 in (280 mm), barbettes 10 in (255 mm), turrets 14 in (356 mm), conning tower 12 in (305 mm)

SPEED: 19 knots (21.8 mph; 35.2 km/h)

CREW: 793

Republique

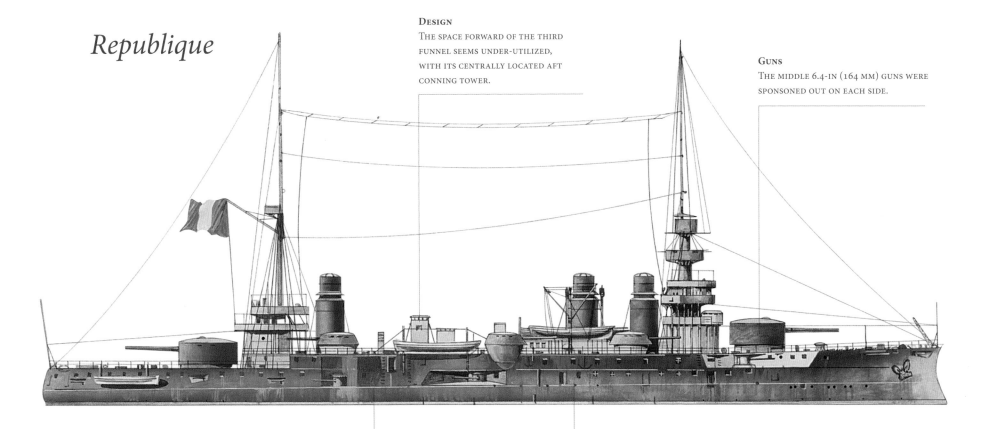

DESIGN
THE SPACE FORWARD OF THE THIRD
FUNNEL SEEMS UNDER-UTILIZED,
WITH ITS CENTRALLY LOCATED AFT
CONNING TOWER.

GUNS
THE MIDDLE 6.4-IN (164 MM) GUNS WERE
SPONSORED OUT ON EACH SIDE.

BUNKER CAPACITY
RÉPUBLIQUE AND ITS SISTER SHIP *PATRIE*
HAD MAXIMUM BUNKER CAPACITY OF 1,825
TONS (1,854 TONNES), ENOUGH TO MAKE A
DOUBLE ATLANTIC CROSSING.

ARMOR
HARVEYIZED NICKEL STEEL WAS USED FOR THE
ARMOR PLATING.

SMS *Schleswig-Holstein* (1908)

UNLIKE THE MAJORITY OF GERMAN BATTLESHIPS, *SCHLESWIG-HOLSTEIN* HAD A LONG CAREER AFLOAT. ON SEPTEMBER 1, 1939, AT DANZIG (NOW GDANSK, POLAND), IT FIRED THE FIRST SHOTS OF WORLD WAR II, AT THE POLISH GARRISON IN THE FORTRESS OF WESTERPLATTE.

Last of the five-strong *Deutschland* class, the ship was laid down at the Germaniawerft, Kiel, Germany, in August 1905, launched on December 7, 1906, and completed on July 6, 1908. Typical of German pre-dreadnoughts of the period, it had no intermediate secondary guns.

On September 21, 1908, it joined the 2nd Squadron, and took part in regular fleet maneuvers. Supplementary oil firing was fitted in 1915, but by the time of Jutland the ships of the 2nd Battle Squadron were considered to be slow and insufficiently armored.

At Jutland it was one of the last in the line and had no opportunities to strike at British ships. Instead it took long-range fire, and a heavy hit left three men killed and eight wounded. On the following day it fired its secondary guns at a British destroyer group that had just torpedoed its sister ship *Pommern*.

In April 1916 two 3.4-in (88 mm) AA guns were mounted. In 1917 it was used as a depot ship at Bremerhaven, Germany, and as an accommodation ship at Kiel in 1918.

In the 1920s, despite its age, it was adapted to act as flagship of the German navy from January 31, 1926. In 1927–28 the fore-funnel was trunked back into the second. From September 22, 1935, it was adapted as a training ship, and as such made some lengthy cruises with 175 cadets, into the South Atlantic and the Indian Ocean.

World War II Surprise Assault

On what was supposedly a ceremonial visit in August 1939, it opened fire on Polish positions with its main guns at 04:47 on September 1. In April 1940 it supported the invasion of Denmark, grounding briefly off the eastern coast, then resumed a training role. Plans were made to convert it into a convoy escort with heavy AA defenses, but on December 18, 1944, it was hit by RAF bombers and sank at Gotenhafen (now Gdynia, Poland) naval base. Raised by the Russians in 1945–46, it was towed to Tallinn, Estonia, and subsequently beached and used as a stationary target.

SPECIFICATIONS

DISPLACEMENT: 12,982 tons (13,190 tonnes); 13,993 tons (14,217.5 tonnes) full load

DIMENSIONS: 418 ft 8 in x 72 ft 10 in x 26 ft 11 in (127.6 m x 22.2 m x 8.2 m)

PROPULSION: Triple shafts, triple expansion engines, 12 boilers, 17,000 ihp (13,000 kW)

ARMAMENT: Four 11-in (280 mm)/ 40-caliber, fourteen 6.7-in (170 mm)/ 40-caliber, twenty-two 3.5-in (88 mm) guns; four 20-in (500 mm) torpedo tubes

ARMOR: Belt 9.4 in (240 mm), turrets 11 in (280 mm), deck 1.6 in (40 mm)

SPEED: 19.1 knots (22 mph; 35.4 km/h)

CREW: 743

SMS *Schleswig-Holstein*

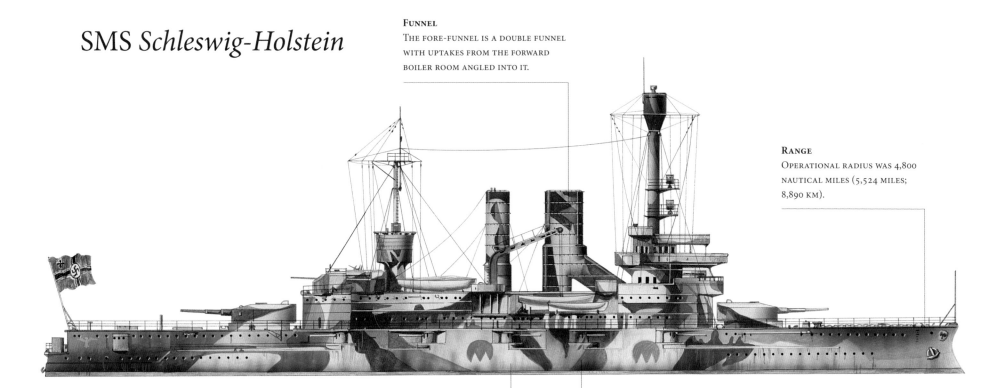

FUNNEL
THE FORE-FUNNEL IS A DOUBLE FUNNEL WITH UPTAKES FROM THE FORWARD BOILER ROOM ANGLED INTO IT.

RANGE
OPERATIONAL RADIUS WAS 4,800 NAUTICAL MILES (5,524 MILES; 8,890 KM).

BUNKERS
STANDARD CAPACITY OF THE BUNKERS WAS 836 TONS (849 TONNES) AND THE SHIP COULD BE COALED FROM EMPTY WITH 700 TONNES IN 85 MINUTES, A GERMAN NAVY RECORD WITH A MAXIMUM OF 1,693 TONS (1,720 TONNES).

BOILERS
THE BOILERS WERE ADAPTED FOR SUPPLEMENTARY OIL FIRING IN 1915.

Vittorio Emanuele (1908)

SECOND OF THE FOUR-STRONG *REGINA ELENA* CLASS, THIS PRE-DREADNOUGHT TOOK
PART IN OPERATIONS IN THE ITALIAN–TURKISH WAR BUT THOUGH ACTIVE ALSO IN
WORLD WAR I, SAW NO FURTHER COMBAT.

Designed by Vittorio Cuniberti, chief constructor of the Italian Navy, a believer in the "all big-gun" battleship concept and a highly influential figure in warship design, it was laid down at Cantieri di Castellammare di Stabia on September 18, 1901, launched on October 12, 1904, and completed on August 1, 1908. Cuniberti modified his principles considerably for the class, which carried only two heavy guns and a large array of "semi-heavy" 8-in (200 mm) guns, rather than his ideal of twelve 12-in (305 mm) guns. The two main guns were carried in single turrets with sloping sides; after 1912 machine guns were mounted on the tops. Two torpedo tubes were fitted below the waterline.

With three tall funnels and a low navigation bridge, the ship had a distinctly old-fashioned appearance even when newly-commissioned. The armor was of Krupp-type steel, manufactured in Italy at the Terni works.

A Preference for Speed

Compared to what was new in Britain and the United States the ship was under-armored and under-gunned, though as far as speed was concerned it could more than hold its own: high speed was another Cuniberti ideal. In the Italian–Turkish war of 1911–12, when Italy seized Libya from the Ottoman Empire, it was the flagship of the Italian Navy's 1st Division. It shelled shore positions at Tobruk and Benghazi in Libya in October 1911, and was off Rhodes on May 4–5 when the island was captured by Italian forces. During World War I Italian naval strategy concentrated on blocking off the Adriatic Sea and the main Austrian naval base at Pola, and *Vittorio Emmanuele* was mostly patrolling between the naval bases at Taranto and Brindisi in Italy, and Volona (now Voltrë,

Albania). With the end of the war, the ship was used for a short time as a training ship, then laid up. On April 1, 1923, it was removed from the naval register, and broken up later that year.

SPECIFICATIONS

DISPLACEMENT: 13,914 tons (14,137 tonnes)

DIMENSIONS: 474 ft x 73 ft x 28 ft 1 in (144.6 m x 22.4 m x 8.58 m)

PROPULSION: Twin shafts, two triple expansion engines, 19,424 ihp (14,484 kW)

ARMAMENT: Two 12-in (305 mm), twelve 8-in (200 mm), sixteen 3-in (76 mm) guns; two 17.7-in (450 mm) torpedo tubes

ARMOR: Belt 9.8 in (248 mm), turrets 8 in (203 mm), conning tower 10 in (250 mm), deck 1.5 in (38 mm)

SPEED: 21.36 knots (24.58 mph; 39.56 km/h)

CREW: 764

Vittorio Emanuele

FUNNELS

THERE WERE SOME DIFFERENCES WITHIN THE *REGINA ELENA* CLASS. *REGINA ELENA* HAD FUNNELS 8 FT (2.5M) SHORTER THAN *VITTORIO EMMANUELE* AND THE LAST TWO, *ROMA* AND *NAPOLI*, HAD NO FOREMAST.

RANGE

CRUISING RANGE WAS 10,000 NAUTICAL MILES (11,500 MILES; 18,500 KM) AT 10 KNOTS (11.5 MPH; 19.5 KM/H).

WATERLINE

FEAR OF TORPEDO STRIKES BELOW THE WATERLINE BELT FROM AUSTRIAN SUBMARINES KEPT THE SHIP OUT OF THE ADRIATIC SEA DURING WORLD WAR I.

GUNS

THE 8-IN (203 MM) GUNS WERE ARRANGED IN THREE TWIN TURRETS ON EACH SIDE, WITH THE SUPERSTRUCTURE CORNERS ANGLED TO INCREASE THEIR FIELD OF FIRE.

HMS *Indomitable* (1908)

THE THREE SHIPS OF THE *INVINCIBLE* CLASS WERE THE FIRST BATTLECRUISERS, POWERED BY TURBINES AND CARRYING EIGHT 12-IN (305 MM) GUNS, BUT WITH RELATIVELY LIGHT ARMOR PROTECTION. THE BATTLECRUISER WAS A NEW CONCEPT IN NAVAL TECHNOLOGY.

Announced first as "armored cruisers" and not officially known as battlecruisers until 1911, the appearance of HMS *Indomitable* and its sister ships started a controversy that has lasted long after the disappearance of battlecruisers from the world's navies: was the concept a useful one, or not? *Indomitable* was laid down at Fairfield's yard on the River Clyde, Glasgow, Scotland, on March 1, 1906, launched on March 16, 1907, and completed on June 25, 1908. The other two, HMS *Inflexible* and *Invincible*, were built with equal speed.

Their appearance, with some individual variations, was highly distinctive. *Indomitable* had three funnels, with the fore-funnel mounted higher than the others, and the after funnel set well behind, almost under the tripod mainmast. Its eight 12-in (305 mm) guns were placed in twin turrets firing over the bow and stern, and in two diagonal midships positions, the port turret placed ahead of the starboard one. Abaft these turrets, the open deck dropped a level, so that the freeboard at the forecastle was much higher than at the stern. As with *Dreadnought*, it was turbine-powered and clean hull lines helped it to a speed well in excess of the battleships of the day.

Action in World War I

Indomitable was commissioned at Chatham, England, on June 25, 1908, and took the Prince of Wales to Quebec for the tercentenary celebrations. It was then assigned to the Home Fleet, Nore Division, until April 1909 when it joined the 1st Cruiser Squadron. Apart from a refit between November 1911 and February 1912, *Indomitable* was variously with the 2nd (as flagship) and 1st Cruiser Squadrons until August 1913, when it joined the 1st Battle Cruiser Squadron in the Mediterranean. In August 1914 it was engaged in pursuit of the German battleships *Breslau* and *Goeben*, then joined the Dardanelles blockade. It was in action at the Battles of the Dogger Bank and Jutland, sustaining no damage, and was with the 2nd Battle Cruiser Squadron from June 1916 to January 1919. Its final role was as flagship of the Reserve Fleet at the Nore until paid off on March 31, 1920. It was sold for scrapping in December 1922.

SPECIFICATIONS

DISPLACEMENT: 17,373 tons (17,652 tonnes); 20,078 tons (20,400 tonnes) full load

DIMENSIONS: 567 ft x 78 ft 6 in x 26 ft 2 in (172.8 m x 22.1 m x 8 m)

PROPULSION: Quadruple shafts, Parsons turbines, 31 Babcock & Wilcox boilers, 41,000 shp (30,570 kW)

ARMAMENT: Eight 12-in (305 mm)/ 45-caliber, sixteen 4-in (102 mm)/45-caliber QF guns; seven Maxim guns; five 18-in (457 mm) torpedo tubes

ARMOR: Belt 6–4 in (152–100 mm), bulkheads 7–6 in (180–152 mm), barbettes 7–2 in (180–50 mm), turret faces 7 in (180 mm), conning tower 10–6 in (250–152 mm), deck 2.5–0.75 in (65–20 mm)

SPEED: 25.5 knots (29.3 mph; 47.2 km/h)

CREW: 784

HMS *Indomitable*

VULNERABLE TURRET
INDOMITABLE'S SISTER SHIP *INVINCIBLE*
WAS DESTROYED AT JUTLAND WHEN "Q"
TURRET (STARBOARD AMIDSHIPS) WAS
STRUCK BY A SHELL FROM *DERFFLINGER*:
1,026 WERE KILLED.

GUNS
FOUR-IN (102 MM) GUNS, COMPLETELY
OPEN UNTIL 1917, WERE MOUNTED ON
TOP OF THE 12-IN (305 MM) TURRETS.

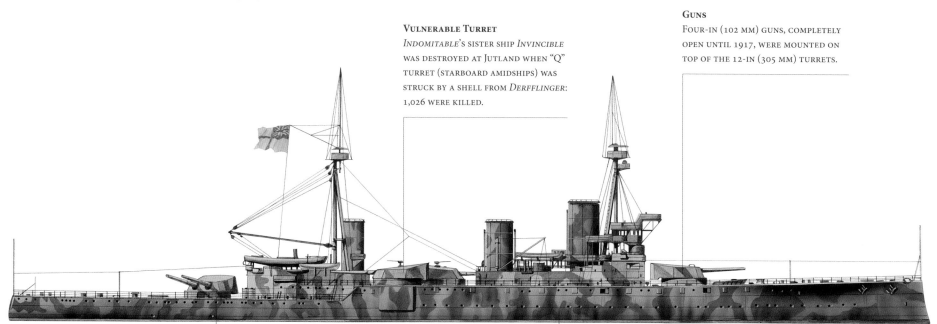

FIREPOWER
AT JUTLAND *INDOMITABLE*'S GUNS
HIT *DERFFLINGER* THREE TIMES,
AND *SEYDLITZ* AND *POMMERN* ONCE
EACH IN THE COURSE OF FIRING ONE
HUNDRED SEVENTY-FIVE 12-IN (305
MM) SHELLS.

ENHANCEMENTS
IN 1917 A DIRECTOR TOWER WAS ADDED,
SEARCHLIGHTS WERE MOUNTED AROUND THE AFT
FUNNEL, AND AIRCRAFT-PLATFORMS INSTALLED
ON THE WING TURRETS.

HMS *Lord Nelson* (1908)

REPRESENTING A SIGNIFICANT IMPROVEMENT IN FIREPOWER OVER ITS PREDECESSORS, *LORD NELSON* WAS ALMOST IMMEDIATELY OUTCLASSED BY *DREADNOUGHT*, BUT GAVE USEFUL WARTIME SERVICE IN THE EASTERN MEDITERRANEAN AND THE DARDANELLES CAMPAIGN.

Lord Nelson was laid down at Palmers' yard on the Tyne on May 18, 1905, launched on September 4, 1906, and completed in October 1908. A rectangular superstructure topped by a flying deck carried both masts and two funnels of the same height, the after one larger. The deckhouse was quite narrow to provide deck space for six 9.2-in (234 mm) turrets on each side, the end ones carrying two guns, and originally had no bridge, only a high conning tower, but after trials, a bridge, with lateral wings, and a charthouse perched above, were added. The superiority in gun power was striking: the 12-in (305 mm) guns could penetrate Krupp cemented armor 12-in (305 mm) thick from 7,600 yards (6,950 m), compared to 7,480 yards (6,840 m) for HMS *Dominion*'s 40 caliber; the 9.2-in (234 mm) guns could penetrate the same thickness from 5,200 yards (4,755 m), compared with 4,550 yards

(4,160 m) for *Dominion*'s 40 caliber. The anti-torpedo boat defense was twenty-four 12-pounders, the largest yet fitted. Excluding the turrets, *Lord Nelson* carried 4,200 tons (4,267 tonnes) of armor. Internally the hull was subdivided into self-contained sections, each with its own drainage, ventilation, and pumping equipment and access lifts, by a series of solid bulkheads. Though doubtless effective, such a design also made the ship difficult to work, and was not repeated.

Flagship of the Channel Fleet

The ship was commissioned in December 1908 in the Home Fleet's Nore Division and served in the Home Fleet until May 1912 when it was attached to the 1st Battle Squadron, and briefly to the 4th Battle Squadron. With the outbreak of World War I it was made flagship of the Channel Fleet until February 1915, when it was sent to the Dardanelles, and remained

in the Eastern Mediterranean area until April 1919. On return to Chatham, it lay in reserve until sold in November 1920.

SPECIFICATIONS

DISPLACEMENT: 15,358 tons (15,604 tonnes); 17,820 tons (18,110 tonnes) full load

DIMENSIONS: 443 ft 6 in x 79 ft 6 in x 26 ft (135.2 m x 24.2 m x 7.9 m)

PROPULSION: Twin shafts, vertical triple-expansion engines, 15 Babcock & Wilcox boilers, 16,750 ihp (12,490 kW)

ARMAMENT: Four 12-in (305 mm)/45 caliber, ten 9.2-in (234 mm)/45-caliber guns; twenty-four 12-pounder QF, two 3-pounder guns; five 17.7-in (450 mm) torpedo tubes

ARMOR: Belt 12–2 in (305–50 mm), bulkhead 8 in (203 mm), barbettes, citadel, conning tower, and main turrets 12 in (305 mm), decks 4–1in (102–25 mm)

SPEED: 18 knots (21 mph; 33 km/h)

CREW: 817

HMS *Lord Nelson*

MAST
THIS WAS THE FIRST BATTLESHIP TO CARRY A TRIPOD MAST.

GUNS
ALL-TURRET GUNS REPLACED THE BATTERY ARRANGEMENT OF SECONDARY GUNS ON PREVIOUS SHIPS.

ENGINE
LORD NELSON AND *AGAMEMNON* WERE THE LAST BRITISH CAPITAL SHIPS TO BE FITTED WITH RECIPROCATING TRIPLE-EXPANSION ENGINES.

TORPEDO NETS
TORPEDO-NET BOOMS WERE REMOVED BY 1917.

SMS *Nassau* (1909)

ONE OF THE FIRST GERMAN BIG-GUN SHIPS TO BE BUILT AFTER *DREADNOUGHT*, *NASSAU* CARRIED A SUBSTANTIAL SECONDARY ARMAMENT AS WELL AS TWELVE MAIN GUNS, AND WAS IN ACTION WITH THE HIGH SEAS FLEET AT JUTLAND.

Plans for ships of this class had been worked on from March 1904 and the final design was completed in 1906. Unlike *Dreadnought* a large-scale secondary armament was also included, with twelve 5.9-in (150 mm) guns mounted in casemates at a level below the port and starboard main turrets, and sixteen 3.4-in (86 mm) guns in side-mounted sponsons on the hull and superstructure. *Nassau*'s masts had high wireless aerial gaffs set at an angle from the mizzen top of both masts; these were removed in 1911 and during World War I a spotting top was fitted on the foremast. Gooseneck cranes at each side of the aft funnel swung out the boats housed amidships. *Nassau* had triple-expansion engines with water-tube boilers. Consequently the three boiler rooms and the engine room occupied most of the hull between the masts. German designers set great store by good

underwater protection and *Nassau*'s hull had sixteen watertight divisions, with the placing of armor on the class done on a scientific basis. But the underwater lines had to be modified after sea experience. It had been supposed that the wide beam and the lateral placing of heavy guns would make a stable ship, but in some North Sea swells they rolled violently and bilge keels had to be fitted.

Taking Fire at Jutland

In August 1914 *Nassau* was one of the eight ships of Battle Squadron I of the High Seas Fleet. The ship saw no action until an unsuccessful sortie off the Dutch coast on March 15–16, 1916. On April 24, 1916 it escorted a squadron of battlecruisers to bombard English coastal towns. In the Battle of Jutland, May 31, it was hit twice by shellfire, and ran against the British destroyer *Spitfire* in an attempt to sink it by ramming, but all damage

was repaired by July 10. Subsequently it made three further sorties into the North Sea without any positive result; on the last occasion, with other ships of the Squadron, reaching the latitude of Stavanger (April 23, 1918). Not among the ships scuttled at Scapa Flow, it was stricken on November 5, 1919. Intended to go to Japan as war reparation, it was sold by the Japanese government to a British company who had it scrapped at Dordrecht in the Netherlands, in June 1920.

SPECIFICATIONS

DISPLACEMENT: 18,900 tons (19,200 tonnes)

DIMENSIONS: 479 ft 4 in x 88 ft 4 in x 27 ft 11 in (146.1 m x 26.9 m x 8.5 m)

PROPULSION: Triple shafts, three vertical triple-expansion engines, 22,000 ihp (16,405 kW)

ARMAMENT: Twelve 11-in (280 mm), twelve 5.9-in (150 mm), sixteen 3.5-in (88 mm) guns; six 17.7-in (450 mm) torpedo tubes

ARMOR: Belt 11.8 in (300 mm), bulkhead 7.8 in (200 mm), tower (forward) 15.6 in (400 mm), aft 7.8 in (200 mm), barbettes and turrets 11 in (280 mm)

SPEED: 19.5 knots (22.4 mph; 36.1km/h)

CREW: 963

SMS *Nassau*

Guns
The main 11-in (280-mm) guns were of a smaller caliber than the 12-in (305-mm) guns being established as the British standard, but extensive testing had convinced the German navy that they were not significantly less effective.

Guns
The main 11-in (280-mm) guns were of a smaller caliber than the 12-in (305-mm) guns being established as the British standard, but extensive testing had convinced the German navy that they were not significantly less effective.

Armor
6,537 tons (6,642 tonnes) of armor were carried (35.2 percent of standard displacement weight).

Torpedo Nets
Torpedo nets, made of steel mesh, were a fixture of all capital ships from the 1890s up to 1916. The net hung from waterline level.

Boilers
In 1915 the boilers were adapted to burn an oil-coal mix, with the oil sprayed above the burning coal.

Satsuma (1909)

SATSUMA WAS THE FIRST LARGE BATTLESHIP TO BE BUILT IN A JAPANESE YARD, AND THE LAST OF THE IMPERIAL NAVY'S BATTLESHIPS POWERED BY RECIPROCATING ENGINES. SHE SAW NO COMBAT DURING WORLD WAR I AND WAS DECOMMISSIONED IN 1923.

Japanese technicians and designers had profited not only from the practice of the British yards where their first battleships were built, but from the climate of ideas in the Royal Navy, where the merits of the "all big-gun" ship were widely discussed. *Satsuma*, laid down at Yokosuka Kaigun Kosho on May 15, 1905—just before the Battle of Tsushima—was intended to be such a ship. It was launched on November 15, 1906, and completed on March 25, 1909—a date delayed by a British refusal to send out its 12-in (305 mm) guns from Armstrong while Japan and Russia were at war. As designed it would have had twelve of these guns, but Japan's lack of capital after the war with Russia allowed for only four of them to be bought, along with eight 10-in (254 mm) QF guns, also from Armstrong.

The engines were vertical triple-expansion type, with 20 Japanese Miyabara boilers, but a sister ship, *Aki*, completed almost a year later, was powered by American Curtis turbines from the Fore River Shipyard in New York (necessitating three funnels to *Satsuma*'s two), giving it an advantage of 1.75 knots (2 mph; 3.2 km/h) over *Satsuma*. Its turbine drive, linked to the substantial armament, even if not as heavy as the original plan, earned the two ships the name of "semi-dreadnoughts." Tall pole masts, with small fighting-top platforms, were fitted.

Service in the South Seas

In World War I, *Satsuma* was assigned to the 1st Battleship Squadron, then the 2nd South Seas Squadron, which seized the Caroline and Palau Islands colonies from German rule in October 1914. It rejoined the 1st Battleship Squadron for the rest of the war. Two 3.1-in (79 mm) AA guns were fitted. Disarmed at Yokosuka in 1922, it was removed from the Navy List on September 20, 1923, and used as a target ship. On September 7, 1924, it was sunk in Tokyo Bay by shells from *Nagato* and *Mutsu*.

SPECIFICATIONS

DISPLACEMENT: 19,372 tons (19,683 tonnes)

DIMENSIONS: 482 ft x 83 ft 6 in x 27 ft 6 in (146.9 m x 25.4 m x 8.4 m)

PROPULSION: Twin shafts, vertical triple-expansion engines, 20 Miyabara boilers, 17,300 ihp (12,901 kW)

ARMAMENT: Four 12-in (305 mm)/45-caliber, twelve 10-in (254 mm)/45-caliber, twelve 4.7-in (120 mm)/40-caliber, four 3.1-in (79 mm)/40-caliber, four 3.1-in (79 mm)/28-caliber guns; five 18-in (457 mm) torpedo tubes

ARMOR: Belt 9–4 in (229–102 mm), barbettes 9.2–7 in (234–178 mm), turrets 9–7 in (228–178 mm), conning tower 6-in (152 mm), deck 2-in (50 mm)

SPEED: 18.25 knots (21 mph; 33.8 km/h)

CREW: 887

Satsuma

DESIGN
IN ITS GENERAL LINES AND
PROPORTIONS, *SATSUMA*
RETAINED THE BRITISH LOOK
OF ITS PREDECESSORS.

GUNS
THE 10-IN (254 MM) GUNS WERE
MOUNTED ABOVE DECK LEVEL, KEEPING
THEM FREE OF WAVE INVASION.

BOILERS
JAPANESE MIYABARA COAL-OIL
BOILERS POWERED THE SHIP,
BUT MANY COMPONENTS WERE
IMPORTED FROM ABROAD.

EMBRASURES
FOUR OF THE 4.7-IN (120-MM) GUNS WERE
MOUNTED IN EMBRASURES TOWARDS THE BOW
AND STERN.

USS *South Carolina* (1910)

THE LEAD SHIP OF TWO IN HER CLASS, THE *SOUTH CAROLINA* MOUNTED A FORMIDABLE
EIGHT-GUN 12-IN (305 MM) BROADSIDE, AND THEIR SUPER-FIRING TURRETS WERE TO
BECOME THE STANDARD ARRANGEMENT FOR CAPITAL SHIPS.

Limitation of standard displacement to 16,000 tons (16,257 tonnes) by Congressional mandate brought out the maximum ingenuity of the American designers in obtaining maximum firepower with a broadside of eight big guns. The details had been fixed before *Dreadnought*'s, but *South Carolina* (BB 25), laid down at Cramp's yard, Philadelphia, on December 18, 1906, launched on July 11, 1908, was not commissioned until March 1, 1910. With these ships, what became the classic gun arrangement of the battleship and battlecruiser was established, with two turrets fore and aft, the inner one raised to fire over the top of the outer one. Tests had been made using the armored turret of an old monitor to establish that blast effects from the super-firing turret would not be detrimental to the lower one.

With all the big guns on the centerline, the balancing of the ship was simplified and the magazines could be located in areas of maximum safety. From the viewpoint of gunnery control—by now a vital aspect of battle management—all the main armament could be given instructions at once when firing salvoes on the beam.

Turbine propulsion had been rejected in favor of reciprocating engines which gave a speed 2.5 knots (2.9 mph; 4.6 km/h) less than HMS *Dreadnought*. But the US Navy command considered speed to be less vital than firepower and armor protection, at least until long-range German U-boats began to reach American waters.

Another consequence of the weight limitation was the sacrificing of a deck level compared with the previous *Connecticut* class. Officers were normally accommodated at the stern but in these ships their quarters were moved to the midships superstructure.

Convoy Escort

South Carolina was deployed to the Atlantic Fleet, based at Key West and Guantanamo. After a refit at Philadelphia, completed in January 1917, it returned to Guantanamo. From the outbreak of war in April 1917 it was used as a gunnery training ship in Chesapeake Bay. In September 1918 it had to return from convoy escort duty for mechanical repairs. From February to July 1919 it made four Atlantic crossings to repatriate American troops from France. With *Michigan* it made a training cruise to Honolulu in 1920 and went on further training and goodwill cruises until paid off at Philadelphia on December 15, 1921. It was stricken from the list on January 13, 1924, and scrapped.

SPECIFICATIONS

DISPLACEMENT: 16,000 tons (16,256 tonnes); 17,900 tons (18,186 tonnes) full load

DIMENSIONS: 452 ft 8 in x 80 ft 5 in x 24 ft 7 in (137.9 m x 24.5 m x 7.49 m)

PROPULSION: Twin shafts, two vertical 4-cylinder triple-acting engines, 12 Babcock & Wilcox boilers, 16,500 hp (12,304 kW)

ARMAMENT: Eight 12-in (305 mm) guns, twenty-two 3.5in (88mm) QF guns, two underwater 21-in (533 mm) torpedo tubes

ARMOR: Belt 12–9in (305–228 mm), casemates and barbettes 10–8 in (254–203 mm), turrets 12-in (304 mm), conning tower 12-in (305 mm), deck 1.5-in (38 mm)

SPEED: 18.5 knots (21.3 mph; 34.3 km/h)

CREW: 869

USS *South Carolina*

MASTS

BB25 AND 26 WERE THE FIRST US SHIPS TO CARRY THE SO-CALLED LATTICE MASTS, OFTEN REFERRED TO AS BASKET MASTS, WHICH WERE TO TYPIFY US BATTLESHIPS UNTIL THE 1930S.

SIGHTS

SIGHTS WERE FITTED ON THE TURRET SIDES RATHER THAN ON THE TOPS, TO AVOID BLAST IMPACT.

GUNS

THE ARC OF FIRE WAS AROUND 270°. THE 12-IN (305 MM) GUNS HAD 45-FT (13.72 M) BARRELS WEIGHING 52.75 TONS (53.6 TONNES) AND FIRED 870-LB (390 KG) SHELLS WITH AN EXTREME RANGE OF 20,000 YARDS (18,000 M) AT THEIR MAXIMUM ELEVATION OF 15°. THE RATE OF FIRE WAS THREE ROUNDS A MINUTE AT PEAK PERFORMANCE.

Minas Gerais (1910)

MINAS GERAIS WAS A DREADNOUGHT BATTLESHIP OF THE BRAZILIAN NAVY. ORIGINALLY PLANNED IN THE PRE-DREADNOUGHT YEARS IN ANSWER TO POWERFUL VESSELS THEN BUILDING FOR CHILE, THE DESIGN WAS MODIFIED TO MAKE IT THE FIRST DREADNOUGHT FOR A SOUTH AMERICAN NAVY.

First proposed in a 1904 program, *Minas Gerais* was ordered from the British Vickers-Armstrong yard at Elswick, and laid down in 1907. It was a complete package deal, with the builders supplying the guns and armor. It is a curious tribute to the openness of the armament industry at that time that the design of HMS *Dreadnought*, then newly commissioned, could be used for a warship for another country, albeit one friendly to Britain. Launched on September 10, 1908, the ship was completed on January 5, 1910. At that time, with twelve 12-in (305 mm) guns compared to *Dreadnought*'s ten, it was the most powerful battleship in the world in terms of destructive capacity.

Though immediately known as a "dreadnought," there were significant variations from the type-ship. *Minas Gerais* had super-firing turrets while *Dreadnought* did not, and its wing turrets were offset diagonally rather than set laterally. Although turbine propulsion had been considered, potential maintenance problems resulted in conventional triple-expansion engines with 18 Babcock coal-burning boilers.

Out of Fighting Form

Battleships required regular exercise cruises in order to maintain high levels of gunnery efficiency and maneuvering capability, but *Minas Gerais* and its sister ship *São Paulo* rarely left port. Maintenance too was carried out on a more limited basis than in larger navies. When Brazil declared war on Germany on October 24, 1917, both ships were in poor condition and incapable of active service. Updated equipment, particularly in fire control, had not been fitted. After the war *Minas Gerais* underwent a refit at the New York Navy Yard and in another major refit at Rio between 1931–37 was converted

to oil-firing, lost a funnel, had the bridge, superstructure, and masts modified, and acquired new fire-control systems. In this form it survived until 1952, though seeing little in the way of sea service. In that year it was sold to Italian shipbreakers. Towed to Genoa in 1954, it was broken up there.

SPECIFICATIONS

DISPLACEMENT: 21,200 tons (21,540 tonnes)

DIMENSIONS: 544 ft x 83 ft x 27 ft 10 in (165.8 m x 25.3 m x 8.5 m)

PROPULSION: Twin shafts, vertical triple-expansion engines, 18 Babcock & Wilcox boilers, 23,500 shp (17,524 kW)

ARMAMENT: Twelve 12-in (305 mm), twenty-two 4.7-in (120 mm) guns

ARMOR: Belt 9 in–4 in (230–102 mm), turrets 9 in–8 in (230–203 mm)

SPEED: 21 knots (24 mph; 38.9 km/h)

CREW: 850

Minas Gerais

MAST
THE ORIGINAL TOPMAST WAS REMOVED,
AND A SHORT POLE-MAST ADDED AFT.

TURRETS
HYDRAULIC POWER TURNED THE GUN
TURRETS. ON COMPLETION, THE SHIP
FIRED THE HEAVIEST BROADSIDE OF ANY
WARSHIP IN THE WORLD.

AFTER 1937
THE ILLUSTRATION SHOWS *MINAS GERAIS* IN
POST-1937 CONFIGURATION. ORIGINALLY A
FORE-FUNNEL HAD BEEN SITUATED FORWARD
OF THE MAST.

ARMOR
THE ARMOR PLATE, FROM ARMSTRONG
WHITWORTH, WAS OF KRUPP CEMENTED
STEEL TYPE.

SMS *Von der Tann* (1911)

THIRD SHIP OF GERMANY'S 1907 BUILDING PROGRAM, *VON DER TANN* WAS GERMANY'S FIRST BATTLECRUISER. MATCHED AGAINST ITS BRITISH COUNTERPARTS, IT SHOWED CONSIDERABLE SUPERIORITY IN COMBAT AT THE BATTLE OF JUTLAND.

Built by Blohm & Voss in Hamburg, the ship was laid down on March 25, 1908, launched on March 20, 1909, and completed on February 20, 1911, at a cost of 36.5 million Goldmarks. It was the exact contemporary of the British *Indefatigable* class, but with armor of sufficient staying power to engage in a fleet battle. Unlike the British battlecruisers it was not planned for long-range missions, and crew quarters were limited. *Von der Tann* was the first German capital ship to be turbine-driven and on occasion could be pushed to 28 knots (32.2 mph; 52 km/h). From 1916 the 18 coal boilers were fitted with tar-oil sprayers to improve combustion.

The eight main guns, with the central turrets offset, could be trained to fire a single broadside and had a range (from 1915) of 22,300 yards (20,400 m) with 670-lb (302 kg) armor-piercing shells. The ship also carried a substantial secondary armament of ten 5.9-in (150 mm) guns. Embrasures in the forecastle sides enabled forward fire against advancing torpedo boats.

Fighting in the German Bight

In August 1914 it was assigned to Admiral Franz Ritter von Hipper's 1st Scouting Group of the High Seas Fleet, and on August 28 took part in an unsuccessful counterattack on British battlecruisers in the German Bight, in the North Sea. In November–December it joined in bombardment of English ports and in 1915 served both in the Baltic and North Seas. At the start of the Battle of Jutland, May 31– June 1, 1916, the 1st Scouting Group opened fire on the British battlecruisers at a range of 15,000 yards (14,000 m) and shells from *Von der Tann* sank HMS *Indefatigable*. Six minutes later a 15-in (375 mm) shell from HMS *Barham* pierced the armor and flooded the steering room. Return fire by *Von der Tann* caused serious damage to *Barham*. It remained in the midst of the battle, despite shell damage and mechanical failures that kept the main guns out of action for 11 hours. Repaired by July 29, *Von der Tann* remained active until Germany's capitulation. Interned with the rest of the Fleet in Scapa Flow, in the Orkney Islands, it was scuttled by its crew on June 21, 1919. Refloated on December 7, 1930, it was towed to Rosyth for scrapping.

SPECIFICATIONS

DISPLACEMENT: 19,064 tons (19,370 tonnes); 21,700 tons (22,048 tonnes) full load

DIMENSIONS: 563 ft 4 in x 87 ft 3 in x 26 ft 7 in (171.7 m x 26.6 m x 9 m)

PROPULSION: Quadruple shafts, Parsons turbines, 18 Schulz-Thornycroft boilers, 43,600 shp (32,512 kW)

ARMAMENT: Eight 11-in (280 mm), ten 5.9-in (150 mm), sixteen 3.5-in (88 mm) guns; four 17.7-in (450 mm) torpedo tubes

ARMOR: Belt 10–3.2 in (250–80 mm), bulkheads 7–4 in (180–100 mm), battery 6 in (152 mm), barbettes 9–1.2 in (230–30 mm), turrets 9–2.4 in (230–60 mm), conning tower 10–3.2 in (250–80 mm)

SPEED: 24.75 knots (28.5 mph; 45.8 km/h)

CREW: 1,174

SMS *Von Der Tann*

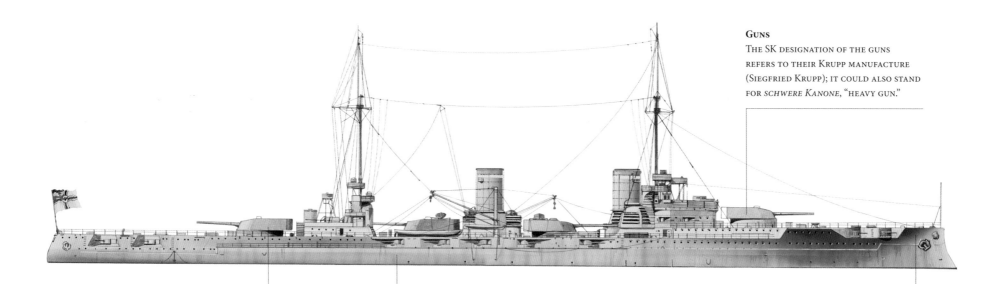

GUNS
THE SK DESIGNATION OF THE GUNS
REFERS TO THEIR KRUPP MANUFACTURE
(SIEGFRIED KRUPP); IT COULD ALSO STAND
FOR *SCHWERE KANONE*, "HEAVY GUN."

TURRETS
THE TURRETS WERE DESIGNATED "A," "B,"
"C," AND "D" (ANTON, BRUNO, CÄSAR,
DORA), WITH THE REAR TURRET AS "C" AND
THE PORT CENTRAL TURRET AS "D."

BILGE KEEL
BILGE KEELS WERE A LATER ADDITION, WHEN THE
ANTI-ROLLING TANKS WERE CONVERTED FOR USE
AS ADDITIONAL COAL BUNKERS.

FORECASTLE
FOR THE FIRST AND ONLY TIME IN A MAJOR
GERMAN WARSHIP THE OFFICERS WERE BERTHED
IN THE FORECASTLE.

HMS *Hercules* (1911)

WITH ITS SISTER SHIP HMS *COLOSSUS*, HERCULES WAS A PRODUCT OF THE BRITISH–GERMAN NAVAL ARMS RACE OF THE PRE-WORLD WAR I YEARS, WHEN BRITISH PUBLIC OPINION INSISTED ON MORE DREADNOUGHTS TO COUNTER RISING GERMAN NAVAL POWER.

Modeled on the hull of HMS *Neptune*, then under construction, but with too many structural variations to be considered in the same class, *Hercules* was laid down on July 8, 1909, at Palmers' yard on the Tyne, launched on April 9, 1910, and commissioned on July 31, 1911, a month after *Colossus*. It cost £1,661,240. Great efforts were made to limit any increase in displacement over *Neptune*, as this would risk putting the waterline belt completely under water. Any increase in weight had to be compensated for by a reduction somewhere else.

Neptune was the first RN ship to have super-firing turrets and this was retained in the *Colossus* class, as was the offset placing of the midships "P" and "Q" turrets. In 1912 the fore-funnel was heightened in an attempt to keep the bridge clear of smoke. Internally the ship was divided into 20 watertight compartments, though interior armor protection was reduced, with the torpedo bulkheads protecting only the magazines and machinery rooms; the armor saved here was used to provide a thicker belt than on *Neptune*. Total armor weight was 6,570 tons (6,675 tonnes).

Fighting at Jutland

Hercules was made flagship of the 2nd Division of the Home Fleet until August 1914 (with a spell from July 1912 to March 1913 as flagship of the 2nd Battle Squadron). In World War I it was part of the 6th Division of the 1st Battle Squadron, and took part in the Battle of Jutland, May 31–June 1, 1916, firing 98 shells and receiving and inflicting (on the battlecruiser *Seydlitz*) only minor damage. During the operation against a potential High Seas Fleet sortie in August 1916 it carried out tests with an unmanned kite balloon. From 1916 to 1918 it was flagship of the 4th Battle Squadron. In December 1918 it carried the Allied Naval Commission to Kiel. In 1919 it was placed in Category C reserve, and in November 1921 was towed to Kiel for scrapping.

SPECIFICATIONS

DISPLACEMENT: 20,225 tons (20,550 tonnes); 23,050 tons (23,420 tonnes) full load

DIMENSIONS: 546 ft x 85 ft x 28 ft 9 in (166.4 m x 25.9 m x 8.8 m)

PROPULSION: Quadruple shafts, Parsons turbines, 18 Yarrow boilers, 25,000 shp (18,642.5 kW)

ARMAMENT: Ten 12-in (305 mm)/50-caliber, sixteen 4-in (102 mm)/50-caliber, four 3-pounder guns; three 21-in (533 mm) torpedo tubes

ARMOR: Belt 11–7 in (280–180 mm), bulkheads 10–4 in (250–102 mm), barbettes, turrets, and tower 11 in (280 mm), deck 4–1.75 in (102–45 mm)

SPEED: 21 knots (24 mph; 38.9 km/h)

CREW: 755

HMS *Hercules*

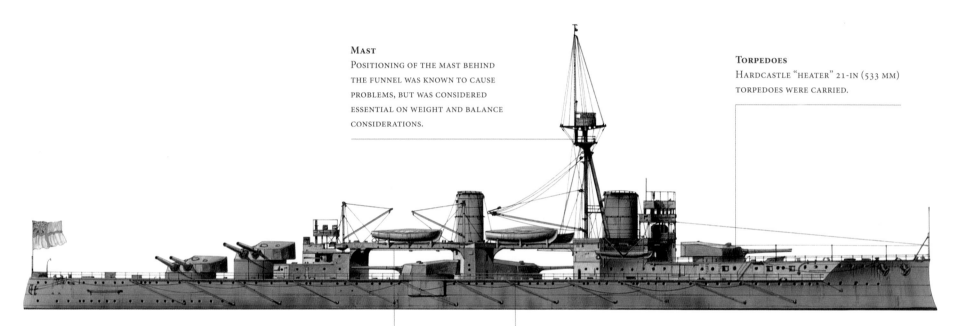

MAST
POSITIONING OF THE MAST BEHIND THE FUNNEL WAS KNOWN TO CAUSE PROBLEMS, BUT WAS CONSIDERED ESSENTIAL ON WEIGHT AND BALANCE CONSIDERATIONS.

TORPEDOES
HARDCASTLE "HEATER" 21-IN (533 MM) TORPEDOES WERE CARRIED.

DECK
THE FLYING DECK OVER THE CENTRAL TURRETS, KNOWN AS THE "MARBLE ARCHES," WAS REMOVED DURING WORLD WAR I.

TURRETS
THOUGH THE PLACING OF "P" AND "Q" TURRETS WAS INTENDED TO ALLOW FULL BROADSIDES, IN PRACTICE SUCH BROADSIDES WERE NOT FIRED BECAUSE OF BLAST PROBLEMS.

USS *Utah* (1911)

Utah and *Florida* were the United States Navy's most powerful battleships when commissioned in 1911, though by that time the USS *Wyoming*, with twelve 12-in (305-mm) guns, was already launched.

Utah and *Florida* were slightly larger versions of the preceding *Delaware* class. *Utah* (BB 31), was laid down at the New York Shipbuilding Yard, Camden, New Jersey, on March 15, 1909, launched on December 23 that year, and completed on August 31, 1911, at a cost of $8 million. Unlike the *Wyoming* class, the funnels were both placed between the narrow basket masts, all concentrated amidships, in order to make room for the triple set of turrets carried aft of the mainmast. The foremast was built up above the bridge. Following criticism of secondary gun protection on *Delaware*, a lightly armored upper casemate protected the secondary 5-in (127 mm) guns on each side.

Utah's war service began with the US occupation of Vera Cruz, Mexico, where it and Florida landed marines on April 21, 1914. From April 6, 1917, it was based at Chesapeake Bay for engineering and gunnery training until August 30, 1918, when it crossed the Atlantic to Bantry Bay, Ireland, as flagship of Battleship Division 6, patrolling the Western Approaches to the British Isles.

After the war it escorted President Woodrow Wilson's ship to the Versailles peace negotiations. From July 1921 until October 1922 it was flagship of US warships in Europe, then on October 21 resumed the role of flagship of Battleship Division 6. *Utah* was extensively rebuilt at the Boston Navy Yard in 1925, with new oil-fired boilers replacing the coal burners, a single large funnel, and the aft cage mast removed and replaced by a light pole. Torpedo protection blisters were fitted to the hull.

Casualty of Pearl Harbor

Decommissioned as a battleship, between July 1, 1931, and April 1, 1932, it was converted into a radio-controlled target ship, as AG-16. Partly as a target vessel, partly as a AA gunnery ship, it participated in many exercises through the 1930s and into the 1940s, all in the Pacific Ocean. In December 1941 it had recently arrived at Pearl Harbor from an overhaul at Puget Sound Navy Yard. In the Japanese surprise attack of December 7 it was struck by two aerial torpedoes and capsized, with the loss of 64 men. Attempts to right and lift the ship failed, and the wreck remains at Pearl Harbor as a war grave.

SPECIFICATIONS

DISPLACEMENT: 22,669 tons (23,033 tonnes)

DIMENSIONS: 521 ft 8 in x 88 ft 3 in x 28 ft 3 in (159 m x 26.9 m x 8.6 m)

PROPULSION: Quadruple shafts, Parsons turbines, 12 boilers, 28,000 shp (20,880 kW)

ARMAMENT: Ten 12-in (305 mm)/ 45-caliber, sixteen 5-in (127 mm)/ 51-caliber guns; two 21-in (530 mm) torpedo tubes

ARMOR: Belt 11 in (279 mm), turret faces 12 in (305 mm), conning tower 11.5 in (292 mm), deck 1.5 in (38 mm)

SPEED: 21 knots (24.2 mph; 39 km/h)

CREW: 1,001

USS *Utah*

TOPS
FIGHTING TOPS WERE MOUNTED ON THE
CRANE TOWERS.

LIGHT POLES
THE ORIGINAL LIGHT POLES ABOVE THE
LATTICE TOWERS HAVE BEEN REMOVED.

RANGE FINDERS
RANGE FINDERS ON THE TURRETS WERE
INSTALLED AFTER 1914.

DESIGN
THE ILLUSTRATION SHOWS *UTAH* AS IT WAS
AROUND 1923. SEVERAL ALTERATIONS WERE
MADE TO CONTROL AND SIGNALING POSITIONS
ON THE MASTS DURING WORLD WAR I.

HMS *Lion* (1912)

THE THREE SHIPS OF THE *LION* CLASS WERE THE FIRST BATTLECRUISERS TO CARRY 13.5-IN (343 MM) GUNS. THEY WERE THE LARGEST, FASTEST CAPITAL SHIPS YET BUILT AND ALSO THE MOST EXPENSIVE. BUT THEY HAD SERIOUS DEFECTS.

The British Navy adopted the super-firing turret arrangement in HMS *Neptune* (1911) and with the *Orion* class (1912) introduced the 13.5-in (343 mm) gun. Both were combined in *Lion*, laid down at Devonport Naval Dockyard on November 29, 1909, launched on August 6, 1910, and commissioned on June 4, 1912. It cost in excess of £2,000,000. As in *Dreadnought* and *Orion,* the fore-funnel was in front of the mast, making the masthead installations often uninhabitable through smoke and heat. In 1912 the original tripod was replaced by a single pole mast with a light spotting top, placed forward of the funnel. The second and third funnels were heightened to be uniform with the fore-funnel.

The ships carried sixteen 4-in (102 mm) guns for anti-torpedo boat defense, their batteries aligned so as to have six firing ahead, eight abeam, and four astern.

Two 21-in (533 mm) torpedo tubes were below the waterline on either side of "A" barbette. The vulnerability of the *Lion* class was more due to insufficient understanding of the flash effects of a shell explosion and the countermeasures necessary, than of lack of armor as such.

Ship Saved by Valiant Action

Lion joined the 1st Cruiser Squadron on commissioning, then was flagship of the 1st Battlecruiser Squadron from January 1913. In World War I it was flagship of the Battlecruiser Fleet, and gave long-range support at the Battle of Heligoland Bight on August 28, 1914.

At the Battle of the Dogger Bank, the only fight involving only battlecruisers, January 24, 1915, a shot from *Lion* knocked out the rear turret of Admiral Hipper's flagship *Seydlitz*, but *Lion* sustained seventeen hits, narrowly avoided flooding of the engine room,

and fell out of the action. Towed back by HMS *Indomitable*, it spent four months under repair.

At the Battle of Jutland, May 31, 1916, *Lion* took a direct hit on "Q" turret, whose officer, Major Francis Harvey, died as he flooded the magazines, saving the ship. Repaired by July 19, *Lion* continued in North Sea operations until the end of the war. In 1921 it was decommissioned, and was sold for breaking up in January 1924.

SPECIFICATIONS

DISPLACEMENT: 30,820 tons (31,314 tonnes) full load

DIMENSIONS: 700 ft x 88 ft 6 in x 32 ft 5 in (213.4 m x 27 m x 9.9 m)

PROPULSION: Quadruple shafts, Parsons direct-drive steam turbines, 42 Yarrow water-tube boilers, 70,000 shp (52,199 kW)

ARMAMENT: Eight 13.5-in (343 mm), sixteen 4-in (102 mm) guns; two 21-in (533 mm) torpedo tubes

ARMOR: Belt 9–4in (229–102mm), bulkheads 4 in (102 mm), barbettes 9–8 in (229–203 mm), turrets 9 in (229 mm), deck 2.5–1 in (64–25 mm), conning tower 10 in (254 mm)

SPEED: 28 knots (33.4 mph; 51.9 km/h)

CREW: 997

HMS *Lion*

FUNNEL
DERRICKS WERE FITTED ON EACH SIDE OF
THE CENTER FUNNEL WHEN THE TRIPOD
MAST WAS REMOVED.

RANGE FINDERS
RANGE FINDERS WERE LOCATED IN "B" AND "Y"
TURRETS AND IN THE CONNING TOWER, WITH
THE FIRE-CONTROL POSITION (THIS WAS LATER
TRANSFERRED TO THE MAST, WHICH WAS REINFORCED
BY STRUTS TO SUPPORT IT).

TURRETS
BY 1918 LION HAD SEARCHLIGHT TOWERS
MOUNTED ON THE AFTER FUNNEL, AND
FLYING-OFF PLATFORMS MOUNTED ON
"Q" AND "X" TURRETS.

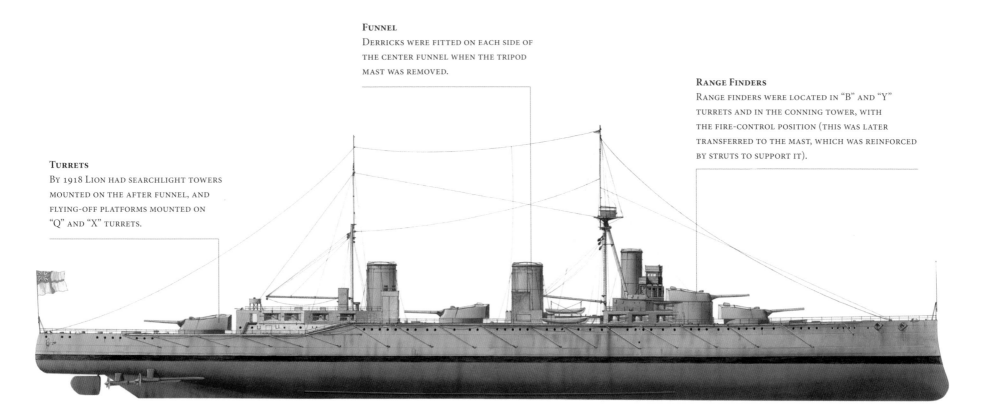

USS *Wyoming* (1912)

WYOMING SERVED IN BOTH WORLD WARS, IN BOTH THE ATLANTIC AND PACIFIC OCEANS, AND WENT THROUGH A SERIES OF CHANGES OF APPEARANCE AND FUNCTION, ENDING UP AS THE "CHESAPEAKE RAIDER" AA TRAINING SHIP.

Wyoming (BB32) was laid down at Cramp's yard, Philadelphia, on February 9, 1910, launched on May 25, 1911, and commissioned at New York Navy Yard in September 1912. It carried twelve 12-in (305 mm) guns in six turrets. The space required by these long guns gave the midships section something of a squeezed-up look, with the two funnels and the basket masts all set close together. Original secondary armament was twenty-one 5-in (127 mm) QF guns. There were two armored decks, above the heavy-gun magazines and the engine room.

World War I Service

Wyoming was assigned to the Atlantic Fleet and operated on routine patrols and exercises, as flagship from December 30, 1912. In 1913 it made a long-range cruise as far as Malta, returning on December 15. Until April 1917 it remained with the Atlantic Fleet. From April to November of that year it was used for engineer training, then joined the British Grand Fleet at Scapa Flow, serving with the 6th Battle Squadron. In June–July 1918 it acted as a guard ship during the laying of the North Sea Barrage, and afterwards was an escort to the surrendered High Seas Fleet on its way to Scapa Flow. In December 1918 it returned to the United States, and from July 19, 1919, until August 1921 was deployed in the Pacific.

Training Ship

A major modernization was done at the Philadelphia Navy Yard in the autumn of 1926. New turbines and four White-Forster oil-burning boilers replaced the originals. These changes made it possible to remove the after funnel, and the ship took on a quite different appearance. Further major modifications were made at Philadelphia from 1930, when *Wyoming* was "de-militarized" and converted to a training ship, designated AG17. This role was maintained and greatly intensified after the Pearl Harbor attack of December 7, 1941, with AA defense training as the prime task.

In early 1944 the fore basket mast was replaced by a pole, and the remaining heavy guns and turrets were taken out, to make room for a wide range of anti-aircraft guns and fire-control equipment. In July 1945 further planned modifications were stopped, and it decommissioned on August 1, 1947, and struck on September 16. In 1947–48 it was broken up at Newark, New Jersey.

SPECIFICATIONS

DISPLACEMENT: 26,000 tons (26,416 tonnes)

DIMENSIONS: 562 ft x 93 ft 2 in x 28 ft 6 in (171 m x 28.4 m x 8.7 m)

PROPULSION: Quadruple shafts, four Parsons turbines, 12 Babcock coal/oil boilers, 28,000 shp (20,880 kW)

ARMAMENT: Twelve 12-in (305 mm), twenty-one 5-in (127 mm) guns; two 21-in (533 mm) torpedo tubes

ARMOR: Belt 11–5 in (279–127 mm), bulkhead 11–9 in (279–229 mm), decks 3–2 in (76–25 mm), turrets 12 in (305 mm), barbettes 11 in (279 mm), funnels 6.5 in (165 mm), conning tower 12 in (305 mm)

SPEED: 20.5 knots (23.6 mph; 37.9 km/h)

CREW: 1,063

USS *Wyoming*

MAST
IN 1926 THE AFT BASKET MAST WAS
REPLACED BY A TRIPOD STRUCTURE, AND
A CATAPULT WAS INSTALLED TO LAUNCH
A FLOATPLANE OFF "C" TURRET.

DECK
THE FLUSH DECK ARRANGEMENT
PLACED THE MIDSHIPS BATTERY ABOUT
4 FT (1.2 M) HIGHER THAN ON PREVIOUS
SHIPS: A MUCH MORE EFFECTIVE POSITION.

GUNS
THE BARREL LENGTH WAS 50 CALIBER,
WEIGHT 56.3 TONS (57.2 TONNES), FIRING
SHELLS OF 868 LB (394 KG) AND WITH A
RANGE OF 27,230 YARDS (24,900 M) WHEN
ELEVATED TO 15°.

SMS *Viribus Unitis* (1912)

THE FIRST TRIPLE-TURRET BATTLESHIP AND THE FIRST AUSTRO-HUNGARIAN DREADNOUGHT OF THE *TEGETTHOFF* CLASS, IT CARRIED THE BODIES OF ARCHDUKE FRANZ FERDINAND AND ARCHDUCHESS SOPHIE BACK TO TRIESTE AFTER THE FATEFUL ASSASSINATION OF JUNE 28, 1914.

Austria-Hungary's only dreadnought class is named for *Tegetthoff*, though *Viribus Unitis* ("with united strength") was first to be laid down, at Stabilimento Tecnico Triestino on July 24, 1910, launched, on June 24, 1911, and completed, on December 5, 1912. The class was designed to counter Italy's triple-turreted *Dante Alighieri*, but in fact *Viribus Unitis* was the first 12 in (305 mm) triple-turret battleship to be commissioned into service. The huge weight of the four turrets required close attention to the metacentric height in design. They were originally conceived for a larger hull, but financial constraints resulted in a reduced freeboard and shorter length. In profile it was a typical dreadnought type.

Bringing Home the Archduke

The ship made its only cruise into the Mediterranean Sea in Spring 1914, with *Tegetthoff* on a training voyage. On June 30 it carried the bodies of Archduke Franz Ferdinand and his wife, assassinated in Sarajevo on June 28, to Trieste. On July 28 it was mobilized with other units to support the German warships *Goeben* and *Breslau* in evading British Navy ships; the Austro-Hungarian squadron came as far south as Brindisi, on the southeastern tip of Italy.

In World War I they formed the 1st Division of the 1st Battle Squadron, based at Pula (now in Croatia), and bombarded Italian coastal positions at Ancona in May 1915. But for most of the war there was no work for the Battle Squadron, beyond AA defense fire against Italian aircraft. The Allied blockade of the Straits of Otranto kept the Austro-Hungarian fleet bottled up in the Adriatic. Under Admiral Miklós Horthy a breakout was planned for June 1918, but the torpedoing of the fourth ship in the class, *Szent István*, by the Italian torpedo boat *MAS 15* on June 10 caused the attack to be aborted. Shortly before the Austrian surrender the ship was handed over to the National Council of the future Yugoslavia (as a neutral force) but Italian frogmen attached a limpet mine to the hull in Pula naval anchorage and sank it, on November 1, 1918.

SPECIFICATIONS

DISPLACEMENT: 20,013 tons (20,426 tonnes); 21,595 tons (21,94 tonnes) full load

DIMENSIONS: 499 ft 3 in x 89 ft 8 in x 29 ft (152.2 m x 27.3 m x 8.9 m)

PROPULSION: Quadruple shafts, Parsons geared turbines, 12 Yarrow boilers, 27,300 shp (20,357.6 kW)

ARMAMENT: Twelve 12-in (305 mm)/45-caliber, twelve 5.9-in (150 mm)/50 caliber, eighteen 2.6-in (66 mm) guns; four 21-in (533 mm) torpedo tubes, 20 mines

ARMOR: Belt 11–6 in (280–152 mm), turrets 11–2.25 in (280–60 mm), casemates 4.75 in (180 mm), conning tower 11–2.25 in (280–60 mm)

SPEED: 20.3 knots (23.3 mph; 37.6 km/h)

CREW: 1,087

SMS *Viribus Unitis*

HEAVY GUNS
EACH OF THE 12-IN (305 MM) GUNS WEIGHED 54 TONS (54.8 TONNES) AND THEIR SHELLS 0.44 TON (450 KG). THERE WERE 76 SHELLS CARRIED FOR EACH GUN. A TRAINED CREW COULD FIRE A SALVO EVERY 40 SECONDS.

SPOTTING PLATFORMS
DUE TO BETTER VISIBILITY IN THE MEDITERRANEAN, THE SPOTTING PLATFORMS WERE INSTALLED HIGHER THAN ON THE BATTLESHIPS OF THE OTHER NAVIES.

TURRETS
FROM 1914 FOUR OF THE 2.6-IN (66 MM) GUNS WERE MOUNTED ON THE SUPER-FIRING TURRETS, FOR AA DEFENSE.

LANDING SUPPORT GUNS
TWO 1.8-IN (47 MM) AND TWO 2.6-IN (66 MM) MOBILE GUNS WERE AVAILABLE FOR LANDING SUPPORT, AS WELL AS TWO 0.3-INCH (8 MM) MACHINE GUNS.

SMS *Derfflinger* (1913)

DIFFERENT IN APPEARANCE FROM ANY PREVIOUS GERMAN CAPITAL SHIP, WITH A FLUSH DECK RISING
GENTLY TOWARDS A STRAIGHT BOW, *DERFFLINGER* WAS GENERALLY CONSIDERED TO BE AMONG THE
MOST HANDSOME-LOOKING WARSHIPS OF ITS TIME.

Laid down at the Blohm & Voss yard in Hamburg, Germany, in January 1912, launched on July 12, 1913 (after sticking on the slipway for a month), and commissioned soon after the outbreak of war, on September 1, 1914, *Derfflinger* cost 56 million Goldmarks. The 12-in (305 mm) guns, used on a German ship for the first time, were placed fore and aft, with super-firing turrets. Rate of fire was one round per minute. Twelve 5.9-in (150 mm) QF guns was fitted in casemates at deck level along the superstructure, and eight 3.4-in (88 mm) QF guns mounted at upper levels. Four of these were removed in 1916 and four AA guns of the same caliber mounted. Armor extended up to deck level between the main turrets and for the full length at waterline level.

Heavy Fighting in World War I

Derfflinger was attached to Rear-Admiral Hipper's 1st Reconnaissance Squadron.

It took part in the bombardment of Scarborough, England, on December 16, 1914, and was at the Battle of the Dogger Bank, January 24, 1915, where it took a shell hit, causing localized flooding in protective coal bunkers.

In August 1915 it was in action in the Gulf of Riga against Russian ships. Back in the North Sea, it made a sortie on March 5–6, 1916, into the southern North Sea; then joined in bombarding Yarmouth and Lowestoft in England on April 24.

At Jutland on May 31 with the battlecruiser *Seydlitz*, *Derfflinger* sank the British battleship *Queen Mary*, and with *Lützow*, sank HMS *Invincible*, itself taking 17 heavy hits and four lesser ones. By the end of the battle, with only two guns still operational, it returned to Wilhelmshaven, Germany, under its own steam, with some 3,000 tons (3,050 tonnes) of water inside the hull. Repairs were completed at Kiel by mid-October, but it remained in port

except for a sortie into the northern North Sea, with other ships, on April 23, 1918.

After the German surrender, it went to Scapa Flow, November 24, 1918, and was scuttled there with the other German ships on June 21, 1919. Raised in 1939, it remained upside down until 1948, when it was towed to Faslane, Scotland, for breaking up.

SPECIFICATIONS

DISPLACEMENT: 26,180 tons (26,600 tonnes); 30,707 tons (31,200 tonnes) full load

DIMENSIONS: 690 ft 3 in x 95 ft 2 in x 30 ft 3 in (210.4 m x 29 m x 9.2 m)

PROPULSION: Quadruple shafts, Parsons turbines, 18 boilers, 63,000 shp (46,979 kW)

ARMAMENT: (1916): Eight 12-in (305 mm), twelve 5.9-in (150 mm), four 3.5-in (88 mm) guns; four 3.5-in (88 mm) AA guns; four 19.6-in (500 mm) torpedoes

ARMOR: Belt 12–6 in (300–150 mm), bulkhead 9.8–3.9 in (250–100 mm), conning tower forward 11.8 in (300 mm), aft 7.8 in (200 mm), barbettes 10.2 in (260 mm), turrets 11 in (270 mm), deck 1.2 in (30 mm)

SPEED: 26.5 knots (30.5 mph; 49.1km/h)

CREW: 1,182

SMS *Derfflinger*

GUNS

WITH A BARREL LENGTH OF 50 FT (15.2 M) AND WEIGHT OF 67 TONS (68 TONNES), THE MAIN GUNS FIRED SHELLS OF 893 LB (405 KG) FOR A DISTANCE OF 17,716 YARDS (16,200 M) AT AN ELEVATION OF 13.5°; LATER EXTENDED TO 22,310 YARDS (20,400 M) AND 16°.

MASTS

ORIGINALLY TWO POLE-TYPE MASTS WERE FITTED; AFTER JUTLAND A BROAD TRIPOD MAST REPLACED THE FORWARD POLE MAST, WITH LARGE VIEWING AND DIRECTION-FINDING STATIONS AND A BRIDGE-PLATFORM BETWEEN ITS AFT PILLARS.

RANGE

OPERATIONAL RANGE WAS 5,300 NAUTICAL MILES (6,099 MILES; 9,816 KM) AT 14 KNOTS (16.1 MPH; 26KM/H).

ANTI-ROLLING TANKS

ANTI-ROLLING TANKS WERE FITTED TO *DERFFLINGER* AS AN EXPERIMENT, PLACED BETWEEN THE FUNNELS IN THE CENTRAL SUPERSTRUCTURE.

Dante Alighieri (1913)

IN TYPICAL FASHION ITALY'S NAVAL ARCHITECTS TOOK THE DREADNOUGHT CONCEPT AND MADE THEIR OWN THING OF IT. THIS WAS THE FIRST BATTLESHIP TO BE DESIGNED WITH TRIPLE TURRETS FOR THE HEAVY GUNS.

Designed on principles set down by Vittorio Cuniberti, *Dante Alighieri* resembled no other big-gun ship of 1912 (though the Russian *Gangut*-class battleships of 1914 would bear a strong resemblance). Laid down at Castellammare on June 6, 1909, launched on August 20, 1910, and completed on January 15, 1913, it had a long, low-set look. Two of the four turrets were placed on the centerline amidships, in a lengthy space between the fore and aft superstructures, each of which had two closely set funnels with a mast rising between them, and each had an armored conning tower.

It was 57 ft (52.1 m) longer than the Austrian *Viribus Unitis*, which also carried twelve 12-in (305 mm) guns, but the Austrian ship made use of super-firing turrets, which Italy's next dreadnoughts, the *Cavour* class, would also use. *Dante's* secondary armament did not match the *Tegetthoff* class's 5.9-in (150 mm) guns but was formed of rapid-firing 4.7-in (120 mm) guns capable of six rounds a minute. They could depress to –10⁰ to aim low, and anti-torpedo-boat defense also included thirteen 3-in (76 mm) guns mounted on the turret tops and capable of firing a shot every six seconds. The four Parsons turbines were placed centrally between the gun turrets, with boilers grouped below the funnels. A complete waterline belt protected the long hull.

Early Testing, Action in World War I

Dante's early career was spent in tests and exercises. A Curtiss reconnaissance floatplane was tested in 1913. From May 1915, when Italy declared war on German and Austria, it was flagship of the 1st Battle Squadron, based at Taranto. From the end of 1916 to the end of the war it was assigned to the Ionian Sea and the Italo-French force guarding the entrance to the Adriatic. In 1923 it was refitted with a tripod foremast, and a flying off platform was mounted on No. 3 turret. The forward pair of funnels were heightened. By 1928, however, the ship was obsolete and expensive to maintain in seagoing condition. It was stricken on July 1 that year, and disposed of for scrap.

SPECIFICATIONS

DISPLACEMENT: 19,552 tons (19,866 tonnes); 21,600 tons (21,947 tonnes) full load

DIMENSIONS: 551 ft 6 in x 87 ft 3 in x 28 ft 10 in (168.1 m x 26.6 m x 8.8 m)

PROPULSION: Quadruple shafts, Parsons geared turbines, 23 Blechynden boilers, 32,190 shp (24,004 kW)

ARMAMENT: Twelve 12-in (305 mm)/46-caliber, twenty 4.7-in (120 mm)/50 caliber, thirteen 3-in (76 mm)/40-caliber guns; three 17.7-in (450 mm) torpedo tubes

ARMOR: Belt and main turrets 10 in (254 mm), secondary turrets and battery 3.8 in (98 mm), conning tower 12 in (305 mm), deck 1.5 in (38 mm)

SPEED: 22.8 knots (26.2 mph; 42.2 km/h)

CREW: 981

Dante Alighieri

MAIN GUNS
THE MAIN GUNS WERE ELSWICK T MODEL 1909 46 CALIBER, MOUNTED IN HYDRAULICALLY POWERED TURRETS.

LIGHT GUNS
THE 3-IN (76 MM) GUNS MOUNTED ON THE TURRET ROOFS COULD NOT BE USED IF THE MAIN GUNS WERE IN USE.

DESIGN
THE RATIO OF LENGTH TO BEAM, 6.32 TIMES, WAS UNUSUALLY LARGE FOR A BATTLESHIP.

BOILERS
SIXTEEN BOILERS WERE FIRED BY COAL WITH OIL SPRAYERS; SEVEN WERE OIL BURNERS.

Kongo *(1913)*

THE LAST JAPANESE CAPITAL SHIP TO BE BUILT OUTSIDE JAPAN, *KONGO* WAS THE FIRST WARSHIP TO CARRY 14-IN (356 MM) GUNS. SHE WAS THE FIRST BATTLECRUISER OF THE *KONGO* CLASS, WHICH WERE AMONG THE MOST HEAVILY ARMED SHIPS IN ANY NAVY WHEN BUILT. IT WAS THE ONLY JAPANESE BATTLESHIP TO BE SUNK BY A SUBMARINE.

Kongo was laid down at the Vickers yard at Barrow in Furness, England, on January 17, 1911, launched on May 18, 1912, and completed on August 16, 1913, to plans drawn up under the direction of Sir George Thurston, Vickers's chief naval architect. In many ways an improved version of the British *Lion* class, it was first of a class of four, with various differences in appearance. *Kongo* had three funnels of equal height, the central one slimmer than the others, and the fore-funnel close to the foremast, giving a more symmetrical look. Armor protection of 6,502 tons (6,606 tonnes) accounted for 23.3 percent of displacement, with an 8-in (203 mm) lower belt of Vickers cemented armor. *Kongo* made regular but uneventful patrols in World War I.

After the war, successive modifications would transform it from a three-funneled battlecruiser to a twin-funneled fast battleship (reclassified as such in March 1931). By January 1937 *Kongo* still had its 14-in (356 mm) guns, now modified to elevate to 43⁰, but little else apart from the basic hull remained unchanged. A redesigned stern added 26 ft (7.9 m) to its length, and the armor was upgraded, though still below normal battleship standard. Catapults were installed between Nos. 3 and 4 turrets. Displacement was raised by over 4,000 tons (4,064 tonnes) chiefly by extra armor, but new direct-drive turbines increased speed to 30 knots (34.5 mph; 55.5 km/h).

Torpedoed in World War II

Kongo participated in campaigns against China in the 1930s. In World War II it was involved in many actions in the Pacific, from the Malayan and Philippines invasions, 1941–42, to the battle of Midway, May 1942, and the Guadalcanal campaign, 1942–43. With reinforced AA armament it participated in the vast-scale battle of Leyte Gulf, October 1944. On November 21, 1944 it was passing through the Formosa Strait, on the way from Brunei to the Kure base, along with *Nagato*, when it was hit by two torpedoes from USS *Sealion*. For two hours it struggled on, before sinking with the loss of 1,200 crew.

SPECIFICATIONS

DISPLACEMENT: 27,500 tons (27,941 tonnes); 32,200 tons (32,717 tonnes) full load

DIMENSIONS: 704 ft x 92 ft x 27 ft 7 in (214.5 m x 28 m x 8.4 m)

PROPULSION: Quadruple shafts, Parsons turbines, 64,000 shp (47,725 kW)

ARMAMENT: Eight 14-in (356 mm)/45-caliber, sixteen 6-in (152 mm)/50-caliber QF, four 3.1-in (79 mm)/40-caliber, sixteen 3-in (76 mm)/28-caliber guns; seven machine guns; eight 21-in (533 mm) torpedo tubes

ARMOR: Belt 8–3in (203–76 mm), barbettes and conning tower 10 in (254 mm), turrets 9 in (227 mm), deck 2.25–1.6 in (57–41 mm)

SPEED: 27.5 knots (31.6 mph; 51 km/h)

CREW: 1,201

Kongo

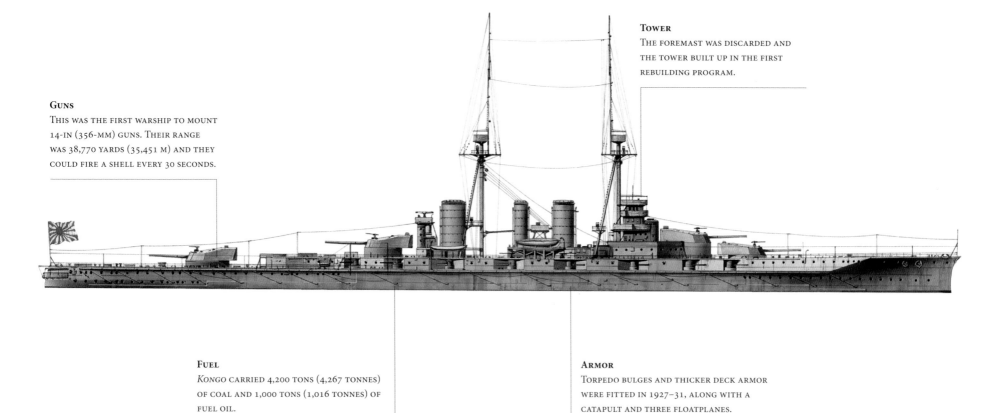

GUNS
THIS WAS THE FIRST WARSHIP TO MOUNT
14-IN (356-MM) GUNS. THEIR RANGE
WAS 38,770 YARDS (35,451 M) AND THEY
COULD FIRE A SHELL EVERY 30 SECONDS.

TOWER
THE FOREMAST WAS DISCARDED AND
THE TOWER BUILT UP IN THE FIRST
REBUILDING PROGRAM.

FUEL
KONGO CARRIED 4,200 TONS (4,267 TONNES)
OF COAL AND 1,000 TONS (1,016 TONNES) OF
FUEL OIL.

ARMOR
TORPEDO BULGES AND THICKER DECK ARMOR
WERE FITTED IN 1927–31, ALONG WITH A
CATAPULT AND THREE FLOATPLANES.

Courbet (1913)

France's first battleship of dreadnought-type, *Courbet* was leader of a class of four, all of which served in the Mediterranean Sea during World War I. *Courbet* was laid down at the Brest Naval Arsenal on September 1, 1910, launched on September 23, 1911, and completed on November 19, 1913.

A three-funneled ship with a straight stem, it had two funnels placed forward of the tubular foremast and the third midway between the two masts. Its main guns were carried in six twin turrets, super-firing fore and aft. The control deck, immediately forward of the fore-funnel and only a little lower, and just above "B" turret, was liable to both smoke and blast effects. *Courbet* was planned with accommodation to serve as a flagship. The secondary guns were rapid-fire, intended to fend off torpedo boats.

Guarding the Otranto Straits

In August 1914 a French and British fleet was in the Adriatic, hoping to draw the Austro-Hungarian fleet into battle, but the Austro-Hungarians stayed in port. The only victim was the light cruiser *Zenta*, caught off Antivari (Montenegro) and sunk by salvoes from *Courbet* and others on August 16. *Courbet* was the flagship of the French squadron engaged in watching the Otranto Straits. Among wartime alterations were the removal of the mainmast for kite-towing gear to be installed, the mounting of a searchlight platform abaft the second funnel, and triple 12-ft (3.6 m) range finders fitted. From the end of the war it served as a gunnery training ship.

A refit from July 9, 1923, to April 16, 1924, following a boiler fire, installed some oil-fired boilers and combined the two forward funnels into one; further modernization was carried out between January 15, 1927, and January 12, 1939. Restored to operational status on May 21, 1940, as part of the 3rd Line Division, in June it supported troop evacuations from Cherbourg, France, and then steamed to Portsmouth, England. Briefly taken over by the Royal Navy, it was handed to the Free French forces and used by them as an accommodation ship and stationary AA platform, downing five enemy aircraft. It was disarmed in 1941 and after three years as a target ship for aircraft, was sunk just off the French coast at Hermanville-sur-Mer on June 9, 1944, as a breakwater to protect the floating "Mulberry Harbour" used for the Allied landings in Normandy. The hulk was scrapped after the war.

SPECIFICATIONS

DISPLACEMENT: 22,189 tons (22,545 tonnes); 26,000 tons (26,417 tonnes) full load

DIMENSIONS: 551 ft 2 in x 91 ft 6 in x 29 ft 6 in (168 m x 27.9 m x 9 m)

PROPULSION: Quadruple shafts, Parsons turbines, 24 Belleville boilers, 28,000 shp (20,879.6 kW)

ARMAMENT: Twelve 12-in (305 mm)/45-caliber, twenty-two 5.4-in (138.6 mm), four 1.8-in (47 mm) guns; four 17.7-in (450 mm) torpedo tubes

ARMOR: Belt 10.6–7 in (270–180 mm), barbettes 10.6 in (270 mm), turrets 12.6 in (320 mm), conning tower 11.75 in (300 mm), deck 2.75–1.1 in (70–30 mm)

SPEED: 22 knots (25.3 mph; 40.7 km/h)

CREW: 1,108

Courbet

MAST
THE POLE FOREMAST WAS REPLACED BY
A TRIPOD IN 1920.

AA GUNS
THE 3-IN (75 MM) AA GUNS FITTED
IN 1930 COULD ELEVATE TO 90° AND
FIRED UP TO 18 ROUNDS A MINUTE, TO A
HEIGHT OF 26,000 FT (8,000 M).

SPEED
COURBET WAS THE FASTEST SHIP OF ITS CLASS,
OUTPACING THE OTHERS BY 0.5 KNOT (0.57
MPH; 0.9 KM/H).

ARMOR
THE WEIGHT OF THE TWO FORWARD TURRETS
DEPRESSED THE BOWS, AND THE BOW ARMOR
WAS REMOVED IN 1923–24.

WATERLINE
THE WATERLINE BELT WAS UNUSUALLY DEEP,
AT 15 FT 6 IN (4.75 M).

HMS *Iron Duke* (1914)

THE FOUR SHIPS OF THE *IRON DUKE* CLASS WERE GREAT BRITAIN'S LAST COAL-BURNING BATTLESHIPS, AND ALSO SHOWED A RETURN TO THE 6-IN (152 MM) GUN AS A USEFUL ADJUNCT TO THE MAIN ARMAMENT. *IRON DUKE* WAS LAID DOWN AT PORTSMOUTH ON JANUARY 12, 1912, LAUNCHED ON OCTOBER 12 THE SAME YEAR, AND COMPLETED IN MARCH 1914.

The ship's cost, averaged out against the four ships of its class, was £1,891,122. Super-firing turrets fore and aft, and one "Q" turret just abaft of midships, held the ten main guns. Admiral John Fisher, "father" of the "dreadnought" type, was no longer at the Admiralty, and a change of opinion there resulted in the installation of twelve 6-in (152 mm)/45-caliber guns. Fisher had considered such guns unnecessary on "big-gun" ships, but at a time when fire control was still a rather rudimentary business, the splashes of 6-in (152 mm) shells were considered useful in confusing enemy controllers and gun-layers, apart from their value at close range.

A single heavy tripod mast was fitted, to carry director and spotting stations, and the superstructure was built up around its base to carry the 6-in (152 mm) gun directors. Ahead of this was a two-level conning tower. The use and value of the conning tower was very much in question at the time. Its limited lookout capacity and poor ventilation against shell-fumes and smoke discouraged its use and officers from admirals down preferred to use the bridge deck. A derrick post of funnel height was placed forward of the after funnel.

Flagship at Jutland

On completion *Iron Duke* was made flagship of the Home Fleet and then the Grand Fleet. At Jutland it was the flagship of Admiral John Jellicoe, and sustained no casualties in the battle. From 1916–19 it was with the 2nd Battleship Squadron, and from 1919 to 1926 it was in the Mediterranean and also the Black Sea, where it was engaged in operations against Bolshevik Russian units.

Its final active spell was with the Atlantic Fleet from 1926 to 1929. A training ship from 1931, it was partially disarmed, and moved to Scapa Flow in 1939 as a shore defense and stores ship. It was sold in 1946.

SPECIFICATIONS

DISPLACEMENT: 25,000 tons (25,401 tonnes); 29,560 tons (30,034 tonnes) full load

DIMENSIONS: 622 ft 9 in x 90 ft x 29 ft 6 in (189.8 m x 27.4 m x 9 m)

PROPULSION: Quadruple shafts, Parsons turbines, 18 Babcock & Wilcox boilers, 29,000 shp (21,625 kW)

ARMAMENT: Ten 13.5-in (343 mm)/ 45-caliber, twelve 6-in (152 mm)/45-caliber guns; two 3-in (76 mm)/20 caliber AA guns; four 3-pounder guns

ARMOR: Belt 12–4 in (305–102 mm), bulkheads 8–1.6 in (203–40 mm), barbettes 10–3 in (254–76 mm), turret faces 11 in (279 mm), deck 2.5–1 in (65–25 mm)

SPEED: 21.25 knots (24.45 mph; 39.3 km/h)

CREW: 1,022

HMS *Iron Duke*

MAST
A SHORT AFTERMAST
WAS FITTED IN 1920 TO
CARRY RADIO AERIALS.

GUN PLACEMENT
PLACING OF THE 6-IN (152 MM) GUNS WAS
CRITICIZED AS TOO CLOSE TOGETHER, TOO
LOW DOWN, AND TOO FAR FORWARD.

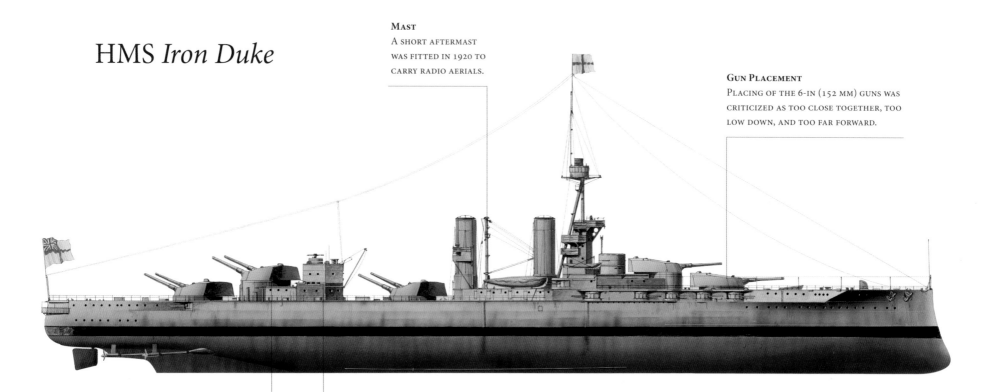

LAUNCHER
IN 1918 A SEAPLANE LAUNCHER WAS
MOUNTED ON "X" TURRET.

AA GUNS
IRON DUKE WAS AMONG THE FIRST
BATTLESHIPS TO CARRY AA GUNS, TWO
3-POUNDERS, THOUGH ITS AA DEFENSES
WERE IMPROVED DURING THE WAR BY
TWO 3-IN (76 MM) AA GUNS ON THE
AFTER SUPERSTRUCTURE.

HMS *Royal Oak* (1914)

ROYAL OAK, OF THE *REVENGE* CLASS, WAS THE FIRST CAPITAL SHIP TO BE SUNK IN WORLD WAR II, TORPEDOED AT ANCHOR IN SCAPA FLOW. *ROYAL OAK* WAS LAID DOWN AT DEVONPORT NAVAL DOCKYARD ON JANUARY 15, 1914, LAUNCHED ON APRIL 29, 1915, AND COMPLETED IN MAY 1916. ITS COST WAS £2,468,269.

The 15-in (381 mm) guns were the same as on the *Queen Elizabeth* class. Secondary armament was fourteen 6-in (152 mm) guns: the last time a main-deck level battery was included on a Royal Navy battleship. The flues from three boiler rooms were trunked into a single massive funnel.

The class were the first battleships to be fitted with anti-torpedo bulges, adding 13 ft (4 m) to the beam, heightened in 1927, almost reaching the battery deck. As on other RN battleships, the original secondary armament was progressively reduced and additional AA guns fitted. Other modernizations included a redesigned bridge structure, improved wireless communications, and improvements to AA defenses. Up to 1938 the mainmast was of pole type, but when gunnery control instrumentation was installed at the crosstrees it was converted to a tripod. Additions to the tower platforms and their combining into a single housing made tower and foremast into an integrated structure. But the extent of modernization was still quite limited. It still had the original engines, and its speed was no longer sufficient to maintain station with the fleet.

Spanish Civil War Patrol

Royal Oak joined the 1st Battle Squadron of the Grand Fleet, took part almost immediately in the Battle of Jutland, May 31, 1916, and remained with the Grand Fleet until 1919, when it moved to the 2nd Battle Squadron and the Atlantic Fleet, until 1922. Between then and 1924 it underwent a refit, then rejoined the 2nd Battle Squadron. From 1926 to 1934 it was flagship of the Mediterranean Fleet based at Malta. A further refit took place from May 1934 to August 1936, after which it returned to the Home Fleet's 2nd Battle Squadron as flagship. From January 24, 1937, it was back with the Mediterranean Fleet, at Gibraltar, and was involved in neutrality patrols off the Spanish coast during the Spanish Civil War, taking two minor hits from incidental firing. From June 4, 1937, it was again deployed with the Home Fleet. With the outbreak of war it was moved to Scapa Flow, where it was torpedoed in a bravura operation on the night of October 14, 1939, by *U47*. It capsized and sank within ten minutes, with the loss of 833 lives.

SPECIFICATIONS

DISPLACEMENT: 28,650 tons (29,110 tonnes); 33,500 tons (34,037 tonnes) with bulges

DIMENSIONS: 620 ft 6 in x 102 ft 2 in x 28 ft 6 in (189 m x 31.2 m x 8.7 m)

PROPULSION: Quadruple shafts, Parsons geared turbines, 18 Yarrow boilers, 40,000 shp (29,828 kW)

ARMAMENT: Eight 15-in (381 mm), twelve 6-in (152 mm), eight 4-in (102 mm) guns; four 21-in (533 mm) torpedo tubes

ARMOR: Belt and turret faces 13 in (330 mm), barbettes 10 in (254 mm), bulkhead 6 in (152 mm), deck 2–1 in (51–25mm)

SPEED: 23 knots (26.5 mph; 42.6 km/h)

CREW: 997

HMS *Royal Oak*

DESIGN
ROYAL OAK WAS THE ONLY SHIP
OF THE *REVENGE* CLASS NOT TO BE
FITTED WITH A FUNNEL COWL.

LAUNCHER
THIS VIEW SHOWS *ROYAL OAK* AS IT LOOKED
IN 1939, WITH AIRCRAFT LAUNCHER ON "X"
TURRET, AND LUFFING CRANE.

TAKEOFF PLATFORM
BETWEEN 1917 AND 1923 ALL SHIPS OF THE
CLASS HAD AIRCRAFT TAKEOFF PLATFORMS
FITTED TO THE SUPER-FIRING TURRETS; AND
IN 1934–35 *ROYAL OAK* HAD AN AIRCRAFT
CRANE WAS PLACED ON THE PORT SIDE OF
THE MAINMAST.

ARMOR
THE BLISTER SHAPE OF THE TORPEDO BULGE
IS APPARENT. TOTAL ARMOR WEIGHT WAS
8,382 TONNES (8,250 TONS)

BATTERY
THIS WAS THE LAST RN BATTLESHIP CLASS WITH
A MAIN DECK SECONDARY BATTERY ON EACH SIDE.

USS *Texas* (1914)

THE FIRST US WARSHIP TO LAUNCH AN AIRCRAFT, USS *TEXAS* SAW SERVICE IN BOTH WORLD WARS, AND STILL SURVIVES AS A MUSEUM SHIP AT LA PORTE, TEXAS, IN ITS NAME STATE. ASSIGNED PENNANT NUMBER BB-35, IT WAS LAID DOWN AT NEWPORT NEWS, VIRGINIA, ON APRIL 17, 1911, LAUNCHED ON MAY 18, 1912, AND COMPLETED IN MARCH 1914.

Costing $4,962,000 (excluding guns), it was the first US battleship to carry 14-in (356 mm) guns. Triple-expansion rather than turbine engines were installed, due to disagreement between the naval authorities and the engine builders over the turbine specification. In the US–Mexican crisis of 1914, *Texas* supported a troop landing at Vera Cruz, Mexico, and was then stationed off Tampico. From 1915 it was part of the Atlantic Fleet. In 1917 it was due to cross the Atlantic to join with the British Grand Fleet, but ran aground at Block Island on September 16 and had to undergo repairs at New York Navy Yard. It finally reached Scapa Flow in the Orkney Islands on February 11, 1918, from where it participated in convoy escort and North Sea patrols.

First Aircraft Launch

On return to the United States, *Texas* became the first US battleship to launch an aircraft, on March 19, 1919. From that year until 1924 it was with the Pacific Fleet, then returned to Norfolk, Virginia, for a major modernization between 1925 and 1927. Six Bureau-Express oil-fired boilers replaced the previous arrangement, with uptakes trunked into a single funnel. Within the hull the torpedo tubes were removed, a new torpedo bulkhead was provided, along with a triple bottom in the midships section, and the horizontal armor was strengthened.

In the 1930s it served with first the Atlantic, then the Pacific fleet, and as a training ship. Further modifications at that time included the removal of the topmasts in 1934–35. In 1938, a compact CXZ radar aerial was fitted above the bridge. During 1940–41 it made patrols in the western Atlantic for protection of US shipping against the belligerents, then after American entry into the war it operated as a convoy escort; and in November 1942 it provided artillery support for Allied landings in Morocco and Algeria, repeating the role in the Normandy landings of 1944 and the landings in southern France in the same year.

In 1942 an SG radar aerial was fitted to a platform on the foremast, and SK radar was added on the aftermast in 1943. Also from 1943 six 0.79-in (20 mm) AA guns were mounted on the top of "B" turret. From late 1944 it was redeployed in the Pacific and saw action at Iwo Jima and Okinawa. *Texas* was the first of several battleships to be transferred by Act of Congress from the Navy to become a museum ship, in 1948.

SPECIFICATIONS

DISPLACEMENT: 27,000 tons (27,433 tonnes)

DIMENSIONS: 572 ft 7 in x 95 ft 3 in x 28 ft 5 in (174.5 m x 29 m x 8.7 m)

PROPULSION: Twin shafts, 14 boilers, two vertical triple-expansion engines, 28,100 ihp (20,954 kW)

ARMAMENT: Ten 14-in (356 mm), twenty-one 5-in (127 mm) guns; four 21-in (533 mm) torpedo tubes

ARMOR: Belt 12–10 in (304–254 mm), turrets 14 in (356 mm), barbettes and conning tower 12 in (305 mm), deck 3 in (76 mm)

SPEED: 21 knots (24.1 mph; 39 km/h)

CREW: 1,530

USS *Texas*

TRIPODS

IN 1925 THE BASKET MASTS WERE REPLACED BY TRIPODS, A CATAPULT WAS FITTED ON THE CENTRAL "C" TURRET, AND CRANES REPLACED THE FORMER DERRICKS ON EACH SIDE OF THE FUNNEL.

GUNS

BARREL LENGTH WAS 45 FT (13.7 M), WITH A WEIGHT OF 63 TONS (64 TONNES), AND FIRING SHELLS OF 1,400 LB (635 KG). EACH TURRET WEIGHED 864 TONS (878 TONNES). THE GUNS ELEVATED TO 30° AND MAXIMUM RANGE WAS 32,800 YARDS (30,000 M).

TAKEOFF PLATFORM

THE "TAKEOFF PLATFORM" WAS ORIGINALLY FITTED TO *TEXAS*'S "B" TURRET DURING THE 1919 REFIT AT THE NEW YORK NAVY YARD. IT WAS USED TO LAUNCH A BRITISH SOPWITH CAMEL AIRCRAFT.

RANGE

TEXAS HAD AN OPERATIONAL RANGE OF 8,000 NAUTICAL MILES (9,206 MILES; 14,816KM) AT 10 KNOTS (11.5 MPH; 18.5KM/H)

Rivadavia (1914)

THE TWO BATTLESHIPS OF THE *RIVADAVIA* CLASS CAUSED CONTROVERSY FIRST BY THE MANNER OF THEIR ORDERING, AND THEN BY A PROPOSAL TO SELL THEM. MILITARILY THEIR CAREERS WERE LONG BUT UNEVENTFUL.

Brazil's ordering of the *Minas Gerais* class prompted Argentina to order two "super-dreadnoughts." After international competition for its construction, *Rivadavia*, almost half as big again as Brazil's *Minas Gerais*, but with the same size and number of main guns, was laid down at the Fore River yard, Quincy, Massachusetts, on May 25, 1910, launched on August 26, 1911, and completed in December 1914. Though rival European and British bidders complained bitterly that their design details had been stolen, the ship looked very much like contemporary US warships, including a basket foremast. When in late 1913 the Argentine government sought to sell both ships, it was the United States' turn to protest, and the plan was dropped.

The machinery layout, with Curtis geared turbines amidships between two boiler rooms, was standard USN practice. An up-to-date electrical plant supplied 4,375 kW from turbogenerators, supplemented by two 75 kW diesel-powered generators. Radio communication was via Telefunken equipment with a range of 932 miles (1,500 km). The two central turrets were offset and could fire across a 180^0 field on their own side and in theory across 100^0 transversely, but potential blast effects made a full broadside impracticable. American levels of protection were provided, with a main belt of 12 in (305 mm) maximum thickness and of 11 ft (3.3 m) vertical height, though the 4 in (102 mm) anti-torpedo boat guns were unprotected.

Neutral in World War I

Argentina's neutrality in World War I kept its battleships out of action. In 1924 *Rivadavia* and *Moreno* were both sent to the United States for upgrading. Oil-fuel boilers were fitted and new fire-control systems installed. Their basket masts were retained long after the US Navy had abandoned them. Both ships made goodwill visits to French and German ports in 1937. Argentina was again a neutral in World War II and *Rivadavia* was kept mainly in harbor. Its last cruise was a goodwill visit to Trinidad, Venezuela, and Colombia in 1946. On February 1, 1957, after ten years' disuse, it was stricken from the navy list and towed to Italy where it was finally scrapped in 1959.

SPECIFICATIONS

DISPLACEMENT: 27,940 tons (28,388 tonnes); 30,600 tons (31,091 tonnes) full load

DIMENSIONS: 594 ft 9 in x 98 ft 5 in x 27 ft 8 in (181.3 m x 30 m x 8.5 m)

PROPULSION: Triple shafts, Curtis geared turbines, 18 Babcock & Wilcox boilers, 40,000 shp (29,828 kW)

ARMAMENT: Twelve 12-in (305 mm), twelve 6-in (152 mm), sixteen 4-in (102 mm) QF guns; two 21-in (533 mm) torpedo tubes

ARMOR: Belt 12–10 in (305–254 mm), casemate 9.3–6.2 in (238–159 mm), turrets and conning tower 12 in (305 mm)

SPEED: 22.5 knots (25.9 mph; 41.7 km/h)

CREW: 1,130

Rivadavia

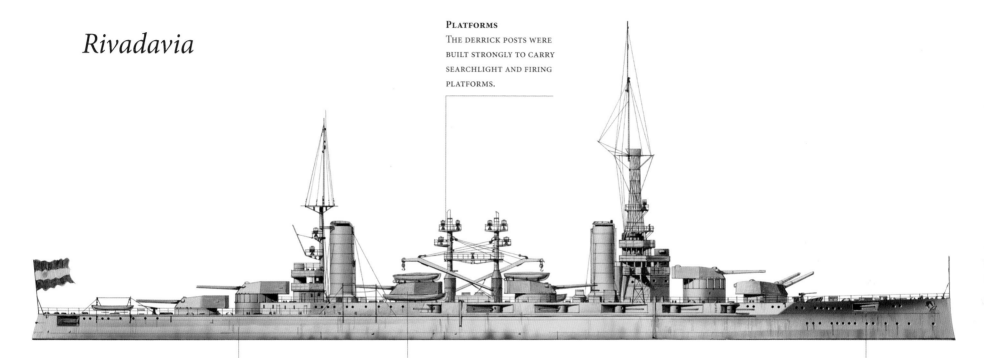

PLATFORMS
THE DERRICK POSTS WERE
BUILT STRONGLY TO CARRY
SEARCHLIGHT AND FIRING
PLATFORMS.

RANGE
WITH A MAXIMUM COAL CAPACITY OF
4,000 TONS (4,064 TONNES), THE SHIP HAD
A RANGE OF 7,000 NAUTICAL MILES (8,055
MILES; 12,960 KM) AT 11 KNOTS (13 MPH;
20 KM/H).

WING TURRETS
RIVADAVIA AND *MORENO* WERE THE ONLY
BATTLESHIPS BUILT IN THE UNITED STATES TO
HAVE MAIN GUNS IN WING TURRETS.

LASTING DESIGN
UNLIKE MOST BATTLESHIPS, THE
SHIP'S APPEARANCE HARDLY CHANGED
THROUGHOUT A LONG CAREER.

HMS *Queen Elizabeth* (1915)

THE *QUEEN ELIZABETH*'S SPEED AND FIREPOWER SET THEM APART AS A SEPARATE BATTLESHIP SQUADRON, INTENDED TO PURSUE AND OUTFLANK AN ENEMY FLEET AND FORCE IT INTO BATTLE WITH THE GRAND FLEET. BUT THEY WERE NOT USED IN THIS WAY AT JUTLAND.

Laid down at Portsmouth Dockyard on October 27, 1912, launched on October 16, 1913, and commissioned on January 19, 1915, *Queen Elizabeth*'s design was influenced by reports and rumors about the battleship designs of other powers, suggesting that the United States and Germany were planning heavier-caliber naval guns.

Consequently, 15-in (381 mm) guns were ordered; and though only eight were to be mounted, it was felt that their weight of impact would more than make up for their number. The gun barrels were 42 ft (12.8 m) long, weighing 95.5 tons (97 tonnes) and firing shells of 1,929 lb (875 kg), the heaviest naval shells used in World War I. The range was 34,995 yards (32,000 m) at an elevation of 30^0 (original maximum elevation was 20^0). Each turret weighed 1,023 tons (1,039 tonnes) and was crewed by 75 men. For the first time in any battleship, only oil fuel was used,

with a bunker capacity of 3,400 tons (3,455 tonnes). On the *Queen Elizabeth* class, maximum armor thickness was applied only in a midships belt 4 ft (1.2 m) wide. Beyond this section, the armor tapered to 4 in (102 mm).

On commissioning *Queen Elizabeth* was immediately deployed to the Mediterranean Fleet and supported the Dardanelles landings, from February to May 1915. It joined the Grand Fleet after Jutland and was flagship from 1916 to 1920. From 1920 it was flagship of the Atlantic Fleet, then from July 1924 of the Mediterranean Fleet.

In 1926–27 it underwent a major conversion following which it returned to the Mediterranean Fleet and thereafter would mostly stay with it until 1942. It was severely damaged at Alexandria on December 19, 1941, along with its sister ship HMS *Valiant*, by an attack from Italian midget submarines.

World War II Service off Burma

After temporary patching-up, it went to Norfolk, Virginia, for a complete repair, returning to the UK in June 1943 to again join the Home Fleet for a few months before being sent in January 1944 as flagship of the Eastern Fleet. Intense activity followed, as escort and support ship for carrier operations and landings in the Indonesian archipelago, followed by a refit in Durban, South Africa, in October–November 1944. It then returned to the Indian Ocean for further service including cover for landings on Ramree, Burma, and action against Japanese-occupied Burma and Sumatra. On July 12, 1945, it returned to Britain and was placed on the reserve list in March 1946. Stricken in June 1948, it was scrapped in the same year.

SPECIFICATIONS

DISPLACEMENT: 27,500 tons (27,940 tonnes); 33,020 tons (33,548 tonnes) full load

DIMENSIONS: 640 ft 11 in x 90 ft 6 in x 30 ft (195.34 m x 27.6 m x 9.1 m)

PROPULSION: Quadruple screws, four Parsons geared turbines, 24 Babcock & Wilcox boilers, 75,000 shp (55,927 kW)

ARMAMENT: Eight 15-in (381 mm), sixteen 6-in (152 mm) guns; two 3-in (76 mm) AA guns; four 21-in (533 mm) torpedo tubes

ARMOR: Belt 13–4 in (330–102 mm), bulkheads 6–4 in (152–102 mm), barbettes 10–4 in (254–102 mm), turrets 13–5 in (330–127 mm), deck upper 1.7–1.2 in (45–32 mm), lower 1 in (25 mm) with 3 in (76 mm) over steering gear

SPEED: 23 knots (26.5 mph; 46.3 km/h)

CREW: 951

HMS *Queen Elizabeth*

GUNS

AA GUNS—0.79-IN (20 MM)—WERE FITTED ON THE
SUPER-FIRING TURRETS; UP TO 52 OF THESE GUNS WERE
INSTALLED DURING WORLD WAR II IN ADDITION TO
THIRTY-TWO 1.6-IN (40 MM) EIGHT-BARRELED AA GUNS
AND SIXTEEN FOUR-BARRELLED HEAVY MACHINE GUNS.

RADAR

FROM 1941 TYPE 273 (SEA SEARCH) RADAR WAS CARRIED
ON THE FOREMAST, THE AERIAL ROTATING WITHIN A
PROTECTIVE PLASTIC CYLINDER.

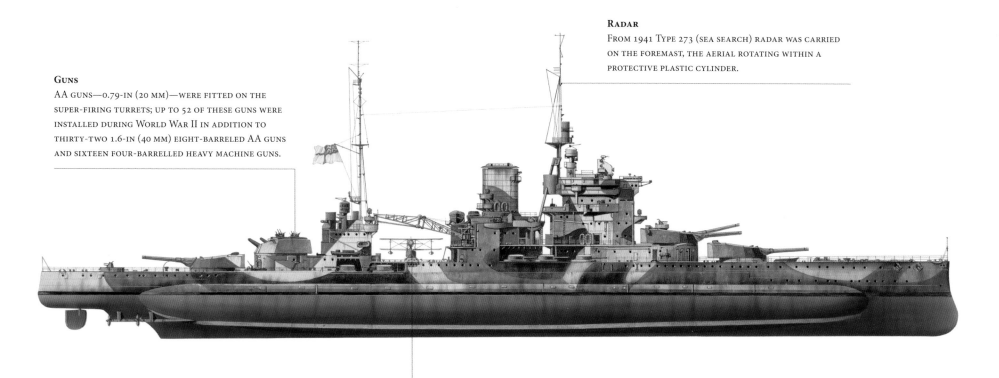

CATAPULT

FROM 1939–43 AN AIRCRAFT CATAPULT WAS INSTALLED
ON THE BOAT DECK. FOUR FLOATPLANES COULD BE
CARRIED. BUT FROM 1943 THE BRITISH DISPENSED WITH
AIRCRAFT ON BATTLESHIPS, RELYING ON CARRIER-BORNE
PLANES FOR SCOUTING.

Fuso (1915)

THE FIRST "SUPER-DREADNOUGHT" OF THE IMPERIAL NAVY TO BE ACTUALLY DESIGNED AND BUILT IN JAPAN, THIS WAS THE WORLD'S LARGEST BATTLESHIP WHEN COMMISSIONED. IN ORIGINAL FORM IT SHOWED A MIX OF BRITISH AND JAPANESE INFLUENCES, BUT LATER MODIFICATIONS CHANGED ITS APPEARANCE DRAMATICALLY.

Fuso's keel was laid at the Kure Naval Base on March 11, 1912, and it was launched on November 8, 1915. Attached to the First Squadron of the First Fleet, it was deployed off the Chinese coast, and from the end of World War I, alternated between first reserve status and patrols off China. On March 12, 1930, a major modernization program began at Yokosuka, Japan. Completed in several phases, with service periods between, it reduced overall weight by 1,270 tons (1,290 tonnes), enabled a single funnel to replace the two funnels, and almost doubled the original power output. A "pagoda" tower was erected, reaching 44 m (144 ft) above the waterline, with navigation bridges, lookout posts and fire-control stations, and the foremast was discarded.

With new 14-in (356 mm) guns, *Fuso* was effectively a new ship in the original hull, with speed boosted by 4.74 knots (5.4 mph, 8.8 km/h). The original 14-in (356 mm) guns elevated from 0^0 to 30^0. Post-1933 elevation was between -5^0 and 43^0, with a maximum range of 38,770 yards (35,450 m). The Tetsukodan armor-piercing shell weighed 1,485 lbs (673.5 kg) and the 01-Shiki Tsujodan high-explosive shell, 1,378 lb (625 kg). By 1933 a catapult and three floatplanes were installed. Further modernizations were mostly concerned with the provision of AA defenses and radar.

In December 1941 *Fuso* acted as a support ship for the Pearl Harbor attack force, and in February 1942 it took part in the failed counterattack on a US carrier force sending bombers over Tokyo (the "Doolittle Raid"). During the war years the AA batteries were built up and by August 14, 1944, *Fuso* had ninety-five 1-in (25 mm) and ten 1.2-in (32 mm) guns in addition to the main and secondary armament.

Battle of Surigao Strait

Fuso and *Yamashiro* left their Brunei base on the October 22, 1944, with the Third Squadron of the First Fleet, under Admiral Shoji Nishimura. Positioned at the north end of the Surigao Strait was a formidable American battle force commanded by Rear-Admiral J.B. Oldendorf: the battleships *California*, *Tennessee*, *Mississippi*, *West Virginia*, *Maryland*, and *Pennsylvania*, plus three heavy cruisers, two light cruisers, and nine destroyers. On the night of the October 23–24, in what was to be the last "classic" sea battle between heavy-gunned battleships, with American torpedo boats and destroyers behind, the Japanese squadron could only advance into devastating firepower. Both battleships were sunk.

SPECIFICATIONS

DISPLACEMENT: 39,145 tons (39,773 tonnes) full load

DIMENSIONS: 672 ft 6 in x 33 ft 1 in x 28 ft (205 m x 10.08 m x 8.6 m)

PROPULSION: Quadruple shafts, six Kampon boilers, four Kampon steam turbines, 75,000 shp (55,927 kW)

ARMAMENT: Twelve 14-in (356 mm), fourteen 6-in (152 mm), eight 5-in (127 mm) guns; sixteen 5.2-in (132 mm) AA guns in quadruple mountings

ARMOR: Belt 12–4 in (305–102 mm), main turrets 11.7–4.5 in (297–114 mm), casemate 6 in (152 mm), deck 5.2–2 in (132–51 mm)

SPEED: 27.74 knots (31.9 mph; 51.4 km/h)

CREW: 1,396

Fuso

CATAPULT

A TYPE KURE SHIKI 2 GO 4 GATA
CATAPULT WAS MOUNTED ON
NO. 3 TURRET IN THE 1930–33
MODERNIZATION.

RADAR

TYPE 21 RADAR WAS FITTED TO *FUSO* AT
KURE IN JUNE 1943, AND TYPES 13 AND
22 ADDED IN AUGUST.

PLANES

JAPANESE CAPITAL SHIPS CARRIED NAKAJIMA
90-11 (1927), NAKAJIMA 90-11B (1933),
KAWANISHI 94-1 (1935), KAWANISHI
95 (1938), OR MITSUBISHI F1 M (1938)
FLOATPLANES. ALL WERE BIPLANES.

Andrea Doria (1915)

ORDERED IN 1912, COMMISSIONED IN 1915, THE ITALIAN NAVY'S *ANDREA DORIA* WAS NOT INVOLVED IN COMBAT UNTIL THE 1940S. AN IMPROVED VERSION OF THE PRECEDING *CAVOUR* CLASS, OF VERY SIMILAR DIMENSIONS AND THE SAME ARMAMENT.

Andrea Doria was laid down at La Spezia naval yard on March 24, 1912, launched on March 30, 1913, and completed on March 13, 1916. The forecastle deck was carried aft as far as the fore-funnel, and the weather deck ran flush to the stern, placing the central triple turret a deck lower than on *Cavour*. The superstructure was of very modest extent, compared to the two massive funnels (increased in height during completion), with an armored conning tower rising just above the super-firing No. 2 turret. The gun layout allowed for a full 13-gun broadside, but the ship played no part in World War I.

Service in the Adriatic

On November 10 it was sent to Corfu, an island claimed both by Greece and Italy, and on December 24, 1920, shelled rebel positions at Fiume (now Rijeka, Croatia), damaging the destroyer *Espero*. In the "Corfu Incident" of 1923 it was again sent to the island. Visits to Spain and Portugal in 1923 and 1925 were followed by a mission to Syria in late 1925. After that the ship had little active life, and from 1932–37 was on reserve at Taranto. From April 8, 1937, to October 26, 1940, it underwent a major reconstruction at Trieste.

Andrea Doria joined the 5th Division of the Italian Navy at Taranto on October 26, 1940, surviving the British attack of November 11–12 unscathed, and moving to Naples on November 12. Movements to intercept British warships, and convoy escort, were its main wartime duties. It was one of the massive Italian force defending Convoys M41 and M42 to Benghazi in December 1941, against British cruisers and destroyers in the brief Battle of Sirte, keeping Italy's convoy route open. After the fall of Italy it was interned at Malta until June 8, 1944, and ultimately returned to Italy. Two spells as flagship of the Italian Navy in 1949–50 and 1951–53 preceded its removal from the list on September 16, 1956, and subsequent scrapping at La Spezia.

SPECIFICATIONS

DISPLACEMENT: 22,956 tons (23,324 tonnes); 24,729 tons (25,126 tonnes) full load

DIMENSIONS: 557 ft 5 in x 91 ft 10 in x 30 ft 10 in (176 m x 28 m x 9.4 m)

PROPULSION: Quadruple shafts, Parsons geared turbines, 20 Yarrow boilers, 30,000 shp (22,371 kW)

ARMAMENT: Thirteen 12-in (305 mm)/46-caliber, sixteen 6-in (152 mm)/45-caliber, thirteen 3-in (76 mm)/50-caliber guns; six 3-in (76 mm) AA guns; three 17.7-in (450 mm) torpedo tubes

ARMOR: Belt 10 in (254 mm), turrets and conning tower 11 in (280 mm), deck 3.9 in (98 mm)

SPEED: 21.3 knots (24.5 mph; 39.4 km/h)

CREW: 1,233

Andrea Doria

MODIFIED DESIGN

ANDREA DORIA AS IT APPEARED AFTER 1937, WITH
THE FORECASTLE DECK EXTENDED AS FAR AS THE
MAINMAST AND THE CENTRAL TURRET REMOVED.

GUNS

TEN 12.6-IN (317 MM) GUNS REPLACED THE ORIGINAL
MAIN GUNS, AND TWELVE 5.3-IN (135 MM) GUNS,
MOUNTED AMIDSHIPS IN TRIPLE TURRETS, REPLACED
THE ORIGINAL 6-IN (152 MM) GUNS; AND 41 AA GUNS
WERE ALSO INSTALLED.

TURBINE

NEW TURBINE MACHINERY WAS INSTALLED
WITH TWIN SHAFTS REPLACING THE
ORIGINAL FOUR.

RESHAPED

BOW AND STERN WERE REBUILT AND RESHAPED.

HMS *Canada* (1915)

ORDERED BY CHILE IN 1911, THE SHIP WAS STILL BEING COMPLETED WHEN IT WAS ACQUIRED BY THE ROYAL NAVY AS AN EMERGENCY WAR PURCHASE TO STRENGTHEN THE GRAND FLEET.

On the outbreak of war in August 1914, three large battleships were being completed at English yards for foreign powers, two for Turkey (which was to become a belligerent on the German side), and one for Chile. Laid down at Elswick in December 1911 and launched as *Almirante Latorre* on November 27, 1913, the ship was completed as HMS *Canada* in September 1915, by which time it had been bought from the Chilean government.

As a longer, more powerfully engined *Iron Duke* type super-dreadnought, carrying ten 14-in (356 mm) guns capable of firing two rounds a minute, it was a welcome addition to the Grand Fleet. Various structural changes were made at a late stage, including removal of bridge and charthouse installation of control platforms on the mast, and the mounting of a boat-launching derrick. A single pole mast was fitted on the aft superstructure,

with a searchlight platform. The 6-in (152 mm) guns were mounted behind shields rather than in turrets or casemates, with a new type of shield intended to allow maximum elevation and depression at all angles of training.

World War I Service, Back to Chile

Canada joined the Grand Fleet in October 1915 and was part of the 4th Battle Squadron at Jutland, firing both its main and secondary guns, and taking no hits. On June 12, 1916, it joined the 1st Battle Squadron, and in 1918 flying-off platforms were mounted on the fore and aft super-firing turrets. In 1919 it was refitted at Devonport and reacquired by the Chilean Navy, assuming its original name of *Almirante Latorre*. On a return to Devonport during 1929–31 it was re-engined and converted to oil firing, the mainmast was raised to 60 ft (18.3 m) and

torpedo bulges were fitted. Back home, its crew led a brief naval mutiny in 1931, and the ship was laid up between 1933 and 1937. During World War II it patrolled Chilean waters to ensure compliance with the country's neutrality. It remained on the active list until 1951, then was disarmed and used as an oil hulk until October 1958. In the summer of 1959 it was towed to Yokohama for breaking up.

SPECIFICATIONS

DISPLACEMENT: 25,000 tons (25,401 tonnes), 32,000 tons (32,514 tonnes) full load

DIMENSIONS: 625 ft x 92 ft 6 in x 33 ft (191 m x 28.2 m x 10 m)

PROPULSION: Quadruple shafts, Brown-Curtis HP and Parsons LP turbines, 21 Yarrow boilers, 37,000 shp (27,591 kW)

ARMAMENT: Ten 14-in (356 mm)/ 45-caliber, sixteen 6-in (152 mm), two 3-in (76 mm), four 3-pounder guns; four 21-in (533 mm) torpedo tubes

ARMOR: Belt 9 in (230 mm), barbettes 10 in (254 mm), turrets 10 in (254 mm), conning tower 11 in (280 mm)

SPEED: 22.75 knots (26.2 mph; 42.1 km/h)

CREW: 1,167

HMS *Canada*

BIG GUNS
THE 14-IN (356 MM) GUNS WEIGHED 85 TONS (86.4 TONNES) AND FIRED A 1,400-LB (635 KG) SHELL, THE SAME WEIGHT AS THE 13.5-IN (343 MM) GUN. AT A MUZZLE VELOCITY OF 2,700 FT (823 M) PER SECOND IT COULD PENETRATE 53.2-IN (135 MM) WROUGHT IRON.

FORWARD GUNS
THE FORWARD 6-IN (152 MM) GUNS WERE MORE EFFECTIVELY ARRANGED THAN ON HMS *IRON DUKE*. THE AFTERMOST GUNS IN THE FORWARD BATTERY WERE REMOVED IN 1917 BECAUSE OF BLAST EFFECTS FROM "Q" TURRET.

RANGE
AFTER 1931 THE SHIP CARRIED 4,300 TONS (4,369 TONNES) OF OIL AND HAD A RANGE OF 4,400 NAUTICAL MILES (5,063 MILES; 8,149 KM) AT 10 KNOTS (11.5 MPH; 18.5 KM/H).

Provence (1915)

FRANCE'S SECOND DREADNOUGHT CLASS, ARMED WITH 13.4-IN (340 MM) GUNS, WAS
INTENDED TO MAINTAIN STRENGTH AGAINST THE NEW GENERATION OF "SUPER-
DREADNOUGHTS" OF THE BRITISH AND GERMAN NAVIES.

Provence and the other ships in the Bretagne class were the least "French-looking" capital ships yet built, with long, elegant lines balanced by the original broad yards on the foremast. It was laid down at the Lorient Arsenal on May 1, 1912, launched on April 20, 1913, and completed in June 1915. The M1912 13.4-in (340 mm)/45-caliber guns were mounted in five center-line turrets. Despite their caliber, they had a shorter range, 15,860 yards (14,500 m) than equivalent heavy guns of the time, with a maximum elevation of 12⁰. It was well armored from the belt up, though the underwater protection was criticized as insufficient.

World War I Flagship, Sunk in World War II

On commissioning on March 1, 1916, Provence became flagship of the French Navy in the Mediterranean and took part in the Salamis and Athens operations against pro-German elements in Greece. It also participated in the blockade of the Straits of Otranto, but remained in port at Corfu for all of 1917. In January and March 1919 it was sent to Cattaro (now Kotor, Montenegro) on the Adriatic to assist with the dispersal of Austrian ships and the repatriation of their crews, then was at Istanbul in 1919–20. In February 1922 it went for refit at Toulon, receiving a large tripod mast carrying a fire-control station and range finder for the four newly installed 2.9-in (75 mm) AA guns. Further modernizations were made in 1925–27 and 1931–34. In the final one, new oil-fired machinery was installed and new main battery guns were mounted.

Thus renewed, the ship was deployed in the Atlantic with the 2nd Squadron. Anti-intervention patrols along the Spanish coast were made in 1936–37 during the civil war. From September 1, 1939, to the French surrender on June 22, 1940, it was engaged on patrols in the Atlantic and Mediterranean. Moored at Mers-el-Kébir, it was bombarded by British warships on July 3 and settled on the harbor floor, but was refloated and moved to Toulon. It was scuttled there on November 27, 1942. The part-dismantled hulk was refloated on July 11, 1943, and sunk again as a blockship in 1944. Raised again in April 1949, it was broken up.

SPECIFICATIONS

DISPLACEMENT: 23,230 tons (tonnes); 25,000 tons (tonnes) full load

DIMENSIONS: 544 ft 7 in x 88 ft 3 in x 29 ft 2 in (166 m x 26.8 m x 8.9 m)

PROPULSION: Quadruple shafts, Parsons geared turbines, 18 Belleville boilers, 29,000 shp (21,625 kW)

ARMAMENT: Ten 13.4-in (340 mm)/45-caliber, twenty-two 5.4-in (139 mm)/55-caliber, four 1.8-in (47 mm) guns; four 17.7-in (450 mm) torpedo tubes

ARMOR: Belt 10.6–6.25 in (270–160 mm), barbettes 9.75 in (248 mm), conning tower 13.4 in (340 mm), decks 3.2–1.6 in (76–40 mm)

SPEED: 20 knots (23 mph; 37 km/h)

Provence

CENTRAL TURRET
THE CENTRAL TURRET WAS MOUNTED ON
THE SUPERSTRUCTURE, WELL ABOVE THE
MAIN DECK.

MAST
FRENCH BATTLESHIPS STILL RETAINED
THE SINGLE POLE-TYPE MAST, THOUGH
NO LONGER IN THE MASSIVE FORM OF
EARLIER DECADES.

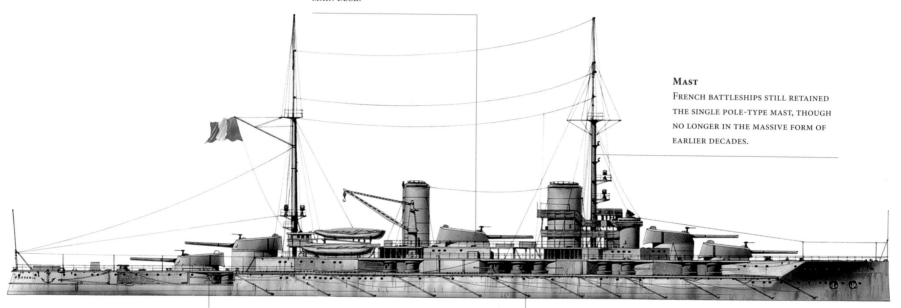

ELEVATION
IN 1918 THE GUN ELEVATION WAS INCREASED
TO 18°, EXTENDING THEIR RANGE TO 19,685
YD (18,000 M).

ANTI-TORPEDO DEFENSES
ON COMMISSIONING THE SHIP WAS FITTED WITH
ANTI-TORPEDO BOOMS AND NETS; THE LIGHT
GUNS ON THE TURRETS WERE INTENDED FOR
ANTI-TORPEDO BOAT DEFENSE.

USS *Nevada* (1916)

THE UNITED STATES' FIRST "SUPER-DREADNOUGHTS," THE TWO SHIPS OF THE *NEVADA* CLASS INCORPORATED A NUMBER OF NEW FEATURES, INCLUDING A REVISED ARMOR ARRANGEMENT, OIL-FIRING, AND TRIPLE TURRETS.

Nevada (BB-36), was laid down at Fore River Shipbuilding Company, at Quincy, Massachusetts, on November 4, 1912, launched on July 11, 1914, and commissioned on March 11, 1916. Firing tests in 1911 showed that light armor was of no value against heavy shells, and instead heavy armor was applied on 400 ft (122 m) of the waterline, and other vital parts only, on the "all or nothing" principle that became standard practice in battleship design after 1918.

Significant alterations were made during 1927–29. The secondary battery, originally in casemates below the forecastle deck, was raised to deck level, with the forward and aft guns removed, which made it more usable in rough conditions. The torpedo tubes were taken out and anti-torpedo bulges applied to the hull. Catapults were mounted on "X" turret and on the fantail, and tripods replaced the basket masts.

World War I Service

Nevada joined the Atlantic Fleet in 1916. From August to December 1918 it was based at Bantry Bay, Ireland, and with the end of hostilities returned to the Atlantic Fleet. From September 17, 1927, to November 26, 1929, it underwent modernization at Norfolk Navy Yard, Virginia, and in early 1930 transferred to the Pacific Fleet. Beached at Pearl Harbor on December 7, 1941, refloated on February 12, 1942, it was repaired at Puget Sound. With a unique rearwards-tilted cap mounted on the funnel, and the rear tripod removed, it joined Pacific operations at the Aleutian Islands in early 1943, then from June was on Atlantic convoy escort duties, followed by support for the Normandy landings in June 1944. In August it was deployed to the Mediterranean.

Modernized for World War II

On return to the United States later that year it had new gun barrels fitted and went again to the Pacific, in action at Iwo Jima and Okinawa between February and June 1945. Hit on March 27, 1945, by a kamikaze aircraft, it was only lightly damaged. It was decommissioned at Pearl Harbor on October 30, 1945. In 1946 it was used as a target in the Bikini Atoll atomic bomb tests but remained afloat, until sunk by an aerial torpedo on July 31, 1948.

SPECIFICATIONS

DISPLACEMENT: 27,500 tons (27,941 tonnes); 28,900 tons (29,364 tonnes) full load

DIMENSIONS: 583 ft 4 in x 95 ft 3 in x 28 ft 5 in (177.8 m x 29 m x 8.7 m)

PROPULSION: Twin shafts, two Curtis turbines, 12 Yarrow boilers, two geared cruising turbines, 26,500 shp (19,761 kW)

ARMAMENT: Ten 14-in (356 mm), twenty-one 5-in (127 mm) guns; two 3-in (76 mm) AA guns; two 21-in (533 mm) torpedo tubes

ARMOR: Belt 13.5–8 in (343–203 mm), bulkheads 1.5 in (38 mm), funnel uptakes 12 in (305 mm), barbettes 13.5 in (343 mm), turrets 18–5 in (457–127 mm), decks 3 in–1.5 in (76–38 mm)

SPEED: 20.5 knots (23.6 mph; 38 km/h)

CREW: 864

USS *Nevada*

FUNNEL
THE FUNNEL WAS HEIGHTENED BY
6 FT 6 IN (2 M) IN 1935; THE DISTINCTIVE
ANGLED SMOKE TUBE WAS ADDED IN
1942.

RADAR
THIS SHOWS *NEVADA*'S 1945
APPEARANCE AFTER THE TOPMAST WAS
HEIGHTENED IN 1943. BOTH MASTS
CARRY SRA AND SK RADAR AERIALS,
THE LATTER BEING ADDED IN 1943.

ANTI-AIRCRAFT GUNS
FORTY-EIGHT 1.6-IN (40 MM) AND TWENTY-SEVEN
0.79-IN (20 MM) AA GUN POSITIONS WERE INSTALLED,
MASSED ON THE SUPERSTRUCTURE, WHICH WAS
REDESIGNED TO GIVE THEM THE WIDEST POSSIBLE
FIRING ARCS.

TURRETS
SIX OF THE MAIN GUNS WERE IN TRIPLE
TURRETS, MOUNTED IN COMMON
CRADLES WHICH MEANT THAT THEY
COULD NOT BE INDIVIDUALLY ELEVATED.

SMS *Bayern* (1916)

BAYERN AND THE THREE OTHERS IN ITS CLASS WERE GERMANY'S EQUIVALENT OF THE BRITISH *QUEEN ELIZABETH* CLASS, WITH THE SAME CALIBER AND LAYOUT OF HEAVY GUNS, BUT WITHOUT THE SAME TURN OF SPEED.

Although the German move to 15-in (380 mm) caliber has been seen as a response to the same guns on the *Queen Elizabeth* class, it seems that the decision was taken before the size of the new British gun was known. *Bayern* was laid down at Howaldtswerke, Kiel, on September 20, 1913. Launched on February 18, 1915, it was completed in March 1916 at a cost of 50 million Goldmarks. Unlike the British *Queen Elizabeths*, they were intended for main fleet service, not as a battle squadron. The German ships' eight 15in (380mm) guns were less effective than the British ones. Their range at first was 22,310 yards (20,400 m), extended to 25,372 yards (23,200 m) when maximum elevation was raised from 16⁰ to 20⁰. They fired a round every 2.5 minutes, compared to 2 minutes for *Queen Elizabeth*. Secondary armament was arranged in traditional style in casemates, all at the same level,

eight on each side. Four continuous longitudinal bulkheads formed the main inner defenses. Five 21-in (533 mm) sea valves were fitted on each side amidships in order to allow for localized flooding of compartments. The outer bottom plating was only 0.6 in (15.8 mm) compared to 1 in (25.4 mm) in HMS *Revenge*.

North Sea Action in World War I

Completed in March 1916, *Bayern* was still running trials during May and was not involved in the Battle of Jutland. On August 19 and October 19, 1916, it made unsuccessful sorties into the North Sea. In 1917 it was in action in the Baltic Sea against Russian units, and struck a mine on October 12. During the repairs, the various modifications noted above were made. It was part of the battle squadron that broke out on April 23, 1918, reaching as far as 58.97⁰N but failing to intercept British convoy escort ships. From

November 26, 1918, it was interned at Scapa Flow, and scuttled there on June 21, 1919. Raised in September 1934, it was broken up at Inverkeithing, Scotland, in the following year.

SPECIFICATIONS

DISPLACEMENT: 31,700 tons (32,200 tonnes)

DIMENSIONS: 590 ft 7 in x 98 ft 5 in x 30 ft 10 in (180 m x 30 m x 9.4 m)

PROPULSION: Triple shafts, three Schichau turbines, 14 marine boilers, developing 52,000 shp (38,776 kW)

ARMAMENT: Eight 15-in (380 mm), sixteen 5.9-in (150 mm), two 3.5-in (88 mm) guns, five 23.6-in (600 mm) torpedo tubes

ARMOR: Belt 13.8–6.7 in (350–170 mm), bulkheads 7.9–6.7 in (200–170 mm), barbettes 13.8 in (350 mm), turrets 13.8–9.8 in (350–250 mm), conning tower 6.7 in (170 mm), deck 5.9–1.2 in (150–30 mm), 13.8 in (350 mm)

SPEED: 22.25 knots (25.6 mph; 41.2 km/h)

CREW: 1,171

SMS *Bayern*

MAST
WHEN COMMISSIONED, *BAYERN* HAD A SINGLE MAST, A TRIPOD WITH FIVE PLATFORMS AND A TALL TOPMAST RISING FROM THE PEAK OF THE TRIPOD. THESE WERE REPLACED IN 1917 BY A RELATIVELY SHORT POLE MAST STEPPED TO THE FUNNEL CASING.

DAVITS
DAVITS ON THE SEARCHLIGHT PLATFORMS WERE USED TO LOWER THE LIGHTS TO PROTECT THEM IN DAYTIME ACTIONS.

FUEL
BAYERN'S COAL CAPACITY WAS A MAXIMUM 3,400 TONNES (3,346 TONS), PLUS 620 TONNES (610 TONS) OF OIL. THE DIFFICULTY OF PROCURING SUFFICIENT OIL SUPPLIES KEPT THE GERMAN NAVY CHIEFLY RELIANT ON COAL WHILE THE BRITISH AND AMERICANS WERE TURNING TO LIQUID FUEL.

TORPEDO TUBES
ORIGINALLY *BAYERN* WAS FITTED WITH FIVE UNDERWATER 23.6 IN (600 MM) TORPEDO TUBES. THE FOUR STERN-MOUNTED TORPEDO TUBES WERE REMOVED AFTER THE SHIP STRUCK A MINE ON OCTOBER 12, 1917, LEAVING A SINGLE BOW TUBE.

HMS *Royal Sovereign* (1916)

FINAL SHIP OF THE *REVENGE* CLASS, *ROYAL SOVEREIGN* SERVED WITH THE GRAND FLEET DURING WORLD WAR I AND WAS EXTENSIVELY USED ON CONVOY ESCORT IN WORLD WAR II. THE FIVE *REVENGE* CLASS WERE THE MAJOR PART OF BRITAIN'S 1913 NAVAL PROGRAM.

Royal Sovereign was laid down at Portsmouth on January 15, 1914, the year after the previous ship of the same name was scrapped; launched on April 29, 1915, and completed in May 1916, just too late to participate in the Battle of Jutland. The ship had an imposing profile with a single large funnel taking the uptakes from 18 boilers. The 15-in (381 mm)/42-caliber guns had already been installed on the *Queen Elizabeths* and *Royal Sovereign* carried the same range of armament and much the same degree of armor protection though with a fully protected main deck (armor was 31.7 percent of displacement in the case of *Royal Sovereign*).

The class was designed with a low metacentric height (GM), the aim being a slower roll period, an easier gunlaying capability, and therefore more accurate long-range accuracy. This was achieved by raising the armored deck to the top of the main belt, which also resulted in better protection against shell-fire, though reducing resistance to underwater damage and making them unstable when subjected to only moderate amounts of flooding. Anti-torpedo bulges were fitted along the flanks during a 1927–28 refit, and the torpedo tubes were removed.

Service in World War I and II

The ship was part of the 1st Battle Squadron from 1916 to 1919, first with the Grand Fleet, then the Atlantic Fleet, and returned to the 1st Squadron after refitting in 1928, remaining until 1935. Following spells in reserve and as a training ship, and a 1937 refit, in which four twin 4-in (102 mm) guns were mounted; also 2-pounder pom-pom guns, housed in sponsons constructed each side of the funnel, it steamed huge distances as a convoy escort both in the Atlantic and Far East.

By this time it was obsolescent, certainly no match for the new Japanese battleships, and unable to maintain the pace of American aircraft carriers. In 1944 it was secretly handed over to the Soviet Navy and operated as *Archangelsk* in Arctic waters, being returned to Britain in February 1949. It was sold for breaking in the same year.

SPECIFICATIONS

DISPLACEMENT: 28,000 tons (28,449 tonnes); 31,000 tons (31,497 tonnes) full load

DIMENSIONS: 624 ft 3 in x 88 ft 6 in x 28 ft 6 in (190.3 m x 27 m x 8.7 m)

PROPULSION: Quadruple shafts, Parsons turbines, 18 Yarrow boilers, 40,000 shp (29,828 kW)

ARMAMENT: Eight 15-in (381 mm)/42-caliber, fourteen 6-in (152 mm)/45-caliber guns; two 3-in (76 mm) AA guns; four 3-pounder guns; four 21-in (533 mm) torpedo tubes

ARMOR: Belt 13–1 in (330–25 mm), bulkheads 6–4in (152–102 mm), barbettes 10–4 in (254–102 mm), turret faces 13 in (330 mm), conning tower 11 in (280 mm)

SPEED: 23 knots (26.5 mph; 42.6 km/h)

CREW: 997

HMS *Royal Sovereign*

TOWER

BY 1939 *ROYAL SOVEREIGN* HAD A BLACK
FUNNEL COWL AND CLINKER SCREEN
FITTED. THE MAST WAS BUILT UP AS A
MULTI-STAGE TOWER.

RUDDER

A SMALLER AUXILIARY RUDDER WAS FITTED
AT FIRST, BUT PROVED OF LITTLE USE AND WAS
REMOVED.

PLATFORMS

FLYING-OFF PLATFORMS WERE FITTED TO "B"
AND "X" TURRETS IN 1917. LATER A CATAPULT
WAS FITTED ON THE QUARTER DECK, BUT THIS
WAS REMOVED EARLY IN WORLD WAR II.

USS *Mississippi* (1917)

REPLACING A PRE-DREADNOUGHT OF THE SAME NAME, *MISSISSIPPI* WAS PART OF THE *NEW MEXICO* CLASS, THE FIRST US BATTLESHIPS FITTED WITH CLIPPER BOWS. THE NAVY BOARD HAD WANTED A COMPLETELY NEW BATTLESHIP DESIGN BUT THE GOVERNMENT OPTED FOR A REPETITION OF THE PRECEDING *PENNSYLVANIA* CLASS, WITH MINOR ALTERATIONS.

Mississippi, (BB-41), was first of the class to be laid down, at Newport News, on April 5, 1915, launched on January 25, 1917, and completed on December 18, 1917. Previous battleships had carried their secondary armament in casemates below the weather deck, conning tower with constant problems of unusability if a high sea was running. In *Mississippi* the batteries were on the weather deck and suffered far less from wetness; lower-level bow and stern guns in the hull were removed and the positions plated over.

In the manner established with USS *Nevada*, the armor was "all or nothing" but the bulkheads and the armored deck were 0.5-in (12.5 mm) thicker as a result of weight savings elsewhere. Like *Pennsylvania* it had four screws rather than *Nevada*'s two. The 14-in (356 mm)/50-caliber guns were of a new (at first not entirely satisfactory) design in which each gun in the triple turrets could be trained independently.

Last Salvo Between Capital Ships

On July 19, 1919, *Mississippi* was deployed to the Pacific Fleet at San Pedro, California, remaining there until a refit at Norfolk Navy Yard in 1931–33 when the original lattice masts were removed and the foremast replaced by a tower structure. From 1934 to 1941 it was back at San Pedro, and after a short spell in the North Atlantic, protecting US shipping, it was dispatched to the Pacific after the Pearl Harbor attack. From 1943 through to 1945 it was engaged in many actions, bombarding shore positions and supporting troops landings.

In the Surigao Strait battle, part of the Leyte Gulf extended battle, as part of Rear-Admiral Oldendorf's force, it was in action against Japanese battleships: its one and only salvo, from all twelve guns, was the last such to be fired in a fight between capital ships. *Mississippi* had a ten-year postwar career as AG-128, an auxiliary ship testing new weapons systems, including the Terrier guided missile, first test-fired from its deck on January 28, 1953. Decommissioned on September 17, 1956, it was sold for scrapping in November of that year.

SPECIFICATIONS

DISPLACEMENT: 32,000 tons (32,513 tonnes); 33,000 tons (33,529 tonnes) full load

DIMENSIONS: 624 ft x 97 ft 5in x 30 ft (190.2 m x 29.7 m x 9.1 m)

PROPULSION: Quadruple shafts, Curtis turbines, nine Babcock & Wilcox boilers, 32,000 shp (23,862 kW)

ARMAMENT: Twelve 14-in (356 mm)/50-caliber, fourteen 5-in (127 mm)/51-caliber, four 3-in (76 mm)/50-caliber guns; two 21-in (533 mm) torpedo tubes

ARMOR: Belt 13.5–8 in (343–203 mm), bulkheads 1.5 in (38 mm), funnel uptakes 12 in (305 mm), barbettes 13.5 in (343 mm), turrets 18–5 in (457–127 mm), decks 3.5 in–1.5 in (89–38 mm)

SPEED: 21 knots (24.2 mph; 38.9 km/h)

CREW: 1,084

USS *Mississippi*

LAUNCHER
THE ORIGINAL AIRCRAFT TEST LAUNCHER WAS SIMPLY A WOODEN PLATFORM ATOP "X" TURRET. BY NOW A CATAPULT AND CRANE ARE FITTED.

GUNS
AA GUNS ARE WIDELY DISTRIBUTED ON THE NEW SUPERSTRUCTURE.

CAMOUFLAGE PAINT
HERE THE *MISSISSIPPI* IS SHOWN IN WORLD WAR II CAMOUFLAGE PAINT.

GUN MOUNTINGS
THE HULL GUN MOUNTINGS WERE PLATED OVER IN WORLD WAR I.

Ise *(1917)*

BEGINNING ITS CAREER AS A WORLD WAR I COAL-BURNING BATTLESHIP, *ISE* PASSED
THROUGH VARIOUS CHANGES TO END UP AS A "BATTLESHIP CARRIER" IN WORLD
WAR II BEFORE BEING SUNK IN JULY 1945.

Ise and its sister ship *Hyuga* were based on a modified *Fuso* design, 10 ft (3 m) longer, with the same beam, and slightly greater draft. Laid down at the Kawasaki yard, Kobe, Japan, on May 10, 1915, *Ise* was launched on November 12, 1916, and completed on December 15, 1917. Other variations from *Fuso* included placing of the after turrets, all abaft of the funnels, a different secondary armament, and a raised fore-funnel. Internally the armored deck sloped down to meet the lower edge of the belt armor over the magazines as well as the boiler rooms, and splinter protection was improved: changes to the armor accounted for the extra tonnage compared with *Fuso*.

Assigned to the Kure Division, the ship saw no action in World War I but supported the Allied "Siberian Intervention" against Bolshevik Russia in 1919–20. Patrols off the Russian and Chinese coasts followed. AA guns were fitted around 1921, and in 1926–27 a pagoda tower was installed, with a flying-off platform on the aftermost super-firing turret. More reconstruction took place in 1931–32 at Kure, Japan, with the fitting of a catapult and crane on the fantail. New machinery was installed between August 1935 and March 1937, the fore-funnel was removed, the stern lengthened by 25 ft (7.62 m), torpedo blisters added and the six underwater torpedo tubes removed.

Battleship-Carrier

After Midway, Japan lacked carrier strength and *Ise* was converted to a hybrid "battleship-carrier," with a hangar and 230 ft (70 m) aircraft deck replacing Nos. 5 and 6 turrets. Twenty-two dive-bombers could be carried. Concrete was used for ballast and steering-gear protection. AA armament was increased and Type 21 air-search and Type 22 surface-search radar fitted. In fact the ship, completed in this form on September 5, 1943, was never used as a carrier, though participating in the Leyte Gulf battle (October 23–26, 1944), when it was damaged by bombs, and it also made a return trip to Singapore for war supplies. From February 1945 it remained docked at Kure, and was sunk by 16 bombs on July 28. Remaining partially above water, it was dismantled on site in 1946–47.

SPECIFICATIONS

DISPLACEMENT: 31,260 tons (31,762 tonnes); 36,500 (37,086 tonnes) full load

DIMENSIONS: 675 ft x 94 ft x 29 ft 1 in (205.8 m x 28.7 m x 8.8 m)

PROPULSION: Quadruple shafts, Curtis turbines, 24 Kampon boilers, 45,000 shp (33,556 kW)

ARMAMENT: Twelve 14-in (356 mm)/45-caliber, twenty 5.5-in (140 mm)/50-caliber guns; four 3.1-in (79 mm) AA guns; six 21-in (533 mm) torpedo tubes

ARMOR: Belt 12–4 in (305–102 mm), barbettes and turrets 12–8 in (305–203 mm), conning tower forward 12 in (305 mm), aft 6 in (152 mm), decks 2.2–1.5 in (55–34 mm)

SPEED: 23 knots (26.4 mph; 42.6 km/h)

CREW: 1,360

Ise

RADAR
TYPE 21 AIR-SEARCH AND TWO SETS
OF TYPE 22 SURFACE-SEARCH RADAR
WERE FITTED.

GUNS
ISE AS A BATTLESHIP-CARRIER
STILL MOUNTED A POWERFUL MAIN
ARMAMENT.

AA GUNS
FINAL AA ARMAMENT WAS EIGHT TWIN-
MOUNT 5-IN (127 MM) GUNS AND FIFTY-
SEVEN TYPE 96 1-IN (25 MM) GUNS,
NINETEEN OF THEM IN TRIPLE MOUNTINGS.

ROCKET LAUNCHERS
FROM DECEMBER 1944 SIX RACKS OF 30-TUBE
5-IN (127 MM) AA ROCKET LAUNCHERS WERE
CARRIED.

HMS *Hood* (1920)

NEWS IN 1915 THAT GERMANY WAS BUILDING BATTLECRUISERS WITH 15-IN (381 MM) GUNS—
THE *MACKENSEN* CLASS—PROMPTED THE BRITISH ADMIRALTY TO COMMISSION DESIGNS FOR
A NEW CLASS OF SHIP THAT COULD OUTPERFORM THEM.

Before anything was finalized, the Battle of Jutland was fought and the inadequacy of the British battlecruisers in a heavy gun battle was clearly revealed. It was evident that the whole concept had to be rethought. On redrawn plans, *Hood* was laid down at John Brown's yard, Clydebank, Scotland, on September 1, 1916, launched on August 22, 1918, and completed on March 5, 1920, at a cost of £6,025,000.

AA armament was steadily increased from 16 quadruple-mount 1.6-in (40 mm) guns added in 1931 to 24 from 1939, along with four 4-in (102 mm) guns (also 1939) increased to eight in 1940. Fifteen machine guns installed in 1939 were supplemented by 20 quadruple-mount machine guns in 1940. Two 21-in (533 mm) underwater torpedo tubes were removed in 1939, but four of the same caliber mounted on the upper deck abreast of the mainmast were retained.

Hood was the first British capital ship to have Yarrow oil-fired small-tube boilers.

From 1920–29 it served with the Home Fleet on exercises and ceremonial duties, including a 10-month world cruise with HMS *Renown* in 1923. A modernization program at HM Dockyard Portsmouth lasted from June 1929 to May 1931, then it rejoined the Home Fleet. On January 23, 1935, it collided with *Renown* and went to Portsmouth for repairs. After a refit between February and September 1939 it went into war service, suffering slight bomb damage in the North Sea on October 23, 1939.

Sinking of HMS *Hood*

Operations included the chase of *Scharnhorst* and *Gneisenau* in the English Channel in November 1939, and in June–July 1940 it was flagship of "Force H" in the Mediterranean, including the attack on the French fleet at Mers-el-Kébir, Algeria, July 3; then returned to the Home Fleet. A further refit was done at Rosyth between January and March 1941. On May 22, 1941, it was flagship of Vice-Admiral Lancelot Holland's Battle Cruiser Force, sent with HMS *Prince of Wales* to intercept *Bismarck* and *Prinz Eugen*, south of Greenland. While exchanging gunfire with the German ships at a range of around 25,000 yards (22,860 m), *Hood* exploded at 06:00 on the May 24 and sank a few minutes later. Only three of the crew survived.

SPECIFICATIONS

DISPLACEMENT: 41,200 tons (41,861 tonnes); 45,200 tons (45,925 tonnes) full load

DIMENSIONS: 860 ft 7 in x 104 ft 2 in x 32 ft (262 m x 31.8 m x 9.8 m)

PROPULSION: Quadruple shafts, 24 Yarrow small-tube boilers, Brown-Curtis geared turbines, 144,000 shp (107,381 kW)

ARMAMENT: Eight 15-in (381 mm), twelve 5.5-in (140 mm) guns; four 4-in (102 mm) AA guns; six 21-in (533 mm) torpedo tubes

ARMOR: Belt 12–6 in (305–152 mm), bulkheads 5–4 in (127–102mm), deck 3–0.75 in (76–19 mm), turrets 15–11 in (381–279 mm), conning tower 11–9 in (279–229mm)

SPEED: 31 knots (35.6 mph; 57.4 km/h)

CREW: 1,433

HMS *Hood*

MAINMAST

THE TOP SECTION OF THE MAINMAST WAS REMOVED BY 1941. *HOOD* WAS THE LAST RN BATTLESHIP TO HAVE MASTHEAD CONTROL TOPS. BY EARLY 1941 IT ALSO CARRIED TYPE 279 RADAR ON THE MAINMAST, TYPES 282 AND 285 ON THE GUNNERY CONTROL EQUIPMENT, AND TYPE 274 ON THE FOREMAST.

GUNS

THE 15-IN (381 MM) GUNS WERE THE SAME AS THOSE FITTED IN THE *QUEEN ELIZABETH* CLASS. SIXTEEN 5.5-IN (140 MM) GUNS WERE PLANNED FOR, BUT ONLY TWELVE WERE INSTALLED, REDUCED TO TEN IN 1939 AND SIX IN 1940.

POOP DECK

IN 1932 AN AIRCRAFT CRANE AND TELESCOPIC CATAPULT WERE EXPERIMENTALLY MOUNTED ON THE POOP DECK, BUT NOT RETAINED.

DEFLECTOR

THE SHIP FLOATED OVER 3 FT 6 IN (1 M) DEEPER THAN ORIGINALLY PLANNED, AND A DEFLECTOR WAS PLACED TO KEEP BOW SEAS CLEAR OF "A" TURRET.

Nagato (1920)

NAGATO AND ITS SISTER SHIP MUTSU (COMPLETED OCTOBER 1921) OUTGUNNED ANY BATTLESHIP IN WESTERN FLEETS. EVEN WITH THE COMPLETION OF USS MARYLAND IN JULY 1921, CARRYING GUNS OF THE SAME CALIBER, THE JAPANESE GUNS FIRED HEAVIER SHELLS AND HAD A LONGER RANGE.

Japanese naval chiefs studied the Battle of Jutland closely when the class was at the design stage, resulting in some delay while the lessons were absorbed. *Nagato* was laid down on August 28, 1917, at the Kure Kaigun Kosho naval basin, launched on November 9, 1919, and completed on November 25, 1920. It was the first ship to be armed with 16-in (406 mm) guns. The armor-plating was on the principle of maximum fortification to the vital areas and little or nothing elsewhere, except that the lower deck was well-armored, with a thickness of 3–2.8 in (76–71 mm). Among the post-Jutland design refinements was better anti-flash protection.

Throughout its career *Nagato* underwent many changes, starting in 1924, when the fore-funnel was trunked back to distance it from the tower. A second floatplane derrick was fixed to the aftermast and in 1925–26 a German Heinkel catapult was fitted to "B" turret and became a prototype for Japanese designs. Large-scale modernization was done in 1934–36. Horizontal armor was reinforced to a maximum 8.15 in (207 mm), torpedo bulges 9 ft 2 in (2.8 m) wide were applied, new boilers and engines were fitted along with a single funnel set well back from the tower, and the hull was lengthened by 28 ft 6 in (8.7 m) at the stern. The torpedo tubes were taken out and new fire control systems were installed. A folding aircraft crane was fitted on the port side of "X" turret. Range-finding equipment was installed, at first on "B" and "X" turrets and later above the bridge. In 1944 a high platform was built between the foremast and the funnel as a deck for further AA guns.

Midway and Leyte

In World War II *Nagato*'s main actions were operations off Midway Island in June 1942, and the Leyte battles of October 22–25, 1944, when it sank the American escort carrier USS *Gambier Bay* and three destroyers. It returned to the Yokohama naval base and remained at anchor there, with the funnel cap and the after topmast taken down. On July 18, 1945, it was heavily damaged by aircraft strikes. After the war it was used as a target ship in the Bikini Atoll atom bomb tests. The second "Baker" test on July 25, 1946, left it a wreck and it sank four days later.

SPECIFICATIONS

DISPLACEMENT: 33,245 tons (32,720 tonnes); 38,500 tons (39,116 tonnes) full load

DIMENSIONS: 708 ft x 95 ft 3 in x 29 ft 9 in (215.8 m x 29 m x 9.1 m)

PROPULSION: Quadruple shafts, four Gihon turbines, 21 boilers, 80,000 shp (59,656 kW)

ARMAMENT: Eight 16-in (406 mm), twenty 5.5-in (140 mm) guns; four 3-in (76 mm) AA guns; eight 21-in (533 mm) torpedo tubes

ARMOR: Belt 12–4 in (305–102 mm), barbettes 11.8 in (300 mm), turrets 14 in (356 mm), conning tower forward 14.6 in (371 mm), deck upper 1.7–1 in (44–25 mm), lower 2.9–2.7 in (75–50 mm)

SPEED: 26.75 knots (30.8 mph; 49.6 km/h)

CREW: 1,333

Nagato

MASTS
FROM 1944 *NAGATO* CARRIED RADAR ANTENNAE ON BOTH MASTS: TYPE 1 MODEL 3 (AIR SEARCH) AND TYPE 2 MODEL 1 (SURFACE SEARCH).

GUNS
THE 16-IN (406 MM) GUN TURRETS WEIGHED 1,025 TONS (1,041 TONNES) EACH, INCLUDING ROTARY ARMOR OF 490 TONS (498 TONNES). IN FINAL FORM THE MAIN GUNS COULD ELEVATE TO 43°.

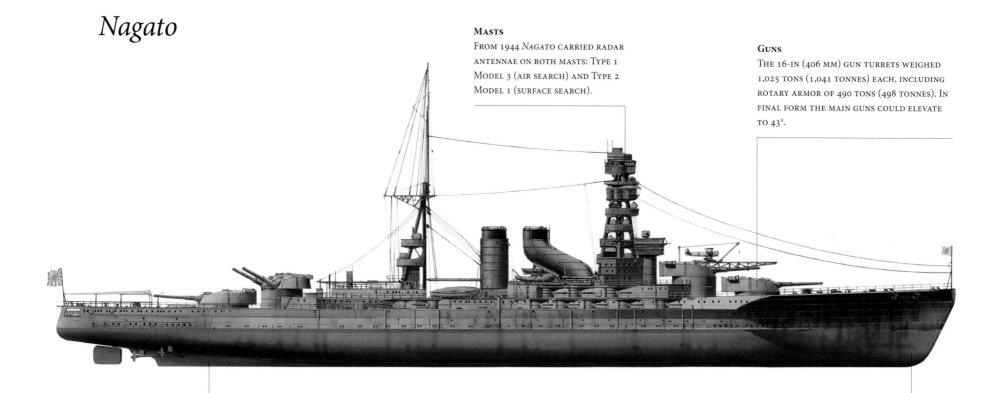

CHANGED DESIGN
FROM 1936 MAXIMUM DISPLACEMENT WAS 42,785 TONS (43,471 TONNES), LENGTH WAS 736 FT 6 IN (224.5 M), BEAM 113 FT 5 IN (34.6 M), AND DRAFT 31 FT 2 IN (9.5 M).

BOW
IN 1934–36 THE ORIGINAL INWARD-CURVING BOW WAS REPLACED BY A STRAIGHT CLIPPER BOW (FIRST TRIED OUT ON *MUTSU*).

Jaime I (1922)

THIRD SHIP IN SPAIN'S LAST CLASS OF BATTLESHIPS, ITS CONSTRUCTION WAS DELAYED BY THE 1914–18 WAR. THOUGH WELL-ARMED, ITS STAYING-POWER UNDER FIRE WAS LIMITED. AS THE SMALLEST DREADNOUGHT-TYPE SHIPS TO BE BUILT, THE *ESPAÑA* CLASS MIGHT BE SAID TO ANTICIPATE THE POCKET BATTLESHIPS OF THE 1930S.

The type's dimensions were restricted by the size of the docks at Spanish naval bases; funds did not allow for new docking facilities and new capital ships. Designed on the "all big-gun" principle, *Jaime I* was laid down at Ferrol, Spain, on February 5, 1912, and launched on September 21, 1914. Construction was in partnership with Vickers-Armstrong of England, and the supply of material and parts was interrupted by the war years; consequently *Jaime I* was not completed until 1922.

The ship was flush-decked, with minimal superstructure, primarily a wide short bridge. Two tripod masts were fitted. Placing of the eight 12-in (305 mm) guns was in an extended echelon with the "B" and "X" turrets mounted laterally, to starboard and port respectively. Lateral casemates below the weather deck carried twenty 4-in (102 mm) guns. The designers' aim was to pack modern guns into a traditional-size hull. It did not lack armor, carrying 4,750 tons (4,826 tonnes), 29.9 percent of displacement, but this was considerably thinner than that of larger dreadnoughts. Though driven by turbines, the power rating was modest and it was not a fast ship.

Action off Spanish Morocco

Jaime I saw action against the Riff revolt in Spanish Morocco in 1922–23, firing against coastal positions and being hit in May 1924 by a coastal battery. At the start of the Spanish Civil War (1936–39) it was based at Santander but was ordered to the Mediterranean. Held by the Republican side, it was based for a time at Tangier, Morocco, then Málaga, Spain. It bombarded Ceuta and Algeciras, Spain, strongpoints of General Francisco Franco's Nationalist forces, setting fire to the gunboat *Eduardo Dato*. On August 13, 1936, it was struck by a bomb at Málaga, and went to Cartagena, Spain, for repairs. While in the dockyard, on June 17, 1937, an internal explosion and fire, apparently accidental, caused major damage, killing around 300 men and leaving the ship unusable. It was scrapped at Cartagena in 1939.

SPECIFICATIONS

DISPLACEMENT: 15,452 tons (15,700 tonnes); 15,700 tons (15,952 tonnes) full load

DIMENSIONS: 459 ft 2 in x 78 ft 9 in x 25 ft 6 in (140 m x 24 m x 7.8 m)

PROPULSION: Quadruple shafts, Parsons turbines, 12 Yarrow boilers, 15,500 shp (11,558 kW)

ARMAMENT: Eight 12-in (305 mm)/50-caliber, twenty 4-in (102 mm), four 3-pounder guns

ARMOR: Belt 8 in–4 in (203–102 mm), upper belt 6 in (152 mm), barbettes 10 in (254 mm), turrets 8 in (203 mm), conning tower 10 in (256 mm), deck 1.5 in (38 mm)

SPEED: 16.75 knots (19.3 mph; 31 km/h)

CREW: 854

Jaime I

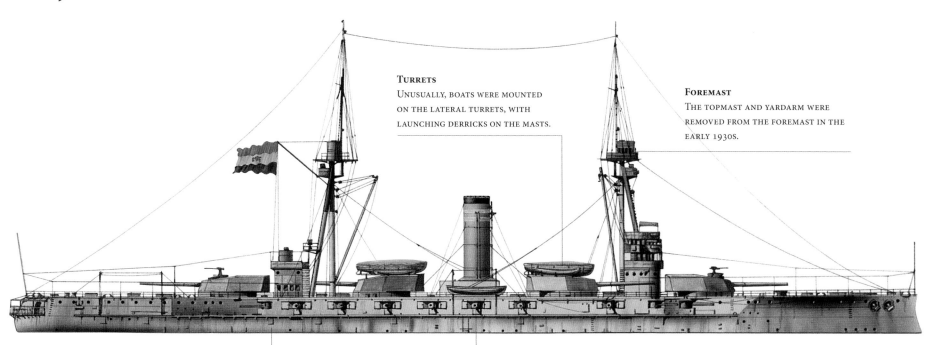

Turrets
Unusually, boats were mounted on the lateral turrets, with launching derricks on the masts.

Foremast
The topmast and yardarm were removed from the foremast in the early 1930s.

Last of the España Class
Jaime I was the last survivor of the class. *España* was wrecked on August 26, 1923, and *Alfonso XIII* (renamed *España* in 1931) was sunk by a mine on April 30, 1937.

Lateral Guns
The lateral guns were carried on different sections of the hull frame, reducing stresses.

HMS *Rodney* (1927)

DESCRIBED AS "UGLY BUT IMPRESSIVE," *RODNEY* WAS ONE OF TWO ROYAL NAVY BATTLESHIPS BUILT UNDER THE TERMS OF THE WASHINGTON NAVAL TREATY OF FEBRUARY 1922, THE ONLY BRITISH WARSHIPS TO CARRY 16-IN (406 MM) GUNS AND THE FIRST TO HAVE TRIPLE TURRETS.

Rodney was laid down on December 28, 1922, at Cammell Laird, Birkenhead, England, launched on December 17, 1925, and completed in August 1927, at a cost of £7,617,799. Lightweight "D" steel was used in hull construction, and fir rather than teak was used for decking, with aluminum and fireproofed plywood for interior fitments.

The Mark I triple-mounted 16-in (406 mm) guns weighed 129 tons (131 tonnes), and had a range of 45,490 yards (41,600 m) at a maximum elevation of 44⁰. Fitted in single cradles, they could be individually aimed. Secondary armament was mounted in individual turrets, the first in the RN to be power-worked.

American-style, the armor protection was "all or nothing." For the first time, side armor was not fitted as an external belt, but on the inner side of the steel hull, angling inwards from the armored deck:

the effect of this was intended to reduce the penetrative power of an incoming shell and also to deflect plunging shells.

On *Bismarck*'s Trail

Rodney was based with the Home and Atlantic Fleets from 1927 to 1939. Its war service was intensive, based first at Scapa Flow, then Rosyth from 13 September 1940. From November 1940 it was on Atlantic convoy escort. On its way to the United States for an engine repair, it was detached to join in the hunt for *Bismarck* in May 1941 and participated in its destruction. It then resumed the voyage to Boston, where engine repairs were carried out during June–September 1941. It then served briefly in the Mediterranean before returning to Britain in November.

A complete refit was done between December 1941 and May 1942, then it returned to the Mediterranean, supporting the North African landings

in November, and remaining until October 1943, when it resumed service with the Home Fleet, bombarding shore targets in France and the Channel Islands, and escorting convoys to Murmansk, Russia. From December 1944 it remained at Scapa Flow, then passed into reserve after the end of the war. In February 1948 it was sold for breaking.

SPECIFICATIONS

DISPLACEMENT: 33,950 tons (34,493 tonnes); 38,000 tons (38,608 tonnes) full load

DIMENSIONS: 710 ft x 106 ft x 30 ft (216.8 m x 32.4 m x 9.1 m)

PROPULSION: Twin shafts, eight Brown-Curtis geared turbines, 3-drum boilers with super heaters, 45,000 shp (33,556 kW)

ARMAMENT: Nine 16-in (406 mm)/ 45-caliber, twelve 6-in (152 mm) guns; six 4.7-in (119 mm) AA guns, eight 2-pounder pom-poms; two 24.5-in (622 mm) torpedo tubes (submerged)

ARMOR: Belt 14 in (356 mm), bulkheads 14–3 in (356–76 mm), turret faces 16 in (406 mm), deck over magazines 6.25 in (158 mm), over machinery 3 in (76 mm)

SPEED: 23 knots (26.5 mph; 42.6 km/h)

CREW: 1,314

HMS *Rodney*

TOWER DESIGN
THE FIVE-DECK TOWER DESIGN,
WITH INTEGRATED MAST, CARRIED
DIRECTORS FOR THE VARIOUS GUN
GROUPS, ADMIRAL'S BRIDGE, TORPEDO
CONTROL STATION, SIGNALING AND
NAVIGATION BRIDGES.

GUN PLACEMENT
ALL *RODNEY*'S MAIN GUNS WERE SITED FORWARD
OF THE TOWER IN ORDER TO CONCENTRATE THE
MAGAZINE ARMOR IN AS LIMITED A SPACE AS
POSSIBLE. IN THEORY THE GUNS COULD FIRE ABAFT
THE BEAM BUT PRACTICE PROVED THIS IMPOSSIBLE,
THE BLAST DAMAGING THE TOWER STRUCTURE.

ELEVATION
THE 40° ELEVATION WAS USED ON OCCASION
TO FIRE 2,641-LB (1,198 KG) SHELLS AT
APPROACHING AIRCRAFT, AT A RANGE OF UP
TO 35,000 YARDS (32,000 M).

TORPEDO TUBES
THE 24.5-IN (622 MM) TORPEDO TUBES WERE
THE ONLY BRITISH USE OF THIS CALIBER.

KMS *Deutschland/Lützow* (1933)

IN 1927, THE CONCEPT OF A FAST *PANZERSCHIFF* (ARMORED SHIP) BEGAN TO CRYSTALLIZE: FASTER
THAN A BATTLESHIP, WITH THICKER ARMOR AND HEAVIER GUNS THAN A CRUISER. IT BECAME THE
"POCKET BATTLESHIP," THE FIRST MAJOR WARSHIP POWERED BY DIESEL ENGINES.

Deutschland was laid down at the Deutsche Werke, Kiel, on February 5, 1929, launched on March 19, 1931, and completed on April 1, 1933, its displacement falsely recorded as 10,000 tons (10,160 tonnes). Every effort was made to save weight, with electric welding resulting in a hull weight 15 percent less than if riveting had been used. The main guns, in two triple turrets, weighed 52.4 tons (53.2 tonnes), firing a shell of 694-lb (315 kg). Secondary armament consisted of eight 6-in (152 mm) quick-firing guns in laterally placed single-mount shields on the forecastle deck (which extended four-fifths of the ship's length) and three 3.5-in (88 mm) AA guns.

In 1934 the port side derrick was replaced by a lattice crane. Further changes in 1937–38 included the fitting of new cranes, a slightly tilted cap to the funnel (considerably heightened at the fore-end in 1942), and large searchlights on a platform round the funnel. In its final form the bridge tower was surmounted by a wide range-finder, in turn topped by a wireless mast.

Twice Torpedoed

On commissioning *Deutschland* became flagship of the German Navy, until 1936. In 1936–37 it made patrols off Spain and took two hits from Spanish Republican aircraft on May 29, 1937, causing considerable damage and 31 deaths. From September 29, 1939, it was engaged in commerce raiding in the Atlantic. Its name was changed to *Lützow* on November 15.

On April 11, 1940, the British submarine *Spearfish* hit it with a torpedo off Norway, and it was towed back to Kiel. On July 13, 1941, attempting an entry to the Atlantic, it was again badly damaged, by a torpedo from an RAF Beaufort, and returned to Kiel for repairs, until January 1942.

Through 1942 and until September 29, 1943, it was based in North Norway, with a return to Kiel for repairs from August 9 to November 9, 1942. In December 1942 it was involved in the Battle of the Barents Sea against the British cruisers HMS *Sheffield* and *Jamaica*. From October 1943 it remained at Gotenhafen (Gdynia). A bomb attack on April 15, 1945, left the ship disabled. Scuttled by its crew on May 4, it was eventually destroyed by Soviet bomb practice and then scrapped.

SPECIFICATIONS

DISPLACEMENT: 11,750 tonnes (11,938 tonnes); full load 15,900 tons (16,154 tonnes)

DIMENSIONS: 610 ft 3 in x 67 ft 6 in x 23 ft 7 in (186 m x 20.6 m x 7.2 m)

PROPULSION: Quadruple shafts, four 9-cylinder double-acting 2-stroke MAN diesel engines, Vulcan gearboxes, 54,000 shp (40,268 kW)

ARMAMENT: Six 11-in (280 mm)/ 54.5-caliber, eight 5.9-in (150 mm), three 3.5-in (88 mm) guns; eight 19.7-in (500 mm) torpedo tubes

ARMOR: Belt 3.1–2.4 in (80–60 mm), bulkheads 1.8–1.6 in (45–40 mm), turrets 5.5–3.3 in (140–85 mm), conning tower 5.9–2 in (150–50 mm), deck 1.8–1.6 in (45–40 mm)

SPEED: 28 knots (32.2 mph; 51.9 km/h)

CREW: 619

KMS *Deutschland/Lützow*

MAINMAST
FROM A 1935 REFIT THE MAINMAST WAS
RIGIDLY CONNECTED TO THE FUNNEL.

ARMOR
DEUTSCHLAND'S SIDE ARMOR WAS
INTENDED TO WITHSTAND FIRE FROM
CRUISERS. IT WAS NOT EXPECTED TO
ENGAGE HEAVY-GUN BATTLESHIPS.

TORPEDO TUBES
EIGHT 19.7-IN (500 MM) TORPEDO TUBES WERE
FITTED IN TWO SETS OF FOUR ON THE UPPER
DECK, WITH ARMORED COVERS; LATER 21-IN (533
MM) TUBES WERE FITTED.

REFITTING
IN 1935 A MAINMAST WAS ATTACHED
ABAFT THE FUNNEL, AA GUN CONTROL WAS
FITTED, AN AIRCRAFT CATAPULT INSTALLED
BETWEEN THE BRIDGE TOWER AND FUNNEL,
AND TWIN-MOUNT 3.5-IN (88 MM) AA GUNS
REPLACED THE ORIGINAL SINGLES.

De Ruyter (1936)

THIS DUTCH LIGHT CRUISER OF THE MID-1930S INCORPORATED MANY ADVANCED FEATURES. IT WAS SUNK IN THE BATTLE OF THE JAVA SEA IN FEBRUARY 1942 AFTER A COMBINED ALLIED FLEET WAS RESOUNDINGLY DEFEATED BY A JAPANESE CRUISER FORCE DURING THE INVASION OF JAVA.

The Royal Netherlands Navy maintained three cruisers on its Far East station based at Batavia (Java) and it was to provide an up-to-date addition to this force that *De Ruyter* was planned. Ordered in 1932, laid down at the Wilton-Fijenoord yard, Rotterdam, on September 16, 1933, launched on May 11, 1935, and commissioned on October 3, 1936, its final specification was different from the original plan which, due to cost limitations, had been strongly criticized as too weak for the ship's purpose. The final version was lengthened to improve the hull lines and thus the maximum speed, and to provide room for a super-firing turret forward, and for a catapult and aircraft hangar abaft of the funnel. The bridge was of tower-type construction, with a conning tower on top. The fire control systems were of advanced type, partly automated in order to provide rapid response and reduce human error.

Torpedoed in the Java Sea

Deployed to Indonesia on January 12, 1937, *De Ruyter* was flagship of the Dutch East India Squadron at Surabaja (Surbaya) and, under Rear-Admiral Karel Doorman, flagship of the combined American-British-Dutch-Australian (ABDA) squadron opposing the Japanese advance on Java. It was in action at the Badung Strait, of the southeast coast of Bali, against Japanese destroyers and transports, on February 19–20, 1942, which was a tactical victory for the Japanese. As a large Japanese convoy escorted by cruisers and destroyers moved towards Java, the regrouped ABDA force set out to intercept it. In the Battle of the Java Sea on February 27, 1942, Doorman's ships failed to break past the escorts to attack the transports. In this battle, torpedoes proved more effective than gunnery. Around 23:30 *De Ruyter*, already hit by shells, was struck by one or more "Long Lance" torpedoes from the Japanese heavy cruiser *Haguro*. Almost at the same time the Dutch cruiser *Java* was hit by a "Long Lance" from the cruiser *Nachi* and sank. Fire broke out on *De Ruyter* and at 02:30 on February 28, it sank with the loss of 345 of its crew. The wrecks were located on December 1, 2002, and named as war graves.

SPECIFICATIONS

DISPLACEMENT: 6,545 tons (6,650 tonnes)

DIMENSIONS: 560 ft 8 in x 51 ft 6 in x 16 ft 9 in (170.9 m x 15.7 m x 5.1 m)

PROPULSION: Twin shafts, Parsons geared turbines, six Yarrow boilers, 66,000 shp (49,216 kW)

ARMAMENT: Seven 5.9-in (150 mm) guns; ten 1.6-in (40 mm) AA guns; eight Browning machine guns

ARMOR: Belt 2 in (50 mm), bulkheads 1.3 in (33 mm), turret faces 3.9 in (100 mm), deck 1.2 in (33 mm)

SPEED: 32 knots (36.8 mph; 59.3 km/h)

CREW: 435

De Ruyter

AA GUNS
THE TEN 1.6-IN (40 MM) BOFORS AA
GUNS WERE DIRECTED BY AN EFFECTIVE
DUTCH HAZEMEYER SIGNAAL CONTROL
SYSTEM.

CATAPULT AND FLOATPLANES
De Ruyter CARRIED A HEINKEL
59-FT (18 M) CATAPULT AND TWO
FOKKER CX1W FLOATPLANES.

TURRET
THE SINGLE-GUN SUPER-FIRING TURRET
COULD FIRE STAR-SHELLS.

GUNS
THE 5.9-IN (150 MM) GUNS FIRED 101.5-
LB (46 KG) SHELLS AT A HIGH MUZZLE
VELOCITY: 2,950 FT (899 M) PER SECOND.

ARMOR
THOUGH THE TOWER LOOKED WELL
ARMORED, IT WAS ONLY LIGHTLY PROTECTED,
LIKE THE REST OF THE SHIP.

Dunkerque *(1937)*

FRANCE'S REACTION TO GERMANY'S *DEUTSCHLAND* WAS TO BUILD TWO "FAST BATTLESHIPS" WITH HEAVIER GUNS. BUILT AT BREST NAVAL ARSENAL, IT WAS LAID DOWN ON DECEMBER 24, 1932, LAUNCHED ON OCTOBER 2, 1935, AND COMPLETED ON DECEMBER 31, 1936.

The sister ship *Strasbourg* was completed in April 1939. The armored protection was intended to withstand 11-in (280 mm) armor-piercing explosive shells, though before it was completed, Germany was building the *Bismarck*, with 15-in (381 mm) guns. All the main guns were mounted forward, like the British *Nelson*, in quadruple turrets, though the design of the after section was quite different. On the long forecastle deck the turrets were widely spaced so that a single shot could not disable both. A tower-type armored bridge rose behind them, incorporating a mast. The single funnel was half-ringed at the aft end by searchlight platforms and the mainmast emerged above triple-tiered control and spotting posts.

Two seaplanes were carried, with the hangar, catapult, and crane all at the stern, on a low afterdeck, fired over by twelve 5.1-in (130 mm) guns, also mounted in quadruple turrets.

Royal Duty and Gold Transport

Commissioned in May 1937, *Dunkerque*'s first duty was representing France at a naval review to mark the coronation of Britain's King George VI. It was not considered fully ready for active service until September 1, 1938, when it was named flagship of the Atlantic Squadron. In the early stages of World War II, it was primarily used as an Atlantic escort, in December 1939 carrying gold bullion from the Bank of France to Halifax, Nova Scotia.

Stationed alternately at Brest and Mers-el-Kébir, *Dunkerque* was at the Mediterranean port when France capitulated in June 1940. On July 3 and 6 it was bombarded with other French ships by British warships and torpedo planes to prevent their being used by the Axis Powers. Though seriously damaged, it was repaired sufficiently to steam to Toulon in February 1942. In November that year, as German forces entered Toulon, it was scuttled in the Vauban basin. It remained there, suffering Allied bomb attacks in 1944, after which it was partially dismantled. With the end of the war it was removed from the dock, and was finally sold for breaking in 1958.

SPECIFICATIONS

DISPLACEMENT: 26,500 tons (26,925 tonnes); 35,500 tons (36,070 tonnes) full load

DIMENSIONS: 704 ft x 102 ft x 29 ft (214.5 m x 31.08 m x 8.7 m)

PROPULSION: Quadruple shafts, Parsons geared turbines, six Indret boilers, 135,585 shp (101,106 kW)

ARMAMENT: Eight 13-in (330 mm)/ 50-caliber, sixteen 5.1-in (130 mm)/ 45-caliber guns; eight 1.5-in (37 mm), thirty-two 0.5-in (13.2 mm) AA guns

ARMOR: Belt 8.9 in (225 mm), turrets 13 in (330 mm), conning tower 11 in (270 mm), deck 4.5 in (114 mm)

SPEED: 31.06 knots (35.7 mph; 57.5 km/h)

CREW: 1,431

Dunkerque

FUNNEL CAP
IN 1938 A LARGER FUNNEL CAP WAS FITTED.

TURRETS
WITH THE WEIGHT OF THE TURRETS, EACH 1,473 TONS (1,497 TONNES), BALANCED BY THAT OF THE MACHINERY, *DUNKERQUE* WAS A HARMONIOUS DESIGN.

GUNS
THE GUNS WERE MOUNTED IN PAIRS AND COULD NOT BE TRAINED INDIVIDUALLY. SHELLS WEIGHED 1,257 LB (570 KG) AND WERE 5 FT 5 IN (1.65 M) LONG.

DESIGN
THOUGH THE BRITISH BATTLESHIPS HMS *NELSON* AND *RODNEY* INFLUENCED THE DESIGNERS OF *DUNKERQUE*, GERMANY'S *DEUTSCHLAND* (LATER *LÜTZOW*) WAS THE SHIP IT WAS DESIGNED TO OUTMATCH.

KMS *Scharnhorst* (1939)

PERHAPS THE MOST EFFECTIVE OF THE REICH'S CAPITAL SHIPS, *SCHARNHORST*'S PART IN GERMANY'S NAVAL ACTIONS DURING WORLD WAR II WAS VERY CONSIDERABLE AND OFTEN DRAMATIC, UNTIL ITS DESTRUCTION AT THE BATTLE OF NORTH CAPE IN DECEMBER 1943.

Scharnhorst was laid down at the Kriegsmarinewerft, Wilhelmshaven, on May 16, 1935, launched on October 3, 1936, and completed on January 7, 1939. Its cost was 143,471,000 Reichsmarks. In July–August 1939, its bow was rebuilt to *Atlantic* form. The hull was built of ST 52 steel, and a new steel armor was introduced, known as type Wh, with a high tensile strength, and Ww, of slightly less. These steels could be welded, with important advantages in construction speed and weight-saving. The armor weighed considerably more than the actual hull, 14,006 tons (14,230 tonnes) compared to 8,233 tons (8,365 tonnes). A pole foremast was attached to the main tower and a tall mainmast abaft the funnel, with the searchlight platform built out round it.

In July–August 1939 alterations, this was changed to a tripod and moved sternwards to a position just forward of the aft control tower, with searchlight and radar platforms. An inclined funnel cap was also fitted.

Damaged in a "Channel Dash"

In the fighting off Narvik, Norway, in April–June 1940, *Scharnhorst* sank the carrier HMS *Glorious*. A torpedo from HMS *Acasta* holed the battleship's side, around 2,500 tons (2,540 tonnes) of water were shipped, and it made for Trondheim, Norway, for emergency repairs, before returning to Kiel for full repair. It remained there until January 22, 1941, then was based at Brest for the commerce raids of January–March which (with *Gneisenau*) accounted for over 105,000 gross tons (106,685 gross tonnes) of Allied merchant shipping. In the "Channel Dash" from Brest to Germany between February 11 and 13, it struck two mines, but made Wilhelmshaven under its own steam.

Repaired again at Kiel, *Scharnhorst* joined with *Tirpitz* in bombarding Spitzbergen (in the Svalbard archipelago) on September 6–8, 1943. By the end of that year it was the Reich's only operational capital ship. Off the North Cape, after an inconclusive encounter with the British cruisers HMS *Norfolk*, *Belfast* and *Sheffield*, *Scharnhorst* came under fire from the radar-directed 14-in (356 mm) guns of HMS *Duke of York*, with four escorting destroyers. A combination of torpedoes and shell-fire at increasingly close range finally destroyed *Scharnhorst*, which fired from the one surviving turret to its last moments. It sank at 19:44 on December 26, in 950 ft (290 m) of water, with the loss of 1,932 men.

SPECIFICATIONS

DISPLACEMENT: 32,100 tons (32,615 tonnes); 38,100 tons (38,711 tonnes) full load

DIMENSIONS: 772 ft x 98 ft 5 in x 31 ft 9 in (235 m x 30 m x 9.7 m)

PROPULSION: Triple shafts, 12 Wagner HP boilers, three Brown-Boveri geared turbines, 160,000 shp (119,312 kW)

ARMAMENT: Nine 11-in (280 mm), twelve 5.9-in (150 mm), fourteen 4.1-in (105 mm) guns; sixteen 1.5-in (37 mm) and ten 0.79-in (20 mm) AA guns; six 21-in (533 mm) torpedo tubes

ARMOR: Belt 13.8–7.9 in (350–200 mm), bulkheads 7.9–5.9 in (200–150 mm), barbettes 13.8–7.9 in (350–200 mm), turrets 13.8–7.9 in (350–200 mm), deck 2–0.8 in (50–20 mm)

SPEED: 31 knots (35.7 mph; 57 km/h)

CREW: 1,968

KMS *Scharnhorst*

AIRCRAFT HANGAR
SCHARNHORST CARRIED AN AIRCRAFT
HANGAR WITH CATAPULT MOUNTED
ON TOP, JUST ABAFT THE FUNNEL. THE
AIRCRAFT CARRIED WERE THREE ARADO
AR196A-3.

EQUIPMENT UPDATES
RANGE-FINDING AND RADAR EQUIPMENT
WAS UPDATED THROUGH 1940–42, AND
BY 1942 IT HAD FuMO 27, FuMB1,
FuMB 4 SAMOS, FuMB7 AND FuMB3
SYSTEMS INSTALLED.

PROPELLERS
THE THREE PROPELLERS WERE TRIPLE-BLADED,
WITH A DIAMETER OF 14 FT 6 IN (4.45 M) AND
SCHARNHORST'S SPEED GAVE IT A DISTINCT EDGE
OVER THE BRITISH *KING GEORGE V* CLASS, WHOSE
MAXIMUM WAS 29.2 KNOTS (33.6 MPH; 54 KM/H).

BOW
THE PEAKED "ATLANTIC" BOW WAS A
DISTINCTIVE FEATURE.

KMS *Bismarck* (1940)

Bismarck REPRESENTED A PEAK OF BATTLESHIP DESIGN—IN TERMS OF SIZE, ARMAMENT, SPEED, AND STAYING POWER. BUT ITS FIRST COMBAT MISSION IN MAY 1941, THOUGH INCLUDING A MAJOR SUCCESS IN SINKING HMS *Hood*, WAS ALSO ITS LAST.

Bismarck was laid down at Blohm & Voss, Hamburg, Germany, on July 1, 1936, launched on February 14, 1939, and completed on August 24, 1940. Its cost was 196,800,000 Reichsmarks. The hull was constructed from ST52 steel and more than 90 percent was of electric welded construction. Armor was of three kinds, Krupp KCn/A face-hardened for belt, turrets, and control towers; Wh—*Wotan hart* ("hard")—for the armored decks; and Ww—*Wotan weich* ("soft")—for the longitudinal torpedo bulkheads. Altogether the armor weight was 17,256 tons (17,533 tonnes), 32.2 percent of total displacement.

The hull was divided into 22 watertight compartments, 17 within the armored zone which accounted for 70 percent of the ship's waterline length. From foretop to keel were 17 levels or decks. In terms of internal layout, levels of protection, and capability in action, this was the most effective battleship yet built. Gunnery control was located in three positions, on the forward conning tower, above the foretop platform, and on the rear conning tower, with communication links to two computation rooms, within the armored zone fore and aft.

Hunting the *Bismarck*

Bismarck and *Prinz Eugen* left Gotenhafen (Gdynia) on May 18, 1941, to raid Atlantic shipping routes, with Admiral Günther Lütjens in command. It was a carefully planned mission, with supply ships and scouting U-boats in position. News of the departure reached the British, and an interception force was mobilized. On May 24 the battlecruiser HMS *Hood* and battleship HMS *Prince of Wales* engaged the German ships, and *Hood* was sunk by *Bismarck*'s fifth salvo. Hits by three 14-in (356 mm) shells from *Prince of Wales* did comparatively little damage.

A huge three-day search and pursuit followed, with some 48 ships involved, including five battleships and two aircraft carriers. *Prinz Eugen* reached Brest safely but *Bismarck*, after almost succeeding in dodging the pursuit, was hit by torpedo bombers from HMS *Ark Royal*, at 20:47 on May 26, jamming the port rudder at 120⁰ to port. On May 27 at 08:47 the battleships HMS *Rodney* and *King George V* opened fire at around 21,900 yards (20,000 m), gradually closing to 8,600 yards (7,860 m). By around 10:00 all *Bismarck*'s guns were disabled and the order was given to scuttle, when three torpedoes from the cruiser HMS *Dorsetshire* struck the armored hull. Even then all the internal equipment continued to operate. *Bismarck* capsized and sank at 10:39, with 1,977 of the 2,221 crew on board.

SPECIFICATIONS

DISPLACEMENT: 41,000 tons (41,700 tonnes); 49,500 tons (50,300 tonnes) full load

DIMENSIONS: 793 ft x 118 ft x 31 ft (251 m x 36 m x 9.3 m)

PROPULSION: Triple shafts, 12 Wagner HP boilers, three Brown-Boveri geared turbines 150,170 shp (111,982 kW)

ARMAMENT: Eight 15-in (381 mm), twelve 5.9-in (150 mm), sixteen 4.1-in (105 mm) guns; sixteen 1.5-in (37 mm), twelve 0.79-in (20 mm) AA guns

ARMOR: Belt 12.6–3.1 in (320–80 mm), bulkheads 8.6–1.7 in (220–45 mm), barbettes 13.4–8.6 in (340–220 mm), turrets 14.2–7 in (360–180 mm), deck 4.3–1.7 in (120–80 mm)

SPEED: 29 knots (33.4 mph; 53.7 km/h)

CREW: 2,092

KMS *Bismarck*

RADAR
BISMARCK CARRIED FuMO RADAR EQUIPMENT ON THE
FORWARD AND AFT RANGE FINDERS AND THE FORETOP,
THOUGH BLAST CONCUSSION DISABLED IT. IT ALSO HAD
HYDROPHONE DETECTORS.

GUNS
THE MAIN GUNS WERE MOUNTED IN TWIN TURRETS,
ARRANGED TO KEEP THE GUNS AS FAR APART AS POSSIBLE
TO AVOID SHOCKS AND INTERFERENCES. RANGE WAS 39,589
YARDS (36,200 M).

BOW
AS WITH *SCHARNHORST*, *BISMARCK*'S
ORIGINAL STRAIGHT STEM WAS REPLACED
BY A MORE SEA PROOF, THOUGH LESS
PRONOUNCED, "ATLANTIC" BOW AFTER
COMMISSIONING.

RANGE
OPERATIONAL RANGE WAS 8,870 NAUTICAL
MILES (10,207 MILES; 16,430 KM) AT 19 KNOTS
(21.8 MPH; 35 KM/H)

Vittorio Veneto (1940)

CLASSIFIED OFFICIALLY AS *CORRAZZATE* (LITERALLY "ARMOR-CLADS"), ITALY'S LAST BATTLESHIP CLASS WAS TO BE FORMED OF FOUR SHIPS, BUT ONLY THREE WERE COMPLETED, OF WHICH TWO SAW ACTIVE SERVICE. *VITTORIO VENETO* WAS LAID DOWN AT CANTIERI RIUNITI DELL'ADRIATICO IN TRIESTE ON OCTOBER 28, 1934, LAUNCHED ON JULY 25, 1937, AND COMPLETED ON APRIL 28, 1940.

The lengthy construction time reflects difficulties in the provision of materials and equipment, and much of the build quality was poor. However, the general appearance was both warlike and elegant. The main guns, in triple turrets, were 50 caliber, and a muzzle velocity of 2,854 ft (870 m) per second led to overstated claims about their penetrative impact. Secondary armament was also in triple turrets. Substantial AA defenses were incorporated from the start, with twelve 3.5-in (90 mm), twenty 1.5-in (37 mm) and sixteen 0.79-in (20 mm) guns providing both long-range and close-in defense.

Total armor weight was 13,331 tons (13,545 tonnes) and protection included massive side armor with internal bulkheads, intended to counter the impact of plunging shells. It was the first Italian battleship to have radar installed: a "Gufo" EC4 device, in 1942.

Convoy Raider

Assigned to the 9th Division of the 1st Squadron, from August 31 to the end of 1940, *Vittorio Veneto* was frequently in action against British convoys to Malta. It survived the raid of November 12 on Taranto and was transferred to Naples, from where it continued to make sorties. It was the Italian flagship in the Battle of Cape Matapan, March 27, 1941, when it was hit by a torpedo launched by a bomber from HMS *Formidable*. Taking on around 3,900 tons (4,000 tonnes) of water, it struggled back to Taranto.

Repaired by August 1, 1941, it was again torpedoed, by the British submarine *Urge* while escorting Convoy M41 to Benghazi, on December 14, and was out of action until June 1942. Its last active service, again against Malta convoys, was in that month. On September 8, 1943, Italy's fleet was surrendered to the Allies. *Vittorio Veneto* was moved first to Malta, then to the Great Bitter Lake in the Suez Canal, for internment. It was returned to Italy in February 1946 and allocated to Great Britain as reparation. Decommissioned on February 1, 1948, it was scrapped at La Spezia between then and 1950.

SPECIFICATIONS

DISPLACEMENT: 41,377 tons (42,040 tonnes); 45,752 tons (46,485 tonnes) full

DIMENSIONS: 778 ft 9 in x 107 ft 9 in x 31 ft 5 in (237.8 m x 32.9 m x 9.6 m)

PROPULSION: Quadruple shafts, eight Yarrow boilers, four Belluzzo geared turbines, 134,616 shp (100,383 kW)

ARMAMENT: Nine 15-in (381 mm), twelve 6-in (152 mm), four 4.7-in (120 mm) guns; twelve 3.5-in (90 mm), twenty 1.5-in (37 mm) and sixteen 0.79-in (20 mm) AA guns

ARMOR: Belt 13.8–2.4 in (350–60 mm), bulkheads 3.9–2.75 in (100–70 mm), barbettes 13.8 in (350 mm), turrets 13.8–3.9 in (350–100 mm), deck 8.1–1.4 in (205–35 mm)

SPEED: 31.4 knots (36.1 mph; 58.2 km/h)

CREW: 1,861

Vittorio Veneto

AIRCRAFT

RO 43 RECONNAISSANCE AIRCRAFT WERE
CARRIED. *LITTORIO* IN 1942 CARRIED
FLOATLESS REGGIANE 2000 FIGHTERS
THAT COULD BE LAUNCHED FROM THE
SHIP BUT HAD TO FIND A LANDING
GROUND ON SHORE.

GUNS

WITH A MAXIMUM ELEVATION OF 35° THE MAIN
GUNS HAD A RANGE OF 46,210 YARDS (42,260 M)
AND FIRED BOTH AP (ARMOR-PIERCING) SHELLS
OF 1,950 LB (885 KG) AND HE SHELLS OF 1,710 LB
(774 KG). THEY FIRED A ROUND EVERY 45 SECONDS.

DESIGN

VITTORIO VENETO AND *LITTORIO* WERE
LAUNCHED WITH SLIGHTLY RAKING STEMS,
GIVING A WATERLINE LENGTH OF 774 FT 3 IN
(236 M). AFTER TRIALS, THEY WERE GIVEN
STRAIGHT STEMS DOWN TO THE WATERLINE,
RESULTING IN AN INCREASE OF 4 FT 6 IN (1.8 M).

TORPEDO DEFENSES

AGAINST TORPEDOES IT HAD THE PUGLIESE
SYSTEM: A LATERAL SPACE BETWEEN THE
TORPEDO BULKHEAD AND THE INNER HULL
BULKHEAD, HOLDING A LONG EMPTY CYLINDER,
MAXIMUM DIAMETER 12 FT 6 IN (3.8 M),
SUSPENDED IN OIL, AND INTENDED TO ABSORB
EXPLOSIVE ENERGY.

Richelieu *(1940)*

THE NEWLY COMMISSIONED *RICHELIEU* WAS ATTACKED BY ALLIED SHIPS AFTER THE FALL OF FRANCE BUT LATER WAS TAKEN OVER BY FREE FRENCH FORCES, AND PLAYED A PART IN STRUGGLE AGAINST THE AXIS POWERS BOTH IN EUROPEAN AND FAR EASTERN WATERS.

Laid down at the Brest Naval Arsenal on October 22, 1935, it was launched on January 17, 1939, and completed on June 15, 1940, a week before the fall of France. The cost was 1,227 million francs. *Richelieu* carried all its main armament forward, mounted in two quadruple turrets, with "B" turret super-firing. The guns were cradled in pairs, and had a range of 49,210 yards (45,000 m) at an elevation of 35⁰. The HE shells weighed 1,940 lb (880 kg) and rate of fire was two rounds a minute.

With only between five and seven battleships in commission through the 1930s, the French Navy saw their role as swift-striking raiders, and *Richelieu* could make a top speed of 32 knots (36.8 mph; 59.2 km/h). During construction numerous changes were made to the original design and the funnel and aft tower were merged into a single structure, with the funnel angled sharply towards the stern.

Under Free French Command

Richelieu was moved from Brest to Dakar (in Senegal) on June 18, 1940, before engine trials were completed. On July 8, as a potential enemy, it was attacked by aircraft from the British carrier HMS *Hermes* and again by gunfire on September 23–25 from HMS *Resolution*.

Following the Allied landings in North Africa (November 1942), French forces joined the Allies, and in January 1943 *Richelieu* was sailed to New York with a Free French crew, for full repairs. On October 14, equipped with new AA defenses, American SF surface and SA-2 air radar, it returned to active service in the Far East and Mediterranean.

After the end of hostilities, it detonated a magnetic mine in the Malacca Straits on September 9, 1945, sustaining some damage. Returned to France on February 11, 1946, *Richelieu* assumed a training role and in 1947–48 was flagship of what was intended as a rapid intervention force, despite obsolescent command systems. From May 1956 it was used as an accommodation ship at Brest, before going into reserve in 1958. Finally stricken on January 16, 1968, it was scrapped at La Spezia that same year.

SPECIFICATIONS

DISPLACEMENT: 43,293 tons (43,987 tonnes); 47,548 tons (48,311 tonnes) full load

DIMENSIONS: 813 ft x 108 ft x 32 ft (247.9 m x 33 m x 9.7 m)

PROPULSION: Quadruple shafts, four Parsons geared turbines, six Indret pressure-fired boilers, 150,000 shp (111,855 kW)

ARMAMENT: Eight 15-in (381 mm), nine 6-in (152 mm) guns; twelve 3.9-in (100 mm) AA guns

ARMOR: Belt 13.5–9.8 in (343–250 mm), bulkheads 15.1–9.9 in (383–251 mm), barbettes 16 in (405 mm), turrets 16.9–7.7 in (430–195 mm), deck upper 6.7–5.1 in (170–130 mm, lower 3.9–1.6 in (100–40 mm)

SPEED: 30 knots (34.5 mph; 56 km/h)

CREW: 1,550

Richelieu

Radar
In 1941 a French surface/air radar system, Directeur electro-magnétique (DEM), was fitted, with two emission antennae on the foremast and two reception antennae on the after tower.

Turrets
Fire from the quadruple turrets was improved from 1948, when retarders were fitted to the outer guns, giving them a delay of 60 milliseconds, enough to avoid mutual dispersional effects of simultaneously fired shells.

Seaplanes
Three Loire 130 seaplanes were carried from July 1941 until late 1942.

AA Guns
Following the 1943 repairs at New York, the aircraft deck was used to house an AA battery.

HMS *Prince of Wales* (1941)

IT WAS *PRINCE OF WALES*'S FATE TO BE FIRST TO REVEAL THE VULNERABILITY OF EVEN A MODERN BATTLESHIP TO INTENSIVE AERIAL ATTACK, WHEN IT WAS SUNK BY JAPANESE NAVAL AIRCRAFT OFF THE COAST OF MALAYA IN DECEMBER 1941.

The *King George V* class was something of a compromise design. Based on a 35,560 tonne (35,000 ton) hull, it was to carry twelve 14-in (356 mm) guns in three quadruple turrets. During design, to save weight for use elsewhere, the super-firing "B" turret was reduced to a twin mounting. All five were laid down in 1937, *Prince of Wales* at Cammell Laird's yard in Birkenhead in January. Launched on May 3, 1939, it was completed in March 1941. The advent of war prompted numerous alterations during completion, including extra ammunition and fuel capacity, and radar antennae, increasing design displacement to 38,000 tons (38,610 tonnes) and deepening the draft from 27 ft 8 in (8.4 m) to 32 ft (9.75 m) with a corresponding reduction in freeboard.

Approximately 12,000 tons (12,190 tonnes) of armor accounted for 40 percent of design displacement, with a high-level armored deck resting on top of the side armor.

With protection on the "all or nothing" principle, careful design of the engine space made it possible to limit the length of the central armored area to 446 ft (136 m). Effective torpedo protection space between hull and bulkhead was 13 ft 4 in (4.1 m).

Still engaged on trials, *Prince of Wales* was ordered out with HMS *Hood* against *Bismarck* and *Prinz Eugen* on May 24, 1941. An early hit knocked out the gunnery control system and it suffered considerable damage, withdrawing from the battle after the sinking of *Hood*. In August 1941 it carried Prime Minister Winston Churchill to meet President Franklin D. Roosevelt at Argentia Bay, Newfoundland. In September it was with Force "H" in the Mediterranean, and after a brief return to Britain was deployed to the Far East, arriving in Singapore on November 27, 1941.

Vulnerable to Air Attack

The ship was regarded at the time as well-equipped to deal with air attack, through its High Angle Control System, linked to long-range air-search radar. From July 1941 it was carrying radar of Types 279 (air-warning), 284 (surface), 282 and 285 (AA control), though on December 10, 1941, the surface-scanning radar was inoperable. On December 8 it fired its AA guns against Japanese aircraft over Singapore. On December 10, 1941, it was off the east coast of Malaya as flagship of Force "Z" with the battlecruiser HMS *Repulse* and four destroyers, when they were attacked by waves of Japanese naval aircraft armed with bombs and torpedoes. Both capital ships were sunk. Destroyer escorts rescued 1,285 men from *Prince of Wales*.

SPECIFICATIONS

DISPLACEMENT: 44,550 tons (45,265 tonnes) full load

DIMENSIONS: 745 ft 1 in x 103 ft 2 in x 34 ft 4 in (227.1 m x 31.4 m x 10.5 m)

PROPULSION: Quadruple shafts, four Parsons geared turbines, eight Admiralty three-drum boilers, 110,000 shp (82,000 kW)

ARMAMENT: Ten 14-in (356 mm), sixteen 5.25-in (133 mm) guns; thirty-two 1.6-in (40 mm) AA guns, 80 UP projectors

ARMOR: Belt 15–4.5 in (381–114 mm), bulkheads 15 in (381 mm), torpedo bulkhead 2 in (51 mm), barbettes 13–11 in (330–280 mm), turrets 13–6 in (330–152 mm), deck 6–5 in (152–127 mm)

SPEED: 28.3 knots (32.5 mph; 52.4 km/h)

CREW: 1,612

HMS *Prince of Wales*

SEAPLANES
FOUR SUPERMARINE WALRUS SEAPLANES
WERE ORIGINALLY CARRIED BY THE *KING
GEORGE V* CLASS.

GUNS
EIGHT UP SMOOTHBORE MULTI-BARREL
AA BATTERIES WERE FITTED, INGENIOUS
BUT NOT VERY EFFECTIVE WEAPONS
INTENDED TO DANGLE SMALL AERIAL
MINES FROM PARACHUTE WIRES.

ARMOR
THIS CLASS WAS FIRST TO HAVE MAIN
HORIZONTAL ARMOR PLACED AT UPPER
DECK, RATHER THAN MAIN DECK LEVEL
OR BELOW.

DESIGN
AN ADMIRALTY DESIGN REQUIREMENT WAS THAT
"A" TURRET SHOULD FIRE FORWARD WITHOUT
REQUIRING ELEVATION, WHICH KEPT THE SHIP'S
BOWS LOW AND OFTEN SEMI-SUBMERGED.

Yamato (1941)

THE *YAMATO* CLASS, THE WORLD'S MOST POWERFUL BATTLESHIPS, WAS INTENDED TO ENFORCE JAPAN'S MASTERY OF THE PACIFIC IN THE FACE OF THE NUMERICALLY SUPERIOR US NAVY, BUT IN FACT MADE A MINIMAL CONTRIBUTION TO THE COUNTRY'S WAR EFFORT.

Three years of intensive planning and modeling preceded *Yamato*'s laying-down in the Kure Kaigun Kosho basin on November 4, 1937. Launched on August 8, 1940, completed on December 16, 1941, it was intended as the first of five "super-battleships." The 18.1-in (460 mm) 45-caliber guns, at 178.6 tons (181.5 tonnes), were the heaviest ever used afloat. Building was done on the raft body principle, with the vital areas contained within side armor of 16 in (410 mm) thickness, tapering towards the bottom to 2.9 in (75 mm), topped by a 7.8 in (200 mm) armored deck and terminated by transverse bulkheads. Only the barbettes, funnel uptakes, and trunks for command systems, all heavily armored, protruded through the "raft." Altogether there were 1,065 watertight compartments below the armored deck, and 82 above. The armored deck was designed so that it could only be pierced by bombs of 2,200 lb (1,000 kg) or more, dropped from a height exceeding 7,800 ft (2,400 m).

Yamato served as flagship of the Combined Fleet, and was command ship in the Battle of Midway at the end of May 1942, in which four Japanese fleet carriers were sunk. *Yamato* was not involved in the fighting. *Yamato* moved between the mid-ocean base of Truk (Chuuk Lagoon) and the home base of Kure, where it underwent a refit in July–August 1943. On December 25 it was torpedoed by the US submarine *Skate*, causing the rear magazine to flood when some 3,000 tons (3,050 tonnes) of water came inboard. Repairs and refitting at Kure lasted until March 18, 1944.

Leyte Gulf and Okinawa

Between October 22 and 25, 1944, it was part of the Japanese Center Force, engaged in the widespread Battle of Leyte Gulf. *Yamato*'s guns sank the US escort carrier *Gambier Bay* and helped sink three US destroyers. It received several bomb and shell hits without sustaining serious damage. On April 6, 1945, it was sent to help repel the American landings on Okinawa in "Operation Ten-go"—in effect a suicide mission. *Yamato* was to be beached on the island to act as a fixed artillery fortress. With no air protection, it was attacked on April 7, southwest of the Kyushu Islands, by three waves of American bombers and torpedo bombers. *Yamato* was progressively disabled, and capsized at 14:23, one of the two fore magazines exploding at the same time. Around 2,055 of the crew were killed or drowned.

SPECIFICATIONS

DISPLACEMENT: 68,010 tons (69,098 tonnes); 71,659 tons (72,806 tonnes) full load

DIMENSIONS: 862 ft 9 in x 121 ft 1 in x 34 ft 1 in (263 m x 36.9 m x 10.39 m)

PROPULSION: Quadruple shafts, four Kampon turbines, 12 Kampon HP boilers, 150,000 shp (111,855 kW)

ARMAMENT: Nine 18.1-in (460 mm), twelve 6.1-in (155 mm), twelve 5-in (127 mm) guns; twenty-four 1-in (25 mm), four 0.52-in (13 mm) AA guns

ARMOR: Belt 16 in (410 mm), barbettes 21.5–2 in (546–50 mm), turrets 19.7–11.8 in (650–193 mm), torpedo bulkhead 11.8–2.9 in (300–75 mm), deck 9.1–7.9 in (230–200 mm)

SPEED: 27 knots (31 mph; 49.9 km/h)

CREW: 2,500

Yamato

TURRETS

THE MAIN TURRETS EACH WEIGHED 2,774 TONS (2,818 TONNES), AND EACH 18.1-IN (460 MM) GUN COULD FIRE TWO 3,240-LB (1,473 KG) SHELLS PER MINUTE OVER A DISTANCE OF 45,000 YARDS (41,148 M).

MAST

INSTEAD OF THE "PAGODA" STYLE SUPERSTRUCTURE OF PREVIOUS JAPANESE BATTLESHIPS, THERE WAS A TALL OCTAGONAL TOWER-MAST, REACHING 28 M (92 FT) ABOVE THE WATERLINE.

BOATS

GAS PRESSURE WHEN THE MAIN GUNS FIRED PREVENTED STOWAGE OF BOATS ON THE MAIN DECK: THEY WERE HOUSED UNDER COVER BELOW THE TOP DECK, ALONGSIDE THE HANGAR AND "C" TURRET.

GUNS

BY APRIL 1945 THE SHIP CARRIED TWENTY-FOUR 5-IN (127 MM) TWIN-BARRELED AA GUNS, 87 TRIPLE-BARRELED AND 63 SINGLE-BARRELED 1-IN (25 MM) AA GUNS.

KMS *Tirpitz* (1941)

SISTER SHIP TO *BISMARCK*, *TIRPITZ* HAD EQUAL QUALITIES OF POWER AND RESISTANCE. ALTHOUGH ITS ACTIVE SERVICE WAS VERY LIMITED, ITS MERE PRESENCE TIED UP SUBSTANTIAL BRITISH RESOURCES UNTIL ITS ULTIMATE DESTRUCTION BY BRITISH AERIAL ATTACK IN NOVEMBER 1944.

Tirpitz was laid down on October 26, 1936, at the Wilhelmshaven Naval Dockyard, launched on April 1, 1939, and completed on February 25, 1941. Its cost was 181.6 million Reichsmarks. Like *Bismarck*'s, its 15-in (380 mm) guns could fire three rounds per minute. *Tirpitz* originally had twelve 0.79-in (20 mm) single-barrel AA guns; this was reduced to ten, but supplemented by forty 0.79-in (20 mm) four-barreled guns. From 1942 it also carried eight 21-in (533 mm) torpedo tubes, in sets of four on the upper deck. Up to six floatplanes could be carried, and a double catapult was fitted.

Numerous modifications were made in the course of 1941–44 to accommodate new radar and telecommunications equipment as well as extending the AA defenses. Turbo-electric drive had been planned originally, but extra-high pressure boilers and steam turbines were fitted. Only *Tirpitz* and *Bismarck* carried a radar aerial fixed on the rotating dome above the command post. From 1941–42 a similar aerial was also placed on the after dome. In 1943–44, a "Würzburg" radar set was installed on the after AA gunnery control position, with a 9 ft 9 in (3 m) parabolic reflector for measuring height, and a Model 30 *Hohentwiel* radar aerial was mounted in the topmast.

Service off Norway

It joined the Baltic Fleet until January 1942, when it was moved to northern Norway as a guard against invasion and in order to attack Russia-bound convoys. From then on it was subject to ceaseless British attacks. On September 6–9, 1942, it bombarded fortifications on Spitzbergen, but on the September 22 sustained serious damage from attack by British midget submarines in Altafjord, Norway, near Narvik, and was out of action until March 1944. Serious damage was again caused on April 3, 1944, when 14 bomb hits were recorded. On September 15, 1944, further bombs left the battleship afloat but unseaworthy. *Tirpitz* was moved under its own power to Tromsö, Norway.

By now the only future that could be prepared for was to use the ship as a floating battery. On November 12, 1944, in "Operation Catechism," 32 Lancaster bombers converged on *Tirpitz* from 09:35. The ship's main guns opened up from long range, but the bombers scored at least two direct hits and four near misses with "Tallboy" 5-ton (5,080 kg) bombs packing 6,614 lb (3,000 kg) of high explosive. The most destructive hit was between the aircraft catapult and funnel, blowing a massive hole in the side armor. *Tirpitz* capsized and at the same time one of the main magazines exploded. Around 1,000 men were lost.

SPECIFICATIONS

DISPLACEMENT: 42,200 tons (42,900 tonnes); 51,800 tons (52,600 tonnes) full load

DIMENSIONS: 823 ft 6 in x 118 ft 1 in x 30 ft 6 in (251 m x 36 m x 9.3 m)

PROPULSION: Triple shafts, three Brown-Boveri geared turbines, 12 Wagner superheated boilers, 138,000 shp (102,906 kW)

ARMAMENT: Eight 15-in (381 mm), twelve 5.9-in (150 mm), sixteen 4.1-in (105 mm) guns; sixteen 1.5-in (37 mm) and twelve 0.79-in (20 mm) AA guns

ARMOR: Belt 12.6–3.1 in (320–80 mm), bulkheads 8.6–1.7 in (220–45 mm), barbettes 13.4–8.6 in (340–220 mm), turrets 14.2–7 in (360–180 mm), deck 4.3–1.7 in (120–80 mm)

SPEED: 30 knots (34.5 mph; 56 km/h)

CREW: 2,065

KMS *Tirpitz*

FUNNEL
AT FIRST BLACK, THE FUNNEL COWLING WAS PAINTED SILVER- OR LIGHT-GRAY FROM 1942. THE CATWALK FROM FUNNEL PLATFORM TO TOWER WAS ADDED IN 1942.

ARMOR
WHEN *TIRPITZ*'S ARMOR WAS DESIGNED, IT WAS ENVISAGED THAT THE MAXIMUM DESTRUCTIVE FORCE WOULD BE AROUND 500 KG (1,100 LB) OF EXPLOSIVE.

STEM
THE REVISED "ATLANTIC" STEM WAS FITTED TO *TIRPITZ* BEFORE LAUNCHING.

USS *Indiana* (1942)

THE SECOND SHIP OF FOUR IN THE *SOUTH DAKOTA* CLASS, *INDIANA* AND ITS SISTER SHIPS
SAW EXTENSIVE ACTION DURING WORLD WAR II, ALL OF IT IN PACIFIC OCEAN CAMPAIGNS,
INCLUDING THE BATTLE OF THE PHILIPPINE SEA.

To a new design, incorporating numerous new features, *Indiana* (BB-58) was laid down at Newport News on November 20, 1939, launched on November 21, 1941, and completed on April 30, 1942, at a cost of around $77 million. Completion was speeded up after Pearl Harbor. These were the first American ships to be given inclined internal side armor, reaching from the armored deck to the inner bottom and 12.2 in (310 mm) thick, tapering to 1 in (25 mm).

The combination of bridge, tower, mast, and funnel was changed on several occasions. Initially all carried a rotating range-finder on the conning tower, and a Type Sra radar antenna was mounted just abaft. The aftermast, mounted on a tripod base, was heightened in 1945. By the end of the war *Indiana* was fitted with SG radar (aft), and SK-2 forward.

Indiana's war service was all with the Pacific Fleet. From August 1942 it was involved in the fighting at Guadalcanal, and from November 28 it was engaged on carrier escort duties. It supported the US landings on the Gilbert Islands and in January 1944 bombarded Kwajalein prior to the landings on the Marshall Islands. On the night of February 1 it collided with USS *Washington*, killing four men. Makeshift repairs were supplemented at Pearl Harbor.

Battle of the Philippine Sea

On April 29–30 it was with Task Force 58 for the Truk Atoll raids, and on June 19 was hotly involved in the Battle of the Philippine Sea, in which it shot down several enemy aircraft. Returning to escort and landing support, at one time it stayed at sea for 64 consecutive days.

In October 1944 it went to Bremerton, Washington, for refit and was back at Pearl Harbor in December. In May 1945 it fought off kamikaze attacks off Okinawa. *Indiana* claimed the downing of 18 enemy aircraft. Having earned twelve battle stars in the war years, it returned to San Francisco on September 29, moving on to Puget Sound Navy Yard. In September 1946 it was placed on the reserve list, was stricken on June 1, 1962, and sold for scrapping on September 6, 1963.

SPECIFICATIONS

DISPLACEMENT: 37,970 tons (38,578 tonnes); 44,519 tons (45,231 tonnes) full

DIMENSIONS: 680 ft x 107 ft 8 in x 29 ft 3 in (210 m x 32.9 m x 8.9 m)

PROPULSION: Quadruple shafts, four Westinghouse geared turbines, eight Foster Wheeler boilers, 130,000 shp (96,941 kW)

ARMAMENT: Nine 16-in (406 mm), twenty 5-in (127 mm) guns; twenty-four 1.6-in (40 mm) and fifty 0.79-in (20 mm) AA guns

ARMOR: Belt 12.2–0.87 in (310–22 mm), bulkheads 11 in (279 mm), barbettes 17.3–11.3 in (439–287 mm), turrets 18–7.25 in (457–184 mm), tower 16–7.25 in (406–184 mm), deck 6–5.75 in (152–146 mm)

SPEED: 27 knots (37 mph; 50 km/h)

CREW: 1,793

USS *Indiana*

BOAT CRANES
THE HEAVY BOAT CRANES BY THE AFT
SUPERSTRUCTURE WERE CARRIED ONLY
ON *INDIANA* AND *MASSACHUSETTS*.

MAIN GUNS
EACH TRIPLE TURRET WEIGHED 1,708
TONS (1,735.4 TONNES). THE MAIN GUNS
WERE 50 CALIBER, THE BARRELS WEIGHED
94.7 TONS (96.2 TONNES), AND HAD A
RANGE OF 42,320 YARDS (38,700 M)
ELEVATED TO 450.

DESIGN
THIS LAYOUT GAVE THE SHIPS A LONG
INDENTED INWARD-ANGLED STRETCH OF
THE CENTRAL HULL, JUST BELOW THE FLUSH
DECK, RATHER REMINISCENT OF THE OLD
CASEMATE STRUCTURE.

PROTECTION DECK
A SPLINTER PROTECTION DECK PLACED 2 FT
7 IN (80 CM) BELOW THE MAIN ARMOR DECK
WAS A NEW FEATURE.

PLANES
A VOUGHT OS 2 U-1 KINGFISHER IS ON THE
CATAPULT. TWO WERE CARRIED.

USS *Missouri* (1944)

THE LAST BATTLESHIP TO BE COMPLETED FOR THE US NAVY, THE *IOWA* CLASS *MISSOURI* WAS ONE OF THE UNITED STATES' FOUR "SUPERSHIPS," SERVING FOR MORE THAN HALF A CENTURY. *MISSOURI* WAS THE LAST BATTLESHIP BUILT BY THE UNITED STATES AND WAS THE SITE OF THE OFFICIAL SURRENDER OF JAPANESE FORCES WHICH ENDED WORLD WAR II.

As BB-63 the ship was laid down at the New York Navy Yard on January 6, 1941, launched on January 29, 1944, and commissioned on June 11, 1944. Building cost was slightly over $100 million.

A large superstructure was topped by a five-decked armored tower and flanked by 5-in (127 mm) guns. Armor protection was kept flush with the hull to reduce drag. Maximum beam was governed by the requirement that the ship should fit the Panama Canal locks.

At the end of the battleship era, the class effectively combined the attributes of battleships and battlecruisers by having the armor of the one and the speed of the other.

The foremast was attached to an upper level of the tower, and an aftermast was mounted on the aft funnel. Mast structures went through significant alterations before final removal of the aftermast in 1984. A crane was mounted on the fantail into the 1950s.

Japanese Surrender

Operational in the Pacific from December 14, 1944, *Missouri* supported the Iwo Jima invasion in February 1945, and the Okinawa landings in March, as well as acting as a carrier escort and bombarding targets on Japan's home islands. On April 11 it sustained slight damage in a kamikaze strike. In May, it became flagship of the Third Fleet, and Japan's formal surrender was signed on its deck on September 2, 1945.

With the end of hostilities, *Missouri* returned to the United States in October 1945. Up to 1950, it operated extensively in the Atlantic area. In January that year it grounded off Hampton Roads, Virginia, and was pulled off by a fleet of tugs. From June 1950, it made two combat deployments in the Korean War,

supporting landings and shelling shore targets. Decommissioned on February 26, 1955, it was in reserve at Bremerton, Washington. With up-to-date sensor, control, and missile systems, it was recommissioned on May 10, 1986. In the next six years it made a world cruise and in January 1991 fired Tomahawk missiles and shells in the Gulf War. Decommissioned again in March 1992, it was stricken from the Naval Vessel Register in 1995. *Missouri* has been a memorial ship at Pearl Harbor, Hawaii, since June 1998.

SPECIFICATIONS

DISPLACEMENT: 52,000 tons (52,834 tonnes); 57,450 tons (58,372 tonnes) full load

DIMENSIONS: 887 ft 2 in x 108 ft 3 in x 38 ft (270.4 m x 33.5 m x 11.5 m)

PROPULSION: Quadruple shafts, four GE steam turbines, eight Babcock & Wilcox boilers, 212,000 shp (158,088 kW)

ARMAMENT: Nine 16-in (406 mm), twenty 5-in (127 mm) guns; sixty 1.6-in (40 mm) four-barrelled AA guns

ARMOR: Belt 12.2-in (310 mm), barbettes 17.3–11.3 in (440–287 mm), turret faces 19.7 in (500 mm), deck 6 in (152 mm)

SPEED: 33 knots (38 mph; 61.2 km/h)

CREW: 1,921

USS *Missouri*

AIRCRAFT
THREE ONBOARD AIRCRAFT WERE
REPLACED BY HELICOPTERS IN 1949,
AND BY UAVs IN 1984.

GUNS AND MISSILES
FROM 1984 *MISSOURI* RETAINED ITS
MAIN GUNS BUT WAS ARMED ALSO WITH
TOMAHAWK AND HARPOON MISSILES.

TURRETS
THE TURRETS WERE DESIGNED TO SLIP
OFF IF THE SHIP WAS ON THE POINT OF
CAPSIZING, WITH THE POSSIBILITY OF
THE HULL RIGHTING ITSELF.

RANGE
MISSOURI'S OPERATIONAL RANGE WAS 12,937
NAUTICAL MILES (14,888 MILES; 23,960KM) AT
12 KNOTS (13.8 MPH; 22.2 KM/H).

USS *Guam* (1944)

One of the US Navy's two World War II battlecruisers, *Guam* had a limited wartime service, being involved in action in the Pacific during 1945. The ship was laid up immediately after the end of the war.

Three battlecruisers were planned in 1940, at a time when the US naval planners had not yet realized that the aircraft carrier was going to be the most strategically useful large warship in a Pacific Ocean war. Only USS *Alaska* and *Guam* were completed, with construction of USS *Hawaii* stopped when 85 percent finished, and they were officially designated as "large cruisers." With pennant number CB 2, *Guam* was laid down at the New York yard on February 2, 1942, launched on November 12, 1943, and completed on September 17, 1944, three months after *Alaska*.

The 12-in (305 mm) guns, mounted in triple turrets, a new design, and the armor protection, with a 9-in (228 mm) side belt inclined at around 10⁰, giving an equivalent of 11 in (279 mm) made it less than a match for the *Yamato* class, though considerably faster. But Japanese battleships were not a threat by the time

Guam came into action. On completion the ship had SG-1 (surface-search) radar, and SK air-search, with the latest fire control systems. The main battery had GFCS (2) with Mk 8 radar on Mk 38 gun directors, as did the secondary guns, with Mk 12 radar on Mk 37 gun directors. The AA guns were directed by Mk 29/34/39 radar on Mk 57 gun directors.

Escort Duty in the South China Sea

In the ship's brief wartime career few modifications were made, though plans were in hand to replace the midships catapults with two twin 5.5-in (137 mm) gun turrets, and have a single catapult on the fantail. Serving mostly with *Alaska*, its missions were primarily as carrier escort in the South China Sea. Laid up after the war, the two ships were considered for conversion to guided-missile cruisers in the late 1950s, but the costs involved

were too great even for a limited Talos and Regulus II armament. Stricken on January 1, 1960, they were sold in 1961 for scrapping.

SPECIFICATIONS

DISPLACEMENT: 29,779 tons (30,257 tonnes); 34,253 tons (34,803 tonnes) full load

DIMENSIONS: 808 ft 6 in x 91 ft 1 in x 31 ft 10 in (246.4 m x 27.8 m x 9.7 m)

PROPULSION: Quadruple shafts, GE turbines, eight Babcock & Wilcox boilers, 153,000 shp (114,092 kW)

ARMAMENT: Nine 12-in (305 mm)/50-caliber, twelve 5-in (127 mm) guns; fifty-six 1.6-in (40 mm) and thirty-four 0.79-in (20 mm) AA guns

ARMOR: Belt 9 in (229 mm), turrets 12.8 in (325 mm), deck 4 in (102 mm)

SPEED: 33 knots (38 mph; 61.1 km/h)

CREW: 1,517

USS *Guam*

CATAPULTS
TWO CATAPULTS WERE MOUNTED AMIDSHIPS. SIX AIRCRAFT WERE ORIGINALLY CARRIED BUT THIS WAS REDUCED TO FOUR, EITHER OS2U KINGFISHER OR SC SEAHAWKS.

RUDDER
THE SINGLE RUDDER GAVE *GUAM* A VERY WIDE TURNING CIRCLE, WITH A TACTICAL DIAMETER OF 870 YARDS (798 M) GREATER THAN THAT OF THE LONGER *IOWA* CLASS.

GENERATORS
EACH OF THE TWO ENGINE ROOMS HAD TWO GE GENERATORS, CAPABLE OF PROVIDING 1,340 SHP (1,000 KW), 450 VOLTS AC, AND THERE WAS ALSO A DIESEL GENERATOR ROOM WITH TWO F-M ENGINES.

UNDERWATER VULNERABILITY
THE GREATEST WEAKNESS OF *GUAM* AND *ALASKA* WAS THEIR LIMITED UNDERWATER PROTECTION, WHICH MADE THEM VULNERABLE TO TORPEDO STRIKES.

Glossary

BL: Breech-loading

BLR: Breech-loading, rifled barrel

Barbette: Open-topped armored enclosure, protecting a gun, with a trunk opening through the armored floor to the magazine

Beam: Width of a ship

Breastwork: An armored area raised above deck level, on which guns could be mounted

Cable: Naval unit of measurement, taken variously as 100–120 fathoms (600–720 ft, 183–219.4 m)

Caliber: 1. An expression of the inside diameter of the barrel (the bore) and projectile, as in a 12-in (305 mm) gun firing a shell of the same diameter. 2. An expression of the barrel's length as a multiple of the bore: a 12-in (305 mm) 40-caliber gun has a barrel length from breech-face to muzzle of 40 times the bore: 480 in (12.2 m).

Casemate: An armored area set in the hull, where guns are mounted

Citadel: An area in the center of a ship, armored on all sides, enclosing machinery, magazines, etc.

Displacement: A measure of the actual weight of a ship and its contents, excluding cargo

Embrasure: An angled opening in the hull side, enabling a gun to fire forwards or aft

Fantail: Extreme afterdeck of an American warship

Flash plate: Metal forecastle deck protection on which the anchor chain rests

Howitzer: A short-barreled gun firing a heavy shell at an elevated angle and relatively low muzzle velocity

Hulk: The hull of a vessel with all rigging and equipment removed

Hurricane deck: A raised deck or walkway above the weather deck

Lay up: To place in a reserve mooring

Magazine: Secure storage room for gunpowder and explosive shells

Metacenter: The point of intersection between two imaginary lines, one drawn vertically through the center of buoyancy when the vessel floats level, the other drawn through the new center of buoyancy when the vessel is tilted

Metacentric height: A measurement of the initial static stability of a floating vessel, calculated as the distance between the vessel's center of gravity and its metacenter

ML: Muzzle-loading

MLR: Muzzle-loading, rifled barrel

QF: Quick-firing: guns firing projectiles that combined the shell and the firing charge

Quarterdeck: The open deck aft of the mainmast

Redoubt: An armored gun emplacement

Reserve: Temporary removal from active service

RB: Rifled bore (gun barrel)

SB: Smoothbore (gun barrel)

Sheer: The fore and aft upward curvature of a ship's hull

Skeg: Sternward extension of the keel as a rudder support

Sponson: A gun-platform extended beyond the side of the hull

Stem: The foremost member of the hull, fixed to the forepart of the keel

Tumblehome: Inward angling of a ship's sides

Turret: An armored construction containing a gun or guns, able to revolve in a partial or complete circle

Transom: A squared-off stern form

UAV: Unmanned aerial vehicle

UP projector: Launcher for "unrotated projectile" AA rockets

Weather deck: The uppermost deck of the ship's hull, open to the sky

Ships Index

General Index

Select Bibliography

Beeler, J. *Birth of the Battleship*. London: Naval Institute Press, 2004.

Breyer, Siegfried. *Battleships and Battle Cruisers*. London: Doubleday & Company, 1973.

Chesneau, R. *Conway's All the World's Fighting Ships, 1860–1905*. London: Conway Maritime Press, 1979.

Gardiner, R. (ed.) *Conway's All the World's Fighting Ships, 1906–1921*. London: Conway Maritime Press, 1985.

Gardiner, R. (ed.) *Steam, Steel and Shellfire: The Steam Warship 1815–1905*. London: Conway Maritime Press, 2001.

Garzke, W.H., and Robert O. Dulin. *US Battleships 1935–92*. Annapolis, Maryland: Naval Institute Press, 1976.

Jenkins, E.H. *History of the French Navy*. London: Macdonald & Jane's, 1973.

Jentschura, H. *Warships of the Imperial Japanese Navy, 1869–1945*. London: Arms & Armour Press, 1977.

McBride, W.M. *Technological Change and the US Navy, 1865–1945*. Baltimore: Johns Hopkins University Press, 2000.

Naval History Center. *Dictionary of American Fighting Ships, 8 vols*. Washington, DC: Department of the Navy, 1959–81.

Paine, Lincoln. *Warships of the World to 1900*. New York: Mariner Books, 2000.

Parkes, Oscar. *British Battleships*. London: Seeley Services & Co., 1966.

Van Oosten, F.C. *HNMS Ship De Ruyter*. Windsor, 1974.

Watts, Anthony. *The Imperial Russian Navy*. London: Arms & Armour Press, 1990.